IDE-JETRO Series

The Institute of Developing Economies, Japan External Trade Organization (IDE-JETRO) series explores the economic issues faced in developing regions globally, providing new research and analysis of these economies, with the aim of creating a more comprehensive understanding of the issues and conditions they are experiencing. With a wide range of volumes covering key economic issues in developing economies, as well as examining the challenges faced as East Asia continues to integrate, the titles in this series are essential companions for academics and policymakers interested in cutting-edge research and analysis of developing economies.

More information about this series at
http://www.springer.com/series/14861

Koji Kubo
Editor

Dollarization and De-dollarization in Transitional Economies of Southeast Asia

palgrave
macmillan

Editor
Koji Kubo
Institute of Developing Economies
Japan External Trade Organization (IDE-JETRO)
Chiba
Japan

IDE-JETRO Series
ISBN 978-3-319-57767-8 ISBN 978-3-319-57768-5 (eBook)
DOI 10.1007/978-3-319-57768-5

Library of Congress Control Number: 2017940375

Printed on acid-free paper

This Palgrave Macmillan imprint is published by Springer Nature
The registered company is Springer International Publishing AG
The registered company address is: Gewerbestrasse 11, 6330 Cham, Switzerland

Preface

This book is a compilation of self-contained accounts of dollarization episodes in four transitional economies of Southeast Asia, Cambodia, Lao People's Democratic Republic (Lao PDR), Myanmar, and Vietnam, which are often collectively referred to as the CLMV countries. There is a large body of literature on dollarization—domestic residents' holding of a significant portion of their financial assets in foreign-currency-denominated assets—in the context of Latin America and the transitional economies of Eastern Europe and the former Soviet Union. Relatively less well understood is dollarization in the transitional economies of Southeast Asia despite its significance. For example, Cambodia is one of the most highly dollarized economies in the world. To the best of my knowledge, this is the first book that dedicates a whole chapter to analyzing dollarization in Myanmar.

In contrast to conventional studies on dollarization that center upon the quantitative examination of the dollarization index, which is the ratio of foreign currency deposits to broad money, this book adopts an analytical narrative approach. Fundamental questions exploring dollarization include *Who holds dollar assets for what purposes*? The chapter on Cambodia reminds us that the prevalence of dollars differs substantially between regions and between various commodity supply chains even in this highly dollarized country. It is also revealed that foreign currency deposits include demand deposits and fixed term deposits that are held for different purposes and that the trends associated with various types of foreign currency deposits exhibit marked differences for the case of Lao PDR. Although crucial for diagnosis and formulation of de-dollarization policies, these features of dollarization are often neglected in existing literature. The studies in this book offer vivid pictures of dollarization in the CLMV countries.

Dollarization has become one of the policy challenges faced by CLMV financial authorities. A comprehensive diagnosis of the phenomena and their backgrounds in one book reveals some similarities but more differences among the dollarization episodes of these countries. The success and/or failure of policy measures against dollarization in one country would provide useful lessons for peer countries. I would be extremely honored if financial authorities and academia interested in these countries would find this book a useful reference.

It was over a decade ago when Shin'ichi Watanabe piqued my interest in the peculiar dynamics of dollarization in these countries in the 1990s and early 2000s; developments that stand in stark contrast with Latin American dollarization episodes. A comparative research project on dollarization in the CLMV countries, which had been one of my research agendas for many years, finally became possible during the 2014–2016 period when I was assigned to the Bangkok Office of the Japan External Trade Organization, an ideal location for conducting a joint research project with experts in the region. I am particularly grateful to Yasuhiro Yamada for giving me the opportunity to station in the hub city of continental Southeast Asia.

A real challenge was finding scholars who would be able to contribute their expertise to this research project. It is fortunate that Ken Odajima, Hidenobu Okuda, and Daiju Aiba brought insights from their ongoing large-scale survey of households and firms on the uses of dollar in Cambodia, a joint research venture involving the Japan International Cooperation Agency and the National Bank of Cambodia. I am particularly indebted to U Myint for introducing Set Aung, who subsequently joined the project. I am also grateful to Ngyuen Anh Duong who participated in the first year of this two-year project and shared his expertise on the Vietnamese dollarization episode. All chapters in this book are based on extensive reviews of the existing literature and novel data pertaining to dollarization.

The various contributors to this project have benefited from comments and suggestions of the participants of seminars and workshops at various places. Prakarn Arphasil, Theerawut Sripinit, Pisut Kulthanavit, and Lim Siphat served as discussants at the workshop at Thammasat University. Chea Serey and Khou Vouthy generously hosted a seminar for us to disseminate our research findings at the National Bank of Cambodia and shared with us their thoughts on dollarization from the viewpoint of practitioners facing the highly dollarized financial system. Earlier drafts of the chapter on Myanmar were presented at numerous venues in Myanmar including the Central Bank of Myanmar. The evolution of that chapter would not have been possible without discussions with Sandar Oo, Win Thaw, Min Han Soe, and their colleagues as well as foreign experts Masaru Tanaka, Shunsuke Yamamoto, and Yasuhisa Ojima.

Many thanks are due to my friends and colleagues in Myanmar including U Than Lwin, Cho Cho Thein, and Khin Thida Maw who always provided me with updates on Myanmar's financial system that were difficult for foreign observers to obtain.

Chiba, Japan

Koji Kubo

Contents

1 **Dollarization and De-dollarization in Transitional Economies of Southeast Asia: An Overview** 1
Koji Kubo

2 **Dollarization in Cambodia: Behavior of Households and Enterprises in a Highly Dollarized Environment** 33
Ken Odajima

3 **Asset Substitution and Currency Substitution behind Dollarization and De-dollarization Policy in the Lao PDR: Evidence from Bank-Level Data** 73
Phetsathaphone Keovongvichith

4 **Dollarization in Myanmar?** 105
Koji Kubo and Set Aung

5 **Dollarization and De-dollarization Policies: The Case of Vietnam** 131
Thi Hoang Anh Pham

6 **Economic Growth, Monetary Policy, and Dollarization in CLMV Countries** 167
Bhanupong Nidhiprabha

7 **Banking and Dollarization: A Comparative Study of Cambodia, Lao PDR, and Vietnam** 197
Hidenobu Okuda

Index 239

Contributors

Phetsathaphone Keovongvichith Bank of the Lao PDR, Vientiane, Lao PDR

Koji Kubo Institute of Developing Economies, Japan External Trade Organization (IDE-JETRO), Chiba, Japan

Bhanupong Nidhiprabha Faculty of Economics, Thammasat University, Bangkok, Thailand

Ken Odajima JICA Research Institute, Japan International Cooperation Agency (JICA), Tokyo, Japan

Hidenobu Okuda Graduate School of Economics, Hitotsubashi University, Tokyo, Japan

Thi Hoang Anh Pham Banking Academy of Vietnam, The State Bank of Vietnam, Hanoi, Vietnam

Set Aung Central Bank of Myanmar, Naypyitaw, Myanmar

List of Figures

Chapter 1 Dollarization and De-dollarization in Transitional Economies of Southeast Asia: An Overview

Fig. 1	Deposit dollarization in the CLMV countries	5
Fig. 2	Trends of consumer price index and exchange rate in the CLMV countries	6
Fig. 3	Monetary aggregate of the CLMV countries	7
Fig. 4	Currency in circulation and income level	14
Fig. 5	Alternative dollarization indices for Cambodia and Vietnam	17
Fig. 6	Prudential regulations and credit creation	23

Chapter 2 Dollarization in Cambodia: Behavior of Households and Enterprises in a Highly Dollarized Environment

Fig. 1	Trend of GDP growth and GDP per capita, Cambodia, 1995–2015	41

Chapter 3 Asset Substitution and Currency Substitution behind Dollarization and De-dollarization Policy in the Lao PDR: Evidence from Bank-Level Data

Fig. 1	Composition of broad money and FCDs in US dollar, Lao PDR, 1988–2013	80
Fig. 2	Composition of deposits by currency and by type of deposits, Lao PDR, 2004–2014	82
Fig. 3	*Ex post* real interest rates on local and foreign currency fixed deposits, Lao PDR, January 1996–December 2014	93

Chapter 4 Dollarization in Myanmar?

Fig. 1	Monetary survey, Myanmar, fiscal years 2000–2014	108
Fig. 2	Composition of deposits in Myanmar, 2000–2014	110
Fig. 3	Deposit dollarization in Myanmar, 2000–2014	111
Fig. 4	Daily official and parallel market exchange rates, Myanmar, April 2012–December 2015	123

Chapter 5 Dollarization and De-dollarization Policies: The Case of Vietnam

Fig. 1	Macroeconomic indicators in Vietnam, 1989–2016	134
Fig. 2	Development of the parallel market premium in Vietnam, 2004–2016 (in percent)	137
Fig. 3	FCD, M2, and FCD/M2 ratio in Vietnam, 1989–Feb, 2016	139
Fig. 4	FC loans, total credit, and FCL/total credit ratio in Vietnam, 1994–2014	140
Fig. 5	Development of deposit dollarization and cash dollarization in Vietnam, 1995–2013	141
Fig. 6	Interest rate differentials between Dong- and Dollar-denominated deposits and deposit dollarization in Vietnam, 1989–2016	145
Fig. 7	Ceiling rate for dong deposits, ceiling rate for US dollar deposits, and depreciation rate in Vietnam, 2011–2016	146

Chapter 6 Economic Growth, Monetary Policy, and Dollarization in CLMV Countries

Fig. 1	Urbanization in the CLMV countries	177
Fig. 2	Declining velocity, output growth, and inflation in Cambodia	178
Fig. 3	Trade openness in the CLMV countries	179
Fig. 4	Financial deepening in the CLMV countries	181
Fig. 5	Real interest rate and financial savings in Vietnam	182
Fig. 6	Vietnam's growth drivers	188
Fig. 7	Synchronization of regional inflation	190
Fig. 8	Growth synchronization: Principal GDP growth components of the CLMV countries and ASEAN-5	191

Chapter 7 Banking and Dollarization: A Comparative Study of Cambodia, Lao PDR, and Vietnam

Fig. 1	Patterns of bank portfolio	207
Fig. 2	Ratios of deposit and loan dollarization	209
Fig. 3	Net foreign assets of banks	210
Fig. 4	Net open foreign exchange position of banks	211

List of Tables

Chapter 2 Dollarization in Cambodia: Behavior of Households and Enterprises in a Highly Dollarized Environment

Table 1	Income dollarization	47
Table 2	Expenditure dollarization	50
Table 3	Households having KHR/USD savings	55
Table 4	Households having KHR/USD deposits	56
Table 5	Loan characteristics by currency	58
Table 6	Loan characteristics by lender	59
Table 7	Choice of loan currency	61
Table 8	Sales dollarization	64
Table 9	Dollarization of expenditure (Production input/wage)	65
Table 10	Loan access and currency choice	69

Chapter 3 Asset Substitution and Currency Substitution behind Dollarization and De-dollarization Policy in the Lao PDR: Evidence from Bank-Level Data

Table 1	Types of deposits and loans of selected commercial banks, Lao PDR, 2000–2013	84

Table 2 Components of deposit accounts by type of account holder of selected commercial banks, Lao PDR, 2002–2014 88

Chapter 4 Dollarization in Myanmar?

Table 1 Trade balance by state and private sectors, Myanmar, fiscal years 2001–2014 114

Chapter 5 Dollarization and De-dollarization Policies: The Case of Vietnam

Table 1 Foreign exchange controls in Vietnam, 1988–2016 148
Table 2 Chronology of interest rate ceiling in Vietnam, 1991–2016 150
Table 3 Interest rate differentials in Vietnam 161
Table 4 De-dollarization and de-goldization policy measures in Vietnam, 1988–2016 162

Chapter 6 Economic Growth, Monetary Policy, and Dollarization in CLMV Countries

Table 1 Top trading partners of the CLMV countries (percentage share of country's total exports/imports) 180

Chapter 7 Banking and Dollarization: A Comparative Study of Cambodia, Lao PDR, and Vietnam

Table 1 Affects of determinants on dollarization 205
Table 2 Macroeconomic environments in Cambodia, Lao PDR, and Vietnam 216
Table 3 Loan to deposit ratios of major banks by currency in Cambodia 222
Table 4 Currency circulation by region in Cambodia 222
Table 5 Composition of deposits and loans by currency for selected banks in Cambodia 223
Table 6 Foreign currency portfolio of banks in Cambodia, Lao PDR, and Vietnam 229
Table 7 Regulations on dollarization in the CLMV countries 231

1

Dollarization and De-dollarization in Transitional Economies of Southeast Asia: An Overview

Koji Kubo

1 Introduction

The transitional economies of Southeast Asia, namely Cambodia, Lao People's Democratic Republic (Lao PDR), Myanmar, and Vietnam, constitute a unique group in terms of diversified experiences of dollarization. Dollarization is the circumstances where domestic residents hold a significant share of their financial assets in foreign-currency-denominated ones (Balino et al. 1999). Foreign-currency-denominated assets are held for different purposes including payments/settlements and for asset portfolio. As purposes of holding foreign-currency-denominated assets differ from one country to another, it is likely that countermeasures for dollarization would differ as well.

Exploring dollarization episodes of these four countries (hereafter CLMV countries), we point out three salient features of dollarization in

K. Kubo (✉)
Institute of Developing Economies, Japan External Trade Organization (IDE-JETRO), Chiba, Japan
e-mail: Koji_Kubo@ide.go.jp

K. Kubo (ed.), *Dollarization and De-dollarization in Transitional Economies of Southeast Asia*, IDE-JETRO Series, DOI 10.1007/978-3-319-57768-5_1

these countries. First, in Cambodia, Lao PDR, and Vietnam, dollarization started in their early stage of financial development unlike in Latin America where dollarization took place in a somewhat developed financial system. Subsequent financial development and economic growth took place under dollarization.

Second, dollarization began in cash-based economies with large inflows of foreign currency banknotes relative to the size of the local economies, notably in Cambodia. This prompted the use of foreign currency as a medium of exchange and unit of account, which makes a contrast with Latin America where foreign-currency-denominated assets functioned more as store of value.

Third, currency convertibility has been limited, and exchange rate and foreign exchange allocation have been heavily managed in Myanmar and Vietnam. The restrictive foreign exchange management is considered to have stimulated the demand for foreign-currency-denominated assets which can be distinguished from asset substitution or currency substitution.

In this volume, we investigate how these three features shaped their dollarization trajectories. We contend that these three features differentiated the pathways of dollarization among them as well as from those of Latin American and Eastern European countries. Given the trajectories of dollarization and their driving forces, we evaluate the validity of de-dollarization measures taken by the authorities of these countries where applicable.

Furthermore, recognition of these salient features of dollarization in CLMV countries leads us to several pertinent questions. With regard to underdevelopment of financial system at the start of dollarization, we ask how the balance between the benefits and costs of dollarization has evolved in CLMV countries in the past three decades. Another question we address is if dollarization subsides or prolongs when financial intermediary becomes capable of savings mobilization on a larger and wider scale.

With regard to large inflows of foreign currency banknotes, we trace how the financial authorities designed regulations to harness foreign currency banknotes outside the banking system toward financial development while managing side effects. We also explore if payment dollarization spreads evenly in the economy or unevenly among regions and economic sectors.

Dollarization in CLMV countries is examined less in the literature compared with cases in Latin America and transitional economies in Eastern Europe. There are, however, still a number of existing studies that examine dollarization in the region, mostly in individual countries. Except for studies on Cambodia (de Zamaroczy and Sa 2002; Duma 2011), studies of dollarization in the region mostly focus on the trends of dollarization index in terms of the ratio of foreign currency deposits (FCDs) over broad money (Ra 2008; Menon 2008; Samreth 2011), or summarize the background of dollarization via a piecemeal approach, including Pani (2002) on Lao PDR and Unteroberdoerster (2002) on Vietnam. In terms of the coverage, the most comprehensive study on dollarization in the transitional economies of Southeast Asia is the edited volume by Capannelli and Menon (2010), but they focus more on monetary and exchange rate policies rather than dollarization itself, and they do not include an analysis on Myanmar.

The research volume contributes to the literature on dollarization by systematically synthesizing the experiences of dollarization in CLMV countries via an analytical narrative approach. We expect that the synthesis of dollarization diagnoses on CLMV countries will provide useful resources for the financial authorities of these economies, particularly for Myanmar—the country still in an early stage of dollarization. The success and failure of de-dollarization policies in peer countries would provide policymakers with valuable lessons.

Furthermore, this research volume complements the four diagnoses of the individual countries with two thematic analyses: one on economic growth and roles of monetary policy under dollarization in CLMV countries (Chap. 6), and the other on the roles of banks as catalysts of dollarization in these economies (Chap. 7).

In the remainder of this introductory chapter, we provide an overview of dollarization in CLMV countries and illustrate key points for analyses in subsequent chapters. In Sect. 2, we present the trends of dollarization in CLMV countries with the conventional metrics and pick up characteristics of dollarization experiences in these countries. In Sect. 3, we review the foundation of the literature of dollarization. The section includes classification of dollarization phenomena and their economic interpretation. In Sects. 4 and 5, we develop analyses about the implications of two salient features of dollarization experiences in CLMV countries, namely, inflows of foreign currency banknotes in the early stage of dollarization, and an underdeveloped banking system at the start of dollarization. In Sect. 6, we argue that dollarization might claim as its costs financial disintermediation and slower growth in credit. In Sect. 7 on measures for de-dollarization, we argue that because of network externalities, elimination of payment dollarization in Cambodia requires holistic measures beyond macroeconomic stabilization. In Sect. 8, we present the outline of this book.

2 Overview of Dollarization in CLMV Countries

2.1 Stylized Facts

We first measure dollarization in CLMV countries in terms of the ratios of FCDs over broad money in Fig. 1. Here, broad money consists of local currency outside banks, local currency deposits, and FCDs. In Fig. 1, we also depict FCDs in terms of US dollars. The dollarization index (FCDs/Broad Money ratio) exhibits a declining trend in recent years in Lao PDR, Myanmar, and Vietnam, but an increasing trend in Cambodia.

A stylized fact in the literature is that the main driver of dollarization is inflation. CLMV countries, to various degrees, experienced high inflation as well as sharp depreciation of the domestic currency in their transition from a planned to a market-oriented economy in the late 1980s and early 1990s. Vietnam experienced inflation of above 400% per annum in 1988–1989, and Cambodia experienced inflation of above 300% in 1993 (Dodsworth et al. 1996). The highest inflation rates in Lao PDR were around 160% per annum in 1989 and 1999, and approximately 70% in Myanmar in 1998 (Fig. 2).

The rise in the dollarization index in Lao PDR in 1997–2000 particularly applies to this inflation–dollarization nexus. As shown in Fig. 2,

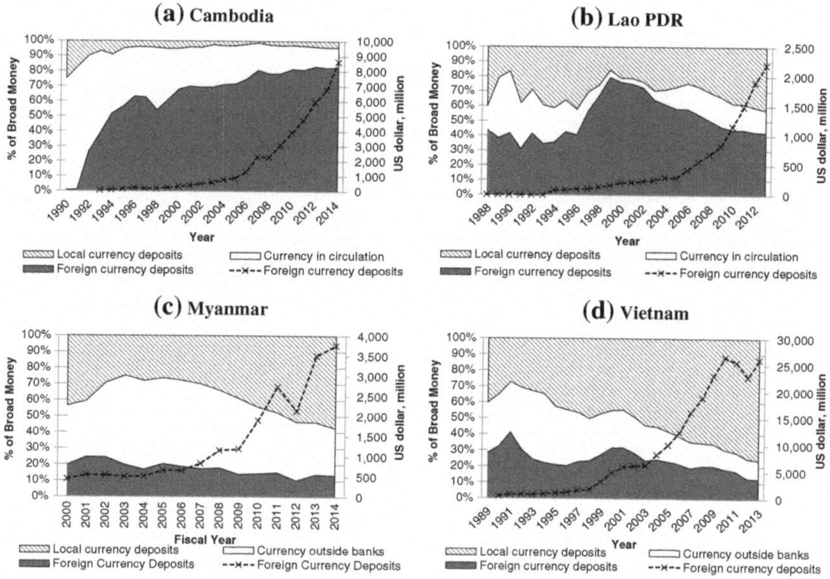

Fig. 1 Deposit dollarization in the CLMV countries. *Sources* IMF Country Report (various issues)

the country experienced a triple-digit high inflation in 1998–1999, which was due to expansionary fiscal and monetary policies to mitigate adverse effects of the Asian financial crisis originated in neighboring Thailand. The exchange rate of Lao kip (LAK) vis-à-vis the US dollar depreciated from LAK 1081 per US dollar in June 1997 to LAK 9430 in June 1999. Then, the dollarization index rose from 56.7% in 1997 to 79.4% in 1999.

Another stylized fact in the literature, which is also applicable to CLMV countries, is persistence or hysteresis of dollarization. Dollarization does not necessarily subside even after successful disinflation. By the mid-2000s, Cambodia, Lao PDR, and Vietnam achieved macroeconomic stability, though they occasionally had moderate inflation. For instance, in Lao PDR the annual average inflation rate has been in single digit since 2005. Regardless of its successful disinflation, the dollarization index in Lao PDR remains around 40%. In Cambodia, the dollarization index has been even rising.

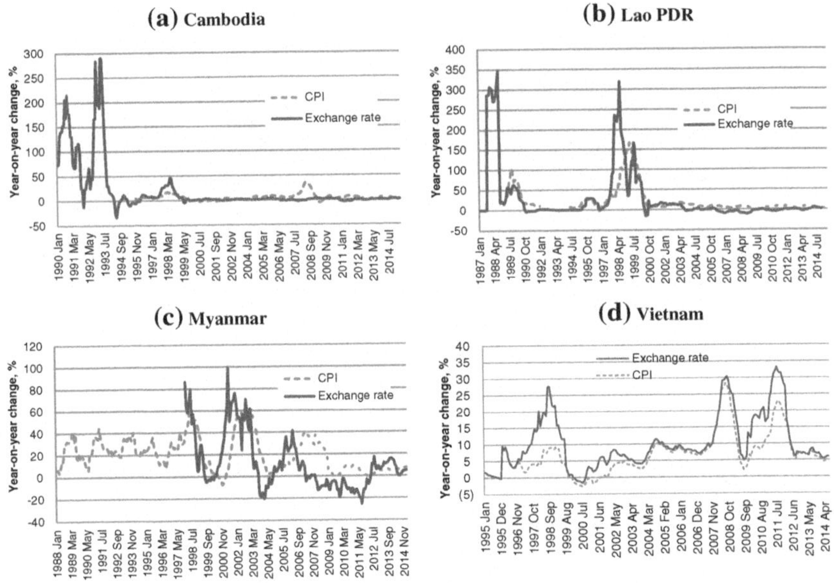

Fig. 2 Trends of consumer price index and exchange rate in the CLMV countries. *Sources* International Financial Statistics, IMF; Survey of parallel foreign exchange market in Myanmar

2.2 Characteristics of Dollarization in CLMV Countries

We list several notable trends of financial statistics which are pertinent to the dynamics of dollarization in CLVM countries. First, as we can observe in Fig. 1, whether the dollarization index declines or not, FCDs in terms of US dollar have been increasing for the most of the periods in all CLMV countries. In Lao PDR, Myanmar, and Vietnam, although FCDs have been rising almost continuously (except 2012 in Myanmar, and until 2010 in Vietnam) , the dollarization index exhibited a declining trend. This signifies that other components of broad money have grown faster than FCDs. In Lao PDR, both local currency deposits and local currency in circulation have grown faster than FCDs since 2002. In Myanmar and Vietnam, the growth in local currency deposits overwhelmed those of the other two components. These suggest that a fall in the dollarization index is mostly attributable not to a shift of existing FCDs to local-currency-denominated assets, but rather to faster growth in local currency components of broad money than that of FCDs.

Second, linked with the above-mentioned first point, our observation window coincides with the period that these countries achieved significant growth in saving mobilization and financial deepening. Figure 3 shows the trend of broad money as a percentage of Gross Domestic Product (GDP) for CLMV countries. For example, in Vietnam, when the dollarization index declined from 31.7% in 2001 to 18.5% in 2010, broad money as a percentage of GDP rose from 58.1 to 129.3%. In the meantime, local currency deposits as a percentage of GDP jumped from 25.9 to 89.6%. Saving mobilization and financial deepening in local currency contributed to a decline in the dollarization index particularly in Vietnam.

Saving mobilization and financial deepening, however, do not always mitigate dollarization. On the contrary, they added to its progress in

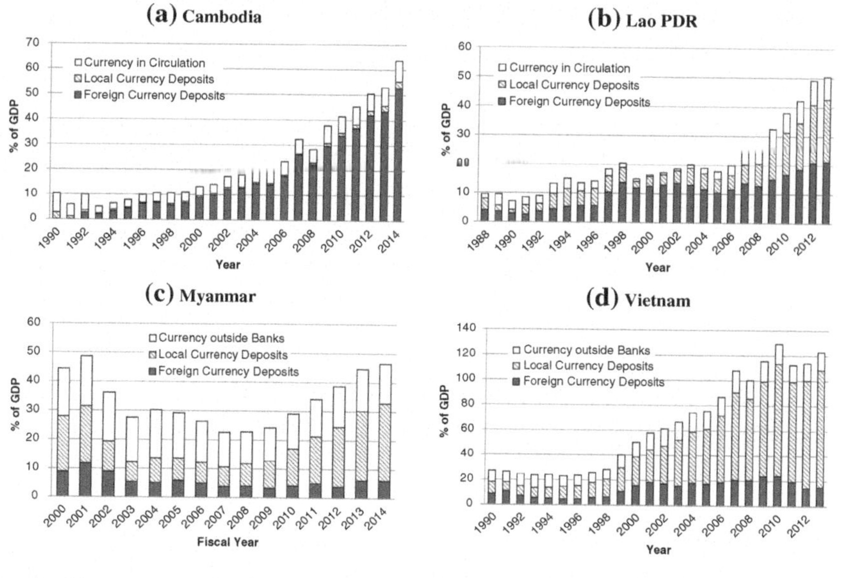

Fig. 3 Monetary aggregate of the CLMV countries. *Sources* International Financial Statistics, IMF; Survey of parallel foreign exchange market in Myanmar

Cambodia. Broad money as a percentage of GDP increased sharply from 13.0% in 2000 to 63.7% in 2014, and this growth is largely attributable to saving mobilization in foreign currency. The growth in FCDs accompanied a rise in the dollarization index from 63.7 to 82.6% during the same period. Therefore, whether saving mobilization and financial deepening take place in local currency or foreign currency has an important implication on trajectories of dollarization.

Third, a low level of local currency in circulation seems to coincide with a large quantity of foreign currency in circulation (FCC) especially in Cambodia and Lao PDR. Local currency outside banks as a percentage of GDP was as low as 2.5% in Cambodia in 1994 and 0.5% in Lao PDR in 2000 (Fig. 3). Due to the underdeveloped financial system and cash-based transaction, foreign currency banknotes have been a possible close substitute for local currency notes in these countries. Furthermore, FCC is an important source of FCD. Savings mobilization translates to absorbing FCC into the banking system.

3 Breaking Down the Dollarization Phenomenon

Even when the same term of dollarization is used in the ongoing analysis, its real content is not always the same. Dollarization refers to various phenomena, and the motives for holding foreign-currency-denominated assets vary among residents and between time periods. We classify reasons of various residents, both corporates and households, for holding various forms of foreign-currency-denominated assets.

3.1 Classification of Dollarization and Motives for Holding Foreign-Currency-Denominated Assets

Dollarization can be classified by several dimensions.[1] First, we can classify dollarization into official (de jure) and partial (de facto) dollarization. Under official dollarization, a country adopts another country's currency—often US dollars but also sometimes Euros or other currencies—as the legal tender. Examples include Ecuador, El Salvador, and Panama. In contrast, under partial dollarization, while a country's domestic currency remains the exclusive legal tender, domestic residents spontaneously use foreign currency as a substitute for local currency for one or all of the three functions of currency (as a medium of exchange, as a unit of account, and as a store of value). All CLMV countries are, to different degrees, operating under partial dollarization.

In partial dollarization, domestic residents hold financial assets in foreign currency, including foreign currency banknotes, FCDs, and cross-border deposits, and use them as a substitute for local-currency-denominated assets. Cross-border deposits are deposits by domestic residents in offshore accounts. Watanabe (2007) notes that gold has been held as a store of value and used as a unit of account especially for real estate transactions in Vietnam, which has been called "goldization" (See Chap. 5 of this volume).

There are three states of partial dollarization. First is "financial dollarization," where financial contracts are written in terms of foreign currency. "Deposit dollarization" and "loan dollarization" are subsets of financial dollarization. The terms "deposit dollarization" and "loan dollarization" describe the situation where FCDs and foreign currency loans (FCLs) account for a significant portion of the balance sheet of the domestic banking system.

Second is "real dollarization," which is the indexing of prices and wages to foreign currency. This includes the situation where prices are quoted in US dollars, but payments can be made in local currency by converting the prices using prevalent market exchange rates.[2]

The third state is "payment dollarization," where foreign currency is used to settle domestic transactions. Foreign currency, although not the legal tender, functions as a medium of exchange alongside the domestic currency. Payment dollarization usually accompanies domestic residents' holdings of foreign currency banknotes. Depending on regulations, FCDs are also used for settling domestic transactions. Both domestic account transfers and checks are available for FCD current accounts in Cambodia, whereas FCDs are banned for uses in settlements of domestic transactions in Vietnam.

Partial dollarization is a response of domestic residents to macroeconomic instability and high inflation (Balino et al. 1999). Foreign-currency-denominated assets offer a means for domestic residents to hedge high inflation. Also, indexing of prices to foreign currency and payments in foreign currency reduce the transaction costs of financial contracts and payments/settlements under inflation.

In addition to classification of dollarization by type into financial, real, and payments dollarization, the literature distinguishes motives of dollarization between asset substitution and currency substitution (Balino et al. 1999).

As for asset substitution, foreign-currency-denominated assets are held for a store of value. Asset substitution results in financial dollarization. FCDs as well as foreign currency banknotes and cross-border deposits offer a means to hedge high inflation. We consider that domestic residents' holdings of foreign currency, motivated from asset substitution, are for an asset portfolio.

As for currency substitution, foreign-currency-denominated assets are used as a medium of exchange and unit of account for domestic transactions. Real dollarization and payments dollarization are equivalent to currency substitution. Pricing and payments in foreign currency reduce transaction costs of settlements in the face of high inflation. We consider that the holdings offoreign currency motivated from currency substitution are for transaction purposes. To limit currency substitution, a modern payment system in local currency that reduces transaction costs would be a policy option; convenient banking services would curtail the demand for foreign-currency-denominated assets for transaction purposes, which is one of the de-dollarization strategies in Lao PDR (Chap. 3).

Asset substitution and currency substitution are not mutually exclusive, and they exist at the same time in FCDs. Although we have described FCDs sweepingly in the ongoing analysis, FCDs are the sum of, for example, current account deposits of corporates for transaction purposes and fixed account deposits of households for asset portfolio. To boost unraveling of FCDs, a combination of de-dollarization policies is required that work on various motivations for holding foreign-currency-denominated assets, either asset substitution or currency substitution, or both.

3.2 International Trade, Convertibility of Local Currency, and Dollarization

Apart from asset substitution and currency substitution, foreign currency is held in the process of settlements of foreign trade, especially informal border trade. When banks do not accommodate settlements of informal trade, some smugglers resort to settlements in foreign currency banknotes and hold cash balance in foreign currency. A good example of this is the holding of Thai baht by domestic residents in Lao PDR in the Thai border areas (Pani 2002). Thai baht is widely accepted in the border areas between Lao PDR and Thailand (Chap. 6).

Furthermore, Lao PDR, Myanmar, and Vietnam once imposed restrictions on convertibility of local currency for foreign exchange and convertibility for current international transactions. As a result, domestic residents maintained foreign-currency-denominated assets to convert their foreign currency revenues at competitive rates in the parallel markets rather than at the officially set exchange rate, as well as to circumvent controls on foreign trade. This was particularly the case for Myanmar (Chap. 4).

3.3 Hysteresis of Dollarization

Persistence or hysteresis is a notable feature of dollarization (Calvo and Vegh 1992), also observed in Cambodia, Lao PDR, and Vietnam. In Cambodia and Lao PDR, dollarization index has remained high for a long period since macroeconomic stabilization. The literature offers two explanations for this phenomenon: expected high inflation and network externalities.

In the case of expected high inflation, domestic residents hold foreign-currency-denominated assets as a hedge against expected high inflation. Even if inflation is stabilized, domestic residents would not return to local-currency-denominated assets until they cease to expect of high inflation. Expected high inflation as a cause of dollarization hysteresis is more to do with asset substitution and financial dollarization.

Network externalities refer to the condition where if more people have been using foreign currency for payments and settlements, it is more convenient to remain holding foreign currency instead of local currency.[3] Network externalities have more to do with currency substitution and payment dollarization.

Balino et al. (1999) argue that dollarization due to currency substitution is more persistent than that of asset substitution, as changing the practices in settlements (i.e., use of US dollar banknotes) would take place only when there are significant benefits of switching from foreign currency to local currency. Regarding the persistence of dollarization in Bulgaria, Valev (2010), using micro-survey data, examines whether the hysteresis of dollarization is attributable to expected high inflation or network externalities, and presents the evidence that the latter is dominant in Bulgaria. In contrast, using cross-sectional data from 45 countries, Ize and Levy-Yeyati (2003) show that the persistence of dollarization is associated with the expected volatility of the inflation rate.

Chapter 2 of this volume on the case study of Cambodia examines the hysteresis of dollarization from the viewpoint of network externalities, and it sheds light on how network externalities work in dimensions of geographical areas and supply chains.

4 Dollarization and Foreign Currency Banknotes in Circulation

4.1 Measurement Issues

The ratio of FCDs over broad money is commonly used as a dollarization index in the literature because of its convenience in terms of data availability. This index does not count FCC (foreign currency in circulation) and cross-border deposits in banks abroad as these data are not readily available. However, convenience comes at some costs. We note at least two drawbacks in this index.

First, foreign currency banknotes and cross-border deposits may be substitutes with FCDs, which means that focusing on FCDs only does not reveal the whole picture of dollarization. Balino et al. (1999) illustrate that easing of restrictions on FCDs resulted in a sharp increase in FCDs in transition economies in Eastern Europe. Such an increase in FCDs would occur when domestic residents replaced foreign currency banknotes in hand and cross-border deposits with FCDs, and it does not necessarily represent a rise in their aggregate foreign-currency-denominated assets. As for CLMV countries, since partial dollarization started in the circumstances where cash-based transactions were prevalent, foreign currency banknotes circulating outside the banking system have been a particularly important component of money.

Second, changes in exchange rate bring in fluctuations in this dollarization index (Mwase and Kumah 2015). A depreciation of the domestic currency against the dollar magnifies the value of FCDs in local currency terms, even though there has been no change in FCDs in US dollar terms. Such valuation effect of currency depreciation on dollarization indices should be differentiated from growth in FCDs due to asset substitution.[4] There are a number of time series econometric analyses with dollarization indices as dependent variables (Ra 2008; Samreth 2011), where changes in the degree of dollarization are not differentiated from the valuation effect of exchange rate changes.

4.2 Local Currency Outside Banks and Foreign Currency in Circulation

To infer the extent of the circulation of foreign currency banknotes in CLMV countries, we compare the size of local currency in circulation of these countries with those of other low-income and lower middle-income countries. On the assumption that low-income and lower middle-income countries are cash-based economies with an underdeveloped banking system, a lower amount of local currency in circulation in a country relative to peer countries implies a larger amount of FCC in that country. Here, we casually examine this hypothesis.

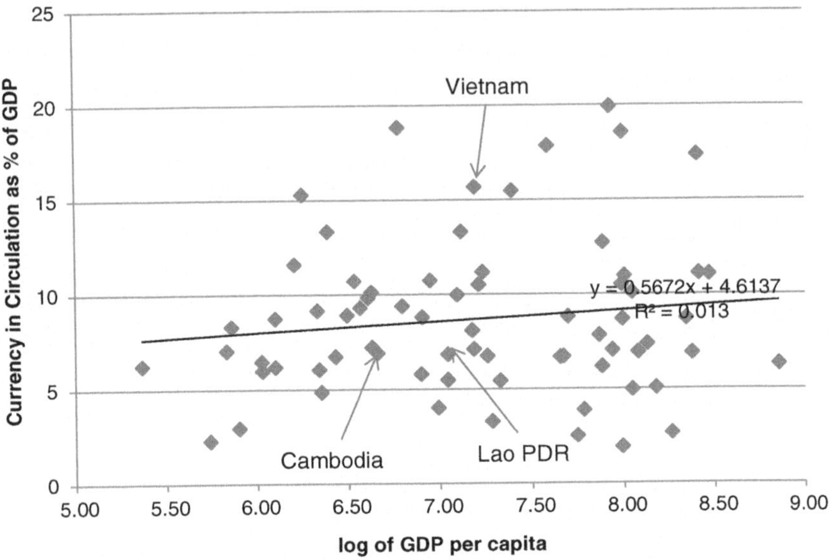

Fig. 4 Currency in circulation and income level. *Sources* International Financial Statistics CD-ROM, IMF; World Development Indicators website, World Bank

Figure 4 summarizes the currency in circulation as a percentage of GDP along with GDP per capita for groups of low-income countries and lower middle-income countries as of 2010. Due to unavailability of data, Myanmar is not included in the sample. There is a weak positive correlation between the amount of local currency in circulation and GDP per capita. Considering the income level, the amount of local currency in circulation as a percentage of GDP is small in Cambodia and Lao PDR.

In fact, the currency in circulation as a percentage of GDP was consistently low in Lao PDR. Before the high-inflation episode of 1998–2000 high inflation, currency in circulation was as low as 2.4% in 1997. During the high-inflation period, currency in circulation further fell to 0.5%. Such an extremely low level of currency in circulation, combined with the nature of a cash-based economy and an underdeveloped banking sector, strongly suggests that a considerable amount of foreign currency banknotes have been circulating in Lao PDR.

Regarding FCC, sources include private transfers (such as migrant workers' remittances) and official transfers from abroad, spending of foreign tourists, and smuggling exports. As for Vietnam, Watanabe (2006, 2007) documents private transfers by overseas Vietnamese are a major source of US banknotes circulating in the economy. Similarly, de Zamaroczy and Sa (2002: 5) illustrate that the administration of the United Nations Transitional Authority in Cambodia (UNTAC) in 1991–1993, with their 22,000 personnel, brought a large stock of US dollar banknotes; the 2-year budget of the UNTAC was close to US$2 billion, which amounted to 75% of the GDP of Cambodia in 1993, and over a half of the budget was spent in cash throughout the country.

4.3 Estimate of Foreign Currency in Circulation and Alternative Dollarization Index

As argued above, FCC has been potentially a significant component of money in CLMV countries. De Zamaroczy and Sa (2002) offer an estimate of dollars in circulation in Cambodia, Watanabe (2006) for Vietnam, and Girardin (2010) for Cambodia, Lao PDR, and Vietnam. According to the estimate of Cambodia by de Zamaroczy and Sa (2002), US dollar banknotes in circulation outside the banking system were estimated to be above 90% of total currency in circulation (sum of local currency in circulation and US dollar banknotes in circulation), and three times larger than broad money (sum of local currency in circulation, local currency deposits, and FCDs). Similarly, Watanabe (2006) argues that in Vietnam the amount of US dollar banknotes held outside the banking system was US$4.9 billion in 2001, whose value in local currency terms was larger than the local currency outside banks at that time. These results imply that the conventional dollarization indices underrate the degree of dollarization for CLMV countries.

Drawing on de Zamaroczy and Sa (2002), Watanabe (2006), and Girardin (2010), we estimate FCC in Cambodia and Vietnam.[5] First, Watanabe (2006) presents an estimate of the stock of FCC as US $2 billion for Vietnam as of 1995, and de Zamaroczy and Sa (2002) as US $1.2 billion for Cambodia as of 1994. Second, Wanatabe (2006) and

Girardin (2010) calculate the increment of foreign currency in circulation by assuming that net private transfer (NPTR) is a major source of foreign currency inflows. Following these two studies, we estimate an increase in the stock of FCC in a country as

$$\Delta FCC_t = NPTR_t - \varphi \Delta FCD_t, \tag{1}$$

where Δ stands for a difference operator ($\Delta FCC_t \equiv FCC_t - FCC_{t-1}$), and φ ($0 < \varphi \leq 1$) is a discount factor. Equation (1) assumes that private transfers are held as either foreign currency banknotes or foreign currency deposits. With the discount factor φ, we take it into account that sources of changes in FCDs are not limited to households' savings; other sources include banks' credit creation which was especially the case for Cambodia. For simplicity, we assume φ is constant over time, and it takes the value of 0.1 or 0.5. Using the estimates of initial stocks and the data of net private transfers contained in the various issues of the *IMF Country Report* for each country, we can compile time series data of FCC for Cambodia and Vietnam.

We should note that our estimates of FCC may not be accurate for at least two reasons. First, net private transfer may not be a major source of FCC. There are other sources of foreign currency including smuggling exports and spending by foreign tourists. Second, the data for private transfers do not include informal remittances. As Freund and Spatafora (2008) illustrate, a large portion of private remittances have been sent via informal channels as the foreign exchange has been heavily regulated and the banking system of these countries has been underdeveloped. Therefore, our estimate of FCC could over- or underestimate the actual amount of foreign currency in circulation.

Based on the estimates of FCC, we present an alternative index of dollarization for Cambodia and Vietnam in Fig. 5. We define the alternative index as the ratio of (FCC + FCDs) to (Broad Money + FCC), where Broad Money consists of local currency in circulation, local currency deposits, and FCDs.

By comparing the trends of the conventional dollarization index with the alternative index incorporating FCC, we can make some notable observations. For Cambodia, the conventional dollarization index

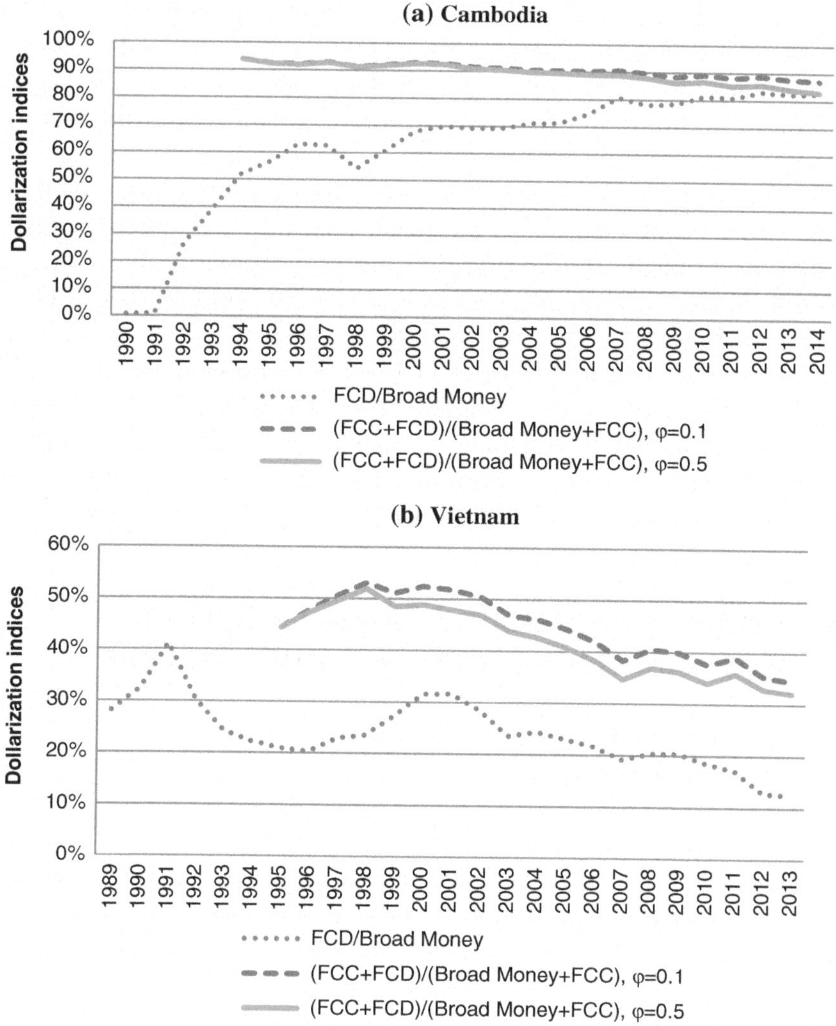

Fig. 5 Alternative dollarization indices for Cambodia and Vietnam. *Sources IMF Country Report* (various issues). *Notes* FCC and FCD refer to foreign currency in circulation and foreign currency deposits, respectively. FCC is calculated using Eq. (1) in Sect. 4.3. For Cambodia, FCC is assumed to be zero from 2011

exhibits an increasing trend despite successful stabilization since 1994, which is puzzling. In contrast, the (FCDs + FCC)/(Broad Money + FCC) index shows that dollarization had its peak of 94% in 1994, and it exhibits a declining trend, which is more compatible with the macroeconomic development in the country.

In Vietnam, FCC has accounted for a considerable portion of monetary assets. As of 1995, FCC was larger than the local currency outside banks. Accordingly, the dollarization index incorporating FCC reached 50% in 1998, and as of 2013 was still hovering around 30%. The FCDs over Broad Money ratio increased from 1998 to 2001, whereas the (FCDs + FCC)/(Broad Money + FCC) index exhibited a decline. This can be interpreted as a shift from FCC to FCDs, which is consistent with the observation by Unteroberdoerster (2002) that such re-intermediation of the foreign currency previously held by households outside the banking system contributed to the sharp rise in FCDs in this period.

5 An Underdeveloped Financial System, Financial Deepening, and Dollarization

5.1 An Underdeveloped Financial System and Dollarization

The banking systems of Cambodia, Lao PDR, and Vietnam began to dollarize when they were still underdeveloped in the late 1980 and early 1990s. The financial authorities of these countries took a liberal attitude toward FCDs and FCLs. When foreign currency banknotes are widely circulating and the banking system is small, it might be a reasonable approach for the authorities to aim at re-intermediation of such foreign currency outside the banking system.[6] In these countries, both households and corporations were permitted to deposit foreign exchange of any sources as an FCD.[7] FCDs and FCLs fostered initial development of the banking systems.

Subsequent trajectories of dollarization on bank balance sheets were substantially different between Cambodia and the other two countries

(See Chaps. 3, 5, and 7 of this volume). In the balance sheet of banks in Cambodia, both deposits and loans remain mostly in foreign currencies. The financial development in Cambodia was that the banks mobilized foreign currency savings, and credit creation in foreign currency accelerated financial dollarization. In contrast, deposit dollarization and loan dollarization have subsided in Lao PDR and Vietnam. Chapter 7 of this volume argues that such divergence in trajectories of financial dollarization cannot be attributable solely to macroeconomic conditions, calling for a holistic approach that takes into consideration differences between payments dollarization and financial dollarization.

5.2 Financial Deepening and Dollarization

Cambodia, Lao PDR, and Vietnam experienced financial deepening in the period from around 2000 through 2015, which might have interacted with dollarization (de-dollarization). One aspect of financial deepening would be an expanding outreach of financial services from urban to rural areas, and from large corporations to poor households. On the assumption that the use of foreign currency would be more prevalent in the corporate sector in urban areas, financial inclusion of rural areas and poor households in the process of financial deepening could alter the composition of banks' deposits and the weight of FCDs in total deposits.

The subsequent chapters of this volume examine the interaction of financial deepening and dollarization. Chapter 2 examines validity of the assumption that dollarization is more prevalent in urban areas, among larger corporations, and among richer households in Cambodia, using the survey data of corporations and households by urban and rural areas. Similarly, Chap. 3 investigates changes in composition of deposits by type of account holders (corporates and households) using bank-level data in Lao PDR. These chapters illuminate how financial deepening effects dollarization, in particular the dollarization index—the ratios of FCDs over broad money.

5.3 Economic Growth and Dollarization

We also consider impacts of dollarization on economic growth. There are indirect and direct channels where dollarization exerts influences on economic growth. Regarding an indirect channel, dollarization works on economic growth via financial development. As argued in Chap. 6, there are interactions between economic growth and financial development. On the one hand, financial development leads to growth in credit to the economy, which is conducive to output growth. On the other hand, the output growth and accompanying growth in per capita income prompt savings mobilization and financial intermediation. Thus, as long as dollarization affects financial development either positively or negatively, dollarization can also exert influences on economic growth.

Regarding a direct channel, we point out fiscal discipline under dollarization (Balino et al. 1999). When the economy is dollarized, residents can hedge inflation by rebalancing their asset portfolio. This would cut inflation tax revenues for the government, which would in turn give fiscal discipline and contain inflation. It is well established that disinflation adds to economic growth. Thus, we can state the disinflationary effect of dollarization contributes to economic growth.

These points remind us that dollarization has benefits and costs on the economy (Chap. 6).

6 Costs of Dollarization

Let us further discuss the costs of dollarization. The full literature on dollarization provides a more extensive list of dollarization's risks and costs versus its benefits. But briefly, first, dollarization leaves the banking system more prone to banking crises (Gulde et al. 2004). Second, the workspace of monetary and exchange policies becomes more complicated in dollarized economies (Balino et al. 1999). We review these risks and costs in some more details below.

6.1 Banking System Fragility and Financial Disintermediation

While FCLs add to financial re-intermediation in the context of Cambodia, Lao PDR, and Vietnam, they bring two types of risks in the financial system: exchange rate risk and liquidity risk (Gulde et al. 2004). Empirical analyses by de Nicolo et al. (2005) and Levy-Yeyati (2006) show that the probability of financial instability is higher in dollarized economies.

Banks with partially dollarized balance sheet are exposed to exchange rate risk in two ways directly and indirectly. One is their open positions, that is, the currency mismatch on their balance sheet. The other is credit risk that arises from exchange rate risk. As for the latter, FCLs ostensibly allow banks to match FCDs. Borrowers of FCLs, however, are exposed to exchange rate risk when their revenues are not in the same currency of FCLs. For banks, extending FCLs to such borrowers merely converts exchange rate risk to credit risk. Thus, the monetary authorities of dollarized countries often restrict banks to extend FCLs only to those whose financial position stands to gain from exchange rate depreciation, so that the balance sheets of banks are not impaired from depreciation.

Liquidity risk arises from maturity mismatch between foreign currency liabilities such as FCDs and foreign currency assets such as FCLs. As long as banks accept foreign currency demand deposits and lend a part of them in a long maturity, it brings in maturity mismatch. Compared with asset-liability maturity mismatch in local currency, the problem is severe since the central bank's function as the lender of last resort to provide foreign currency liquidity is limited. To prevent a run on FCDs, individual banks as well as the central bank have to maintain ample foreign currency liquidities. In Latin American, the regulatory authorities of Honduras and Peru set the reserve requirement ratio on FCDs at as high as 50 and 45%, respectively (Balino et al. 1999). However, unless FCDs are fully covered with the sum of foreign currency liquidities in the consolidated financial sector, the central bank cannot act as the lender of last resort.[8]

Moreover, dollarization of deposits brings in a concern about financial disintermediation (Watanabe 2006). To mitigate liquidity risk due to dollarization of deposits, the authorities set a higher statutory liquidity ratio (reserve ratio) on FCDs than those on local currency deposits. Reserve requirements on FCDs are higher than, and often twice as high as, those on local currency deposits. Banks hold liquidity in foreign assets such as deposits in banks abroad and US treasury bonds. This in turn hampers credit creation in the economy.

With a numerical example, we illustrate the adverse effect of high liquidity ratio control on credit growth in the context of the underdeveloped banking system. Suppose that a simplified balance sheet of a bank is depicted as $R + L \equiv D + K$, where R stands for reserves, L for loans, D for deposits, and K for bank capital. We consider two prudential regulations; one is capital adequacy ratio control,

$$K/L \geqslant \gamma, \tag{2}$$

where γ stands for the minimum capital adequacy ratio. The other is liquidity ratio control, $R \geq \alpha D$, where α refers to the statutory reserve requirement ratio or liquidity ratio. Using the balance sheet identity, we can rewrite the liquidity ratio control as

$$L \leqslant (1 - \alpha)D + K \tag{3}$$

As for Eqs. (2) and (3), we divide both hand sides of inequality by D. With this setting, we can depict the impact of these two regulations on credit creation as in Fig. 6. In this figure, the vertical axis represents the loans to deposit ratio, and the horizontal axis represents the bank capital to deposit ratio. The shaded area is where a bank can operate under the two prudential controls.

In Fig. 6, we depict two types of banks. The bank in Point A absorbs larger deposits relative to its capital. The bank in Point B has smaller deposits relative to its capital. We consider banks in the underdeveloped financial sector are close to Point B as they are still in the early stage of savings mobilization. For banks around Point B, the liquidity ratio control binds the loans while the capital adequacy ratio control is slack.

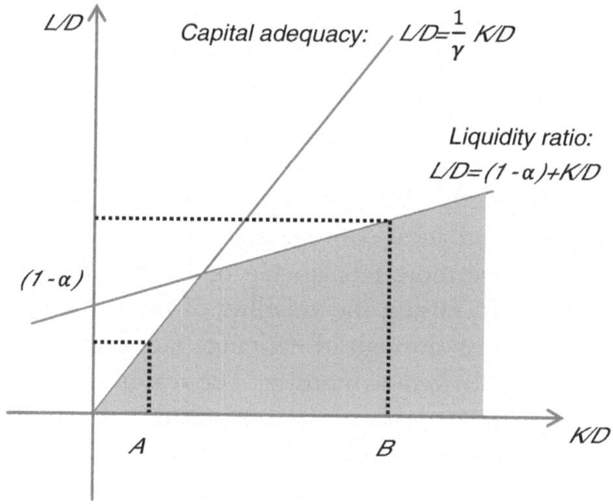

Fig. 6 Prudential regulations and credit creation. *Source* Author

Then, arise in α has contractionary effect on loans, as it lowers the intercept term $(1-\alpha)$ of the liquidity ratio control, which compresses the upper bound of loans. The contractionary effect of a higher liquidity ratio is thus more prominent in the underdeveloped banking system.

Comparison of the banking sector of Cambodia, Lao PDR, and Vietnam in Chap. 7 illustrates that disintermediation due to dollarization of the bank balance sheet is a threat. As for highly dollarized Cambodia, the authorities impose high liquidity requirements on banks in the face of the central bank's impaired lender-of-last-resort capacity. While the high liquidity of banks can be attributed to other factors such as stagnant demand for loans and lack of creditworthy borrowers, it can be also associated with the prudential regulation under dollarization.

6.2 Constraint on Monetary and Exchange Rate Policies

When exchange rate volatility translates into fragility of the dollarized banking system due to currency mismatch on bank balance sheets, there is a greater need for the monetary authorities to stabilize the exchange rate. This imposes a constraint on the flexibility of monetary and exchange rate policies in a dollarized economy.

At the same time, without interventions from the monetary authorities, the exchange rate *ceteris paribus* could be more unstable in partially dollarized economies (Balino et al. 1999). As foreign-currency-denominated assets and local-currency-denominated assets are a close substitute, there can be more rebalancing of an asset portfolio between the two types of assets, raising the volatility of the exchange rate.[9]

Furthermore, the pass-through of exchange rate change into inflation could be higher in dollarized economies. The reason is that, in addition to tradable goods, non-tradable goods are priced in foreign currency in countries with currency substitution.[10] Alvarez-Plata and Garcia-Herrero (2010) present the empirical evidence that the pass-through of currency depreciation to inflation is more significant and persistent in highly dollarized economies than in countries with moderate or low degrees of dollarization. Analogously, Goujon (2006) argues that, in the face of pass-through due to dollarization in Vietnam, disinflation required a stable nominal exchange rate. A rigid nominal exchange rate, however, leaves the money supply more like an endogenous variable rather than a policy target, which would undermine price stability.

Finally, in CLMV countries, the scope of monetary policy is narrow in the first place owing to the two below factors. First, because of the underdeveloped financial market, the transmission channel of monetary policy is limited, so the monetary authorities must rely on monetary (reserve money) targeting. Second, due to dollarization, the portion of the monetary aggregate that the monetary authorities can control directly (i.e., reserve money and local currency deposits) is narrow as well; this is especially the case for Cambodia (de Zamaroczy and Sa 2002).

7 Measures for De-dollarization

'The most effective "de-dollarization" measures are likely to be those that limit the *need* for dollar instruments' (Balino et al. 1999: 24). As inflation erodes the value of local-currency-denominated assets and raises the transaction costs for a settlement that stimulates the needs for foreign-currency-denominated assets, macroeconomic stabilization is considered to be indispensable for de-dollarization. Apart from that, de-dollarization measures listed in the literature[11] include development of financial instruments alternative to foreign-currency-denominated assets, exchange rate policy and exchange rate volatility, prudential banking regulations to create gaps in price/yield between local- and foreign-currency-denominated liabilities/assets, and nonmarket-based measures such as restrictions forcing vendors to price goods in local currency.

Based on the contrasting trajectories of dollarization in Cambodia with those of its peers, we contend that macroeconomic stabilization affects asset substitution and currency substitution differently. Macroeconomic stabilization reduces the need for instrument to hedge inflation, giving impetus to unraveling asset substitution. In contrast, while macroeconomic stabilization also reduces the transaction costs of pricing and settlements in local currency, network externalities of payment dollarization require more incentives for corporations and households to switch their currency for settlements from foreign currency to local currency. As far as more people use foreign currency for payments and settlements, it is more convenient to continue to hold and use foreign currency. Therefore, to unravel payments dollarization, in addition to macroeconomic stabilization, additional measures would be required to give incentives for currency switching, or disincentives for making settlements in foreign currency.

Regulations on the use of foreign currency for settlements of domestic transactions might mitigate payment dollarization. Cambodia's peer countries have prohibited settlements of domestic transactions using foreign currency, though not always fully enforced, whereas Cambodia has not. As conditions were different among the CLMV countries, especially the size of foreign currency in circulation, we cannot easily prove the impact of prohibition of domestic transaction settlement in foreign currency on payments dollarization. However, we still contend that it is useful to overview what measures these countries have taken to control dollarization. Chapters 3 and 5 present comprehensive lists of de-dollarization measures taken in Lao PDR and Vietnam, respectively.

Regarding dollarization that is potentially attributable to restrictions on convertibility for current international transactions, addressing the need for foreign currency is the basis of a de-dollarization policy. Elimination of restrictions on currency convertibility is essential for unraveling this form of dollarization. If network externalities take root into this form of dollarization, liberalizing the current international transactions, however, might not be enough to dissolve dollarization, as has proven to be the case in Myanmar (Chap. 4).

8 Outline of This Book

By exploring dollarization episodes of individual countries, the four-country study chapters illustrate some similarities and more differences of dollarization features among the CLMV countries. As for Cambodia, Lao PDR, and Vietnam, large inflows of foreign currency banknotes in the underdeveloped financial system characterized dollarization differently as follows.

In Cambodia, large inflows of US dollar banknotes prompted payment dollarization. The data from the survey of households and firms, however, indicate that the use of US dollar for payments varied between urban and rural areas, and across supply chains (Chap. 2). In addition, by comparing Cambodia with Lao PDR and Vietnam, we could attribute the widespread use of US dollar to accommodating foreign exchange management regulations (Chap. 7).

In Lao PDR, macro-level and micro-level data on deposits indicate that significant saving mobilization and financial deepening coincided with a decline in dollarization (Chap. 3). Saving mobilization is most attributable to local currency fixed deposits which grew much faster than foreign currency fixed deposits. In contrast, growth in foreign currency current deposits kept pace with local currency current deposits. These imply that financial dollarization as seen in fixed deposits subsided in the process of financial deepening, whereas payment dollarization as seen in current deposits prolonged. In addition, in line with observations of Cambodia, deposit dollarization is more pronounced for the urban-based banks than the rural-based bank.

In Vietnam, the monetary authority initially resorted to liberal policies to harness foreign currency in circulation to financial intermediation and accommodated dollarization, and it later tried to manage dollarization with various administrative controls (Chap. 5). In comparison with exchange rate and price stability, de-dollarization appeared to be a subordinate policy target of the monetary authority. Analogous to Lao PDR, dollarization subsided along with financial development. Vietnam's experiences offer a useful case study to overview possible de-dollarization measures.

As for Myanmar, in contrast to the other three countries, holding of foreign-currency-denominated assets has been more associated with limited currency convertibility and administrative controls on foreign exchange (Chap. 4). Strict controls on foreign exchange, relatively large stock of local currency in circulation, and the correlation between regulatory changes and trends of monetary aggregates suggest that asset substitution and currency substitution are not still prevalent in this country.

Finally, two thematic studies complement the country case studies. First, by focusing on the roles of banks in dollarization, Chap. 7 draws salient characteristics of the banking systems under dollarization in Cambodia, Lao PDR, and Vietnam. Unlike banks in Eastern Europe, dollarization in Cambodia, Lao PDR, and Vietnam was not driven by a rapid inflow of overseas dollar funds intermediated through banks. Rather, the banks in these countries raised foreign currency deposits domestically and channeled in the local market, which may add to persistence of dollarization. In addition, accommodative regulations are also considered to exacerbate payment dollarization in Cambodia.

Second, Chap. 6 reconsiders the relationship among economic growth, monetary policy, and dollarization in the context of the CLMV countries. The balance between the benefits and costs of dollarization may not be constant along the way of financial development. Dollarization can be conducive to saving mobilization at least in the circumstance where the banking system faces difficulties in mobilizing savings in local currency. Chapter 6 further alerts that the costs of dollarization in terms of loss of the effectiveness of monetary policy may be over-stated for the CLMV countries. The underdeveloped financial markets in these countries do not allow the authorities to conduct monetary policy in the first place, and increasing economic integration to the global economy in recent years would erode the autonomy of monetary policy.

Notes

1. The definition of dollarization in this section draws on Gulde et al. (2004).
2. During the author's visit to National Bank of Cambodia (NBC) in December 2015, the officials of NBC stressed that pricing in US dollar is highly compatible with settlements in US dollars. Although sellers accept payments in Khmer Riel, they offer an exchange rate that undervalues the Khmer riel, giving incentives for buyers to pay in the currency that the goods are priced, namely US dollars. Interestingly, the same issue is raised in Lao PDR in Chap. 3 of this volume.
3. Dowd and Greenaway (1993) offer a formal model to show that network externalities lead to persistence in the choice of currency that people use.
4. Menon (2008) presents an intuitive numerical example of this valuation effect of depreciation on dollarization indices.
5. We cannot present the estimate for Lao PDR and Myanmar as there are no data on initial stock of foreign currency in circulation for them.
6. Another positive effect of FCLs is that from the viewpoint of exporters, FCLs present to them a convenient scheme to hedge exchange rate risk. Exporters are usually exposed to currency mismatch as their income is in foreign currency and their expenditure is in local currency. An appreciation of the local currency against foreign currencies reduces their export revenues in terms of local currency, and worsens their financial position. FCLs serve as a substitute for foreign exchange forward contracts; by borrowing in foreign currency, exporters can match the denomination of liabilities with their forthcoming export revenues.
7. In Myanmar the authorities in principle restricted sources of FCDs to formal export revenues of corporations.
8. When banks undertake credit creation in dollars, the foreign-currency-denominated assets and liabilities of the banking system inevitably expand larger than the net foreign assets of the banking system. This leaves the banking system vulnerable to runs on FCDs.

9. One episode that shows the sudden rebalancing from foreign-currency-denominated assets to domestic-currency-denominated assets is the disposal of government properties in Myanmar before the turnover of the military junta to the new government in 2011. When the junta underwent large-scale sales of blue-chip state assets, it required that buyers pay in local currency. This reportedly caused repatriation of cross-border deposits and led to a sharp appreciation of the domestic currency against the dollar.
10. However, very highly dollarized economies like Cambodia, where local currency is used only for settlements in small-scale non-tradables, are insulated from the adverse effects of exchange rate fluctuations (de Zamaroczy and Sa 2002).
11. It includes Balino et al. (1999), Ize and Levy-Yeyati (2005), Galindo and Leiderman (2005), Erasmus et al. (2009), Kokenyne et al. (2010), and Garcia-Escribano and Sosa (2011).

References

Alvarez-Plata, P., and A. Garcia-Herrero. 2010. Dollarization and monetary stability. In *Dealing with multiple currencies in transitional economies,* ed. G. Capannelli and J. Menon. Manila: Asian Development Bank. http://www.adb.org/publications/dealing-multiple-currencies-transitional-economies-scope-regional-cooperation-cambodia.

Balino, T.J.T., A. Bennett, and F. Borensztein. 1999. Monetary policy in dollarized economies. Occasional Paper 171. Washington, DC: International Monetary Fund.

Calvo, G.A., and C.A. Vegh. 1992. Currency substitution in developing countries: An introduction. *Revista de Analisis Economico* 7 (1): 3–28.

Capannelli, G., and J. Menon (eds.). 2010. *Dealing with multiple currencies in transitional economies*. Manila: Asian Development Bank. http://www.adb.org/publications/dealing-multiple-currencies-transitional-economies-scope-regional-cooperation-cambodia.

de Nicolo, G., P. Honohan, and A. Ize. 2005. Dollarization of bank deposits: Causes and consequences. *Journal of Banking & Finance* 29 (7): 1697–1727.

de Zamaroczy, M., and S. Sa. 2002. Macroeconomic adjustment in a highly dollarized economy: The case of Cambodia. IMF Working Paper WP/02/92. Washington, DC: International Monetary Fund.

Dodsworth, J.R., A. Chopra, C.D. Pham, and H. Shishido. 1996. Macroeconomic experiences of the transition economies in Indochina. IMF Working Paper WP/96/112. Washington, DC: International Monetary Fund. http://papers.ssrn.com/sol3/papers.cfm?abstract_id=883008.

Dowd, K., and G. Greenaway. 1993. Currency competition, network externalities and switching costs: Towards an alternative view of optimum currency areas. *Economic Journal* 103 (420): 1180–1189.

Duma, N. 2011. Dollarization in Cambodia: Causes and policy implications. IMF Working Paper WP/11/49. Washington, DC: International Monetary Fund.

Erasmus, L., J. Leichter, and J. Menkulasi. 2009. Dedollarization in Liberia—lessons from cross-country experience. IMF Working Paper WP/09/37. Washington, DC: International Monetary Fund.

Freund, C., and N. Spatafora. 2008. Remittances, transaction costs, and informality. *Journal of Development Economics* 86 (2): 356–366.

Galindo, A., and L. Leiderman. 2005. Living with dollarization and the route to dedollarization. Research Department Working Paper #526. Washington, DC: Inter-American Development Bank. http://papers.ssrn.com/sol3/papers.cfm?abstract_id=1818726.

Garcia-Escribano, M., and S. Sosa. 2011. What is driving financial de-dollarization in Latin America? IMF Working Paper WP/11/10. Washington, DC: International Monetary Fund.

Girardin, E. 2010. Measuring dollarization. In *Dealing with multiple currencies in transitional economies,* ed. G. Capannelli and J. Menon. Manila: Asian Development Bank. http://www.adb.org/publications/dealing-multiple-currencies-transitional-economies-scope-regional-cooperation-cambodia.

Goujon, M. 2006. Fighting inflation in a dollarized economy: The case of Vietnam. *Journal of Comparative Economics* 34 (3): 564–581.

Gulde, A.M., D. Hoelscher, A. Ize, D. Marston, and G. de Nicolo. 2004. Financial stability in dollarized economies. IMF Occasional Paper 230. Washington, DC: International Monetary Fund.

Ize, A., and E. Levy-Yeyati. 2003. Financial dollarization. *Journal of International Economics* 59 (2): 323–347.

Ize, A., and E. Levy-Yeyati. 2005. Financial de-dollarization: Is it for real? IMF Working Paper WP/05/187. Washington, DC: International Monetary Fund.

Kokenyne, A., J. Ley, and R. Veyrune. 2010. Dedollarization. IMF Working Paper WP/10/188. Washington, DC: International Monetary Fund.

Levy-Yeyati, E. 2006. Financial dollarization: Evaluating the consequences. *Economic Policy* 21 (45): 61–118.

Menon, J. 2008. Dealing with multiple currencies: What options for the transitional economies of Southeast Asia? *Journal of the Asia Pacific Economy* 13 (2): 131–146.

Mwase, N., and F.Y. Kumah. 2015. Revisiting the concept of dollarization: The global financial crisis and dollarization in low-income countries. IMF Working Paper WP15/12. Washington, DC: International Monetary Fund.

Pani, M. 2002. Dollarization in the Lao PDR. In *Lao People's Democratic Republic: Selected issues and statistical appendix*. IMF Country Report No. 02/61. Washington, DC: International Monetary Fund.

Ra, H.R. 2008. Modeling the dollarization: A case study for Cambodia, Laos and Vietnam. *Global Economic Review* 37 (2): 157–169.

Samreth, S. 2011. An empirical study on the hysteresis of currency substitution in Cambodia. *Journal of Asian Economics* 22 (6): 518–527.

Unteroberdoerster, O. 2002. Foreign currency deposits in Vietnam—Trends and policy issues. In *Vietnam: Selected issues and statistical appendix*. IMF Country Report No. 02/5. Washington, DC: International Monetary Fund.

Valev, N. 2010. The hysteresis of currency substitution: Currency risk vs. network externalities. *Journal of International Money and Finance* 29 (2): 224–235.

Watanabe, S. 2006. Dollarization, remittances and monetary policies in Cambodia, Lao PDR and Vietnam. Paper presented at the workshop of Asian Development Bank Institute: Enhancing Banks' Intermediation Role, April 17–19, 2006, Tokyo. http://www.adbi.org/files/2006.05.10.cpp.dollarization.paper.pdf

Watanabe, S. 2007. De facto dollarization and its effect on financial development and economic growth of Cambodia, Lao PDR and Vietnam. Paper presented at the conference: Policy options and challenges for Developing Asia–Perspectives from the IMF and Asia, April 19–20, 2007, Tokyo. https://www.imf.org/External/NP/seminars/eng/2007/jbic/pdf/s3/03_2%20paper.pdf.

2

Dollarization in Cambodia: Behavior of Households and Enterprises in a Highly Dollarized Environment

Ken Odajima

1 Introduction

Although the Cambodian government never officially adopted dollarization, Cambodia has become one of the most dollarized economies around the world. The US dollar (USD) is the most common foreign currency (FC) not just for commercial transactions, but for everyday transactions in general. In spite of the stabilized macroeconomic conditions and solid economic development for the past decade, dollarization never abated. According to the National Bank of Cambodia, the ratio of foreign currency deposits (FCDs) to broad money reached around 83% in 2015 from 56% in 1995, and FCD accounted for 95% of total deposits by the end of 2015. Normally, dollarization may cease or decline in pace during times of economic and political stability. Given the stable

K. Odajima (✉)
JICA Research Institute, Japan International Cooperation Agency (JICA), Tokyo, Japan
e-mail: Odajima.Ken@jica.go.jp

K. Kubo (ed.), *Dollarization and De-dollarization in Transitional Economies of Southeast Asia*, IDE-JETRO Series, DOI 10.1007/978-3-319-57768-5_2

macroeconomic conditions as well as the political situation in recent years, the persistence or even progress of dollarization is a puzzling phenomenon.

In the literature, the persistence of dollarization is associated with network externalities (Valev 2010). Network externalities refer to conditions where it is convenient for all households or firms to have foreign currency when a large number of people use and accept foreign currency for payments. However, to our knowledge, there are not many empirical studies that illustrate how network externalities work in the context of dollarization. For instance, do "networks" mean geographical boundaries, or do they mean supply chain linkage to international trade?

To shed light on network externalities of dollarization in Cambodia, a large-scale survey on dollarization of households and enterprises was conducted by Japan International Cooperation Agency Research Institute (JICA-RI) in collaboration with the National Bank of Cambodia (NBC), the central bank, in late 2014. Using data collected during a survey conducted from October 2014 to January 2015, we aim to draw a detailed picture of dollarization to infer the underlying mechanisms.

For the Cambodian government or the NBC, such unintended dollarization poses many challenges to the management of monetary policies. With the heavy use of foreign exchange, the NBC has only limited control over the effective level of the money supply. In addition, dollarization undermines the development of financial markets including the stock market and the interbank market. Underdevelopment of the interbank market and low demand for governmental bonds quoted in the local currency, the Khmer riel (KHR), also impairs the scope of monetary and exchange rate policies of the NBC.

The unique circumstances surrounding the introduction of the dollar to the Cambodian economy, combined with a very high level of dollarization, suggests that the process of de-dollarization is likely to be more protracted than it would otherwise be (Menon 2008). Based on the analysis made using the survey data, the present study attempts to draw implications to manage this dollarization.

This chapter is organized as follows. Section 2 overviews the relationship between economic/financial development and dollarization since 1995. Section 3 explains the trend of dollarization. Sections 4 and 5 explain household/enterprise behaviors using survey micro-data. Section 6 concludes the chapter.

2 Review on Studies Used Micro-Surveyed Data

The studies on dollarization began by investigating the determinants using macro-level aggregated data. For example, in the case of foreign currency borrowing, factors in concern have been changes in inflation rates, changes in exchange rates, and its volatility, the volume offoreign currency deposits in the banking sector, and differences in interest rates between domestic- and foreign-currency-denominated loans (interest rate differentials). Ize and Yeyati (2003) and Ize (2005) have developed important theoretical foundation framing financial dollarization, which is called the "minimum variance portfolio (MVP) hypothesis." There have been a number of studies which applied the MVP hypothesis (Luca and Petrova 2008; Basso et al. 2011; Steiner 2011; Csajbok et al. 2010; Rosenberg and Tirpak 2008). These studies attempted to find evidence of the influence of interest rate differentials on foreign currency borrowing both theoretically and empirically though their findings are still ambiguous.

As regard for network externality, Samreth (2011), using macro- and financial sector data published by the National Bank of Cambodia, showed that there is evidence supporting the existence of network externality. Due to data limitation, he approximated the accumulated experience of foreign currency usage which reflects the network externality by the past peak value of currency substitution calculated using nominal exchange rate, foreign currency deposit, and money stock (M1). As he mentioned, his study had its limitation that further detailed study was needed in order to design appropriate policies and mechanisms for de-dollarization under the existence of network externality since he could not examine its detail background. Most of the previous studies have investigated the factors relating to dollarization using macro-level aggregated data. Even when investigating dollarization in relation to behavior of economic agents, the macro-aggregated data has been used due to lack of survey-based micro-data.

In contrast to the aggregated data, micro-data is suitable for researchers to use when analyzing the behavior of economic agents in detail, particularly when looking at the motive behind their currency choice. As clearly stated by Fidrmuc et al. (2013), the analysis of macroeconomic data cannot fully investigate all factors raised in theoretical models of foreign currency borrowing for two main reasons. First, with aggregate data, it is difficult to empirically separate demand from supply effects. This problem can to some extent overcome with the usage of micro-data. Second, many theoretical assumptions are based on expectations for which ex-post values of exchange rate data have been used as a proxy in current literature. By employing the expectation data by household, it is possible to overcome this issue. Micro-data would tell researchers the real picture of how economic agents are involved in dollarization process and which supply or demand factor is an important driver of dollarization.

Under such understanding, in recent years there has been an increase in literature using micro-data, particularly on foreign currency borrowing within households and firms, though most of their concerned countries were in Europe (Pellényi and Bilek 2009; Beer et al. 2010; Brown et al. 2011; Fidrmuc et al. 2013; Beckman and Stix 2015). Pellinyi and Bilek (2009) exploited survey-based data of Hungarian households to investigate determinants of foreign currency borrowing. They found that foreign currency borrowing appeared to be a universal phenomenon in the case of Hungary, and driven by persistently large interest rate spreads and massive underestimation of currency risk. Beer et al. (2010) investigated characteristics of foreign currency (Swiss franc) borrowers in Austria. They found that less financially literate and less risk-averse households were more likely to take out a housing loan in foreign currency. From those findings, the authors concluded that Swiss franc borrowing might be driven by households which involved in the carry trade.

Using survey-based data of households from nine Central and Eastern European countries (CEECs), Fidrmuc et al. (2013) have studied the determinants of foreign currency borrowing by households. Exploiting rich data, they have used both macroeconomic and household-specific variables to test the hypotheses. Beckmann and Stix (2015) have further investigated households' foreign currency borrowing behaviors, in particular, the relationship between the exchange rate risk and foreign currency borrowing, using the same data from Central and Eastern European countries as Fidrmuc et al. (2013). They showed that knowledge about the exchange rate risk enhances the impact of a household's expectations of depreciation on their choice of loan currency.

By and large, previous empirical studies on household borrowing have showed mixed results relating to the relationship between foreign currency borrowing and household characteristics. For example, Pellényi and Bilek (2009) found that households with a high income are less likely to borrow in a foreign currency. In contrast, Beer et al. (2010) and Fidrmuc et al. (2013) found that households with a higher income are more likely to take out foreign currency loans, especially in non-EU and heavily "euroized" countries. Brown et al. (2011) examined the firm- and country-level determinants of foreign currency borrowing by small firms, using detail information on loan extended to firms. They found that foreign currency borrowing is significantly related to firm-level foreign currency revenues. Their findings suggested that borrowers of foreign currency loans were in better position to manage currency risks than is commonly thought.

In terms of network externalities, as far as the author's best knowledge, only Valev (2010) used surveyed data to examine factors for persistent use of foreign currency. Using survey data in Bulgaria he showed that foreign currencies were preferred in transaction if they were widely used already and if local currency was expected to depreciate, confirming the hysteresis of dollarization.

In this manner, until recent, to best of the author's knowledge, usage of micro-evidence has been limited to cases in European countries and scarce in the other regions. However, there were only two cases done by Khou (2012) and Siregar and Chan (2014). They tried to identify driving factors behind the holding of foreign currency by households in Cambodia. Using their unique dataset, they identified key features and characteristics of household's holding patterns of foreign currencies. Their results suggested that factors such as income level, economic sector, or access to finance determine the level of foreign currency holding.

Siregar and Chan (2014) mentioned some shortcomings of their study. It is ideal to extend the survey at the firm level to gain better understanding of firms by industry and area. Moreover, as for household survey, it would be better to cover remaining seven provinces, not covered in their survey. Those provinces are mainly located in either Thai bordered or Vietnamese bordered areas where residents are expected to hold not only USD but also Thai Baht or Vietnamese Dong as foreign currencies. It would have enriched the results. It should also be extended to currency holding not only "at home" but also at bank/MFI accounts or other formal/informal mode to get better pictures of currency choice of people. If their resource constraint allows it, questionnaire would have covered not only just cash holding but also income currency, expenditure currency, or borrowing currency so as to get more comprehensive pictures of household behavior. Though they had done the first step in the context of Cambodia, there are several rooms for improvement.

The questionnaire of the survey conducted by JICA and NBC covers incomes by currencies, expenditures by items and by currencies, saving by modes of holding and by currencies, borrowing details including currencies, and perceptions for usage of foreign currencies. The data allows us to control a broad set of explanatory variables, including their expectation, observed at individual household level. For instance, it contains detailed information about loans taken out by households, which allows us to examine risk-hedging behaviors of households in currency choice when borrowing. The dataset allows us to investigate the households' characteristics in more detail, especially in currency composition of income stream, financial assets, and loans. Such detailed dataset may develop a deeper understanding of households' behaviors in foreign currency borrowing.

3 Development of Dollarization and the Financial Sector

After independence from France in 1953, Cambodia experienced a relatively short period of peace, political stability, and stable but fragile economic conditions. From 1970, increasing strife in the region led to internal turmoil. The following two decades could be illustrated as continuous process for eroding confidence, trust, and credibility on the riel given the political instability. The period 1970–1975 was characterized by a civil war, when Cambodia had its first experience with limited dollarization during the LunNol regime (1970–1975), as increases in US military personnel and assistance brought dollars into the country (De Zamaroczy and Sa 2002).

When the civil war ended with the Khmer Rouge taking office in April 1975, the Khmer Rouge regime introduced an extreme revolutionary program. It included bans on banking and even on money, and therefore the riel. The central bank was closed and the financial infrastructure was completely destroyed. Once the Khmer Rouge regime was ended in 1979, the central bank was reestablished, and in March 1980, the riel was reintroduced.

Since the reestablishment of the NBC, the banking system had been a mono-banking system, that is, a state-owned mono-bank with central, commercial, and development banking roles. The Foreign Trade Bank was established simultaneously inside the NBC to provide commercial banking services. Dollars started to flow into the country in the mid-1980, as the United Nations (UN) dispatched humanitarian and emergency aid, international non-governmental organizations (NGOs) were allowed to operate, and remittances from abroad resumed. During the 1980s, the country achieved only limited monetization and most domestic transactions were based on barter, with gold being the universal commodity for transacting and hoarding (De Zamaroczy and Sa 2002).

From 1989, the country started to seek the two-tier banking system, which was a gradual reform to separate the commercial banking function from the NBC. Nonetheless, lack of confidence in local currency, hyperinflation, and massive exchange devaluation of the riel against the dollar during 1988–1991 pushed the public to sell their riel-denominated assets in exchange for gold and dollars (Pum and Vanak 2010).

The use of the dollar was further facilitated by large inflows during the operation of the United Nations Transitional Authority in Cambodia (UNTAC). During 1991–1992, UNTAC; brought US $1.7 billion, equivalent to about 75% of GDP at that time, mostly spent for rent and local services for its peacekeeping operation (De Zamaroczy and Sa 2002). FCDs became an important component of the bank deposit base

(Rumbaugh et al. 2000). Under the two-tier banking system, the first privately owned commercial bank, Cambodian Commercial Bank, was established as a joint venture between Siam Commercial Bank and the NBC in July 1991 to attract investors and serve the activities of UNTAC (Pum and Vanak 2010).

From 1993, the political regime was officially transformed into a democratic framework, and the economy was transformed from the centralized and planned system to a market-oriented economy, and property rights were gradually strengthened. However, the legal foundation for two-tier banking system was established only after promulgation of the Law on the Organization and Operations of the NBC (January 26, 1996), the Law on the Foreign Exchange (August 22, 1997), and the Law on Banking and Financial Institutions (November 18, 1999).

Based on this foundation, the NBC started a series of important reforms from 1998 to 2001. It abolished of the requirement of 15% NBC stake in all private banks, introduced a new classification of financial institutions into commercial banks, specialized banks and microfinance institutions (MFIs), and increased minimum capital requirement of commercial banks (Praka[1] on Commercial Bank's Minimum Capital, February 9, 2000).

By the Law on Banking and Financial Institutions, re-licensing process was implemented to restructure the banking system. At that time several commercial banks had unstable financial positions, while others had insufficient solvency ratios. The re-licensing process resulted in a significant reduction in the number of banks in the system to ensure that those that remained were strong enough to make a meaningful contribution to the development of the economy (NBC 2005). In other words, the re-licensing was designed to establish viable banks, foster public confidence in the banking system, and promote savings.

The spread between official and market exchange rates in Cambodia averaged 20% during 1989–1992. From November 1992, the NBC began maintaining the official rate within a 5-% margin of the average parallel market rate over the previous 2-week period. The spread between the two rates was subsequently narrowed further, so that from March 1994 the official exchange rate was generally maintained in the vicinity of

1% of the market rate on a daily basis (Dodsworth et al. 1996). Until now, we can observe that the divergence between official and market rates has been kept marginal regardless of their fluctuation.

There are two recent initiatives to developing the financial market of Cambodia: establishing a stock exchange market and introducing Negotiable Certificates of Deposit (NCDs). As for security exchange, the market began trading with one listing in April 2012. Listing is only allowed in KHR, but transactions can be made in either KHR or USD. To make any settlements in USD, the buyer and seller must have an agreement as to the exchange rate to be used; otherwise, the settlement must be done in riel. As of the end of 2015, only three companies[2] are listed, and traded volume is quite low. NCDs were introduced in September 2015 to promote the development of a money market and interbank lending on a secured basis (securities can be used as collateral for repo-transactions). NCDs are currency neutral and can be issued in either riel or USD.

The Cambodian economy enjoyed steady growth, resulting in per capita GDP at the level of over US $1000 (Fig. 1). At the same time, it attained low inflation, averaging 4.1% from 2009 to 2013, and the

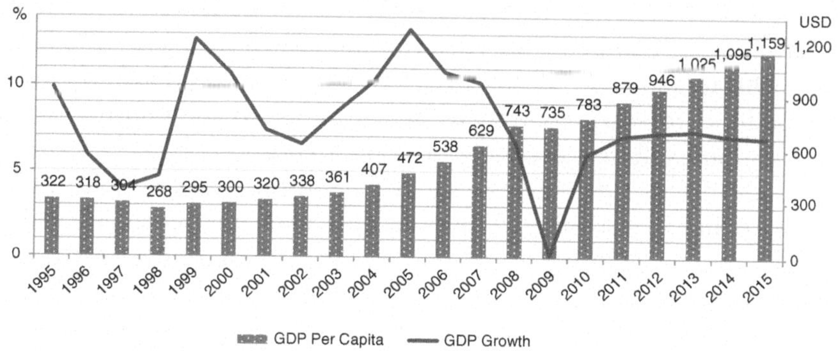

Fig. 1 Trend of GDP growth and GDP per capita, Cambodia, 1995–2015. *Sources* International Financial Statistics, International Monetary Fund (IMF); National Bank of Cambodia

exchange rate was kept stable (Fig. 2(A), Chap. 1). However, the Cambodian economy exhibits structural vulnerability. According to Duma (2014), Cambodia economy has two parallel worlds: One is a dollar-based urban economy comprising a flourishing garment sector, tourism, construction, foreign direct investment, and aid. The other is a generally riel-based rural economy that is dependent on agriculture. Although the garment and services sectors, including tourism, are driving the economic growth, the exports base remains narrow and backward linkages of the manufacturing and service sectors to the rural economy are very limited. Moreover, the banking system is heavily concentrated in urban areas but is lacking an efficient network between the urban and rural branches. This concentration and fragmentation of the system imposes risks to economic stability (Duma 2014).

4 Degree of Dollarization

4.1 Measuring Dollarization

Cambodia became a*de facto* dollarized economy during 1991–1995 (De Zamaroczy and Sa 2002), and it is still as dollarized, if not more so, than it was 10 years ago. Measured as the ratio of FCDs to broad money, dollarization in Cambodia has risen continuously from about 60% in the late 1990s to about 85% in 2013 (Fig. 1(A), Chap. 1). Dollarization in Cambodia is in sharp contrast to that in other Asian countries, where dollarization exhibits a declining or stable trend.

From 1997 to 1998 there was a decline in the ratios of dollarization due to political instability. However, this may not be interpreted as de-dollarization. During this period, the composition of dollar-denominated assets held by agents still changed (De Zamaroczy and Sa 2002) through withdrawal of dollar deposits. Though the ratio of FCDs to domestic currency deposits shows several fluctuations over decades, other ratios show a constant increasing trend (Fig. 1(A), Chap. 1).

4.2 Motives for Holding Foreign Currencies

As noted in the introductory chapter of this volume, there are three motives for holding foreign-currency-denominated assets: precautionary demand under foreign exchange restrictions, currency substitution, and asset substitution. Because foreign exchange is freely available through the parallel market, in Cambodia precautionary demand is rather limited. There are demands for foreign currency in terms of the latter two motives, however.

4.2.1 Financial Dollarization, Asset Substitution, and Currency Substitution

Several studies suggest that financial dollarization may occur in periods of macroeconomic turbulence, in particular under high inflation, as the confidence in the local currency deteriorates. If the usage of foreign currency spreads out further, then dollarization may develop into payment dollarization. The environment that brought about dollarization to Cambodia is somewhat different from other dollarized economies. As Okuda (2013) noted, in case of Cambodia, payment dollarization started before financial dollarization, or at least developed simultaneously. The Khmer Rouge regime Cambodia was without a monetary system, or indeed, money. Even after the regime, in the 1980s, the country achieved only limited monetization and most domestic transactions were based on barter, with gold being the universal means of transacting and hoarding (De Zamaroczy and Sa 2002). Therefore, when there was a surge in dollar inflow during UNTAC operations, in fact there was virtually nothing that could perform the function of money, payment, widely accepted by the public. In other words, payment dollarization (means of payment) and real dollarization (unit of account) developed before financial dollarization (store of value). As Duma (2014) and Menon (2008) noted, the rise in dollarization, particularly from 2000, has not necessarily come about through substitution of local currency for foreign currency, but rather replacement of FCDs with foreign currency cash outside the banking sector.

In terms of financial dollarization, through strong and continuous inflow, the dollar became a major depositary base in the banking system. Financial deepening was advanced using dollar deposits. Riel deposits have grown eightfold from 2005 to 2013. During the same period, FCDs have grown at about the same rate. The riel deposit remains only around 2% of GDP in 2013, while the FCDs have expanded beyond 40% of GDP. Although financial intermediation using the riel has increased, mainly in rural areas, dollar intermediation was by far larger, advancing financial dollarization.

4.2.2 Persistence of Dollarization: Hysteresis and Network Externalities

Samreth (2011) showed that dollarization in Cambodia has reached the state of hysteresis. Currency substitution develops further when there is evidence supporting the existence of network externalities, implying the hysteresis of the currency substitution in Cambodia. The concept of hysteresis extends all the way from simple inertia to path-dependence to rigid irreversibility. Basically, it suggests that Cambodian-specific history matters, and that there can be nonlinearity, or stickiness, in the system, that must be taken into account to understand the process of dollarization, or its unraveling (Menon 2008).

Reconstruction of the economy after the destruction of the economic and financial system in the late 1970s and economic mismanagement in the 1980s took place using the dollar, which had high confidence from the public. As the reconstruction process started to move, a monetization process and reestablished of banking system began. In this manner, the number of people using the dollar for transaction increased along with recovery and development progress of the financial system. During this process, externalities for usage of the dollar emerged, developed, and enhanced. If transactions in the dollar had been prohibited at that time, the development of externalities would have faced strong restrictions. However, an environment with no exchange control including purchases and sales of foreign exchange on the foreign exchange market, transfer, international settlements, and capital flows in foreign currency enabled the expansion of network externalities in the country (Okuda 2013).

5 Household Survey

The survey on dollarization of households in Cambodia was conducted in late 2014. The survey collected information on attributes of households, investigated currency usage in all 25 provinces, covering 2273 households, with stratified sampling in accordance with the General Census 2008 (covering 2,841,897 households). From each of the 25 provinces, district/communes were selected based on the location (district/communes) and representativeness. Also, we purposely selected district/communes close to the border for those provinces bordering Thailand or Vietnam to see the usage of foreign currency other than USD. The classification and selection of urban and rural communes/villages are based on the Reclassification of Urban areas of the National Institute of Statistics. Questionnaire covers relevant aspects of activities including income (revenue), expenditure, saving (assets), and borrowing.

5.1 Income

5.1.1 General View of Income Dollarization

The dataset contained not only the ratio of foreign-currency-denominated income, but also the total income of an individual household. Therefore, it is possible to calculate the general aggregated level of foreign-currency-denominated income of the household sector. Using all 25 province samples, the dollarization ratio inclusive of income denominated in any foreign currency (not only in US dollars but also in Thai baht and Vietnamese dong), was around 38%, while around 62% of total household income was denominated in local currency, KHR. For households, on an aggregate basis, KHR was the dominant currency for income.

First, we classify income sources of households into salary/wage income, income from business ownership, and income from agriculture.

When looking into the foreign-currency-denominated income by source of income, we can observe that salary/wage income had highest ratio of foreign currency, at around 50%, while those from business ownership and from agriculture were around 25 and 10%, respectively. Thus, at the aggregate level, salary/wage payment was a key driver for income dollarization. Specifically, the data suggested that among wage earners, those engaged in the garment/shoe sector, which was the major export sector of the country, had the highest foreign currency ratio of income.

It is possible to observe a somewhat positive relationship between income level and dollarization. The lowest group of income (less than US $300 equivalent) had a relatively low level of income dollarization, around 25%. From the second-lowest group (US $300–500) to the fourth-lowest group (US $1000–5000) income dollarization ratios stay around 30–35%. The highest-income group showed the highest dollarization ratio, which was double the level of the lowest group.

The level of income dollarization differed by source (agriculture, business ownership, and wage/salary) and by level of income. Income from agriculture had the lowest ratio in all categories of income levels. Income from wage/salary showed the highest ratio in all level of income except for the highest category of more than US $5000. Dollarization of income from business ownership had a clear increasing trend with the level of income, and was highest in the highest-income category. Dollarization of income from wage/salary was highest in all categories of income level, except for in the highest group of more than US $5000.

5.1.2 Micro-Level of Income Dollarization

While aggregated figures suggest a general picture of income dollarization, micro-level data tells us that there was a significant difference between those who are in Phnom Penh and those who are not (Table 1).

Mean of income dollarization ratios of the total 2164 effective samples was 21.6%. If we divide the samples into Phnom Penh and the rest of the country, the mean values become 44.4 and 20.0%, respectively. It is clear that income dollarization was prevalent in the capital city. When we further divide each area category by income level, the highest-income

Table 1 Income dollarization

Area	Phnom Penh		Other regions	
Monthly income	N	% of FC income to total income	N	% of FC income to total income
Below USD 300	11	33.5	586	17.0
Between USD 300 and 500	19	56.4	350	21.4
Between USD 500 and 1000	33	50.8	467	22.1
Between USD 1000 and 5000	73	37.5	557	19.5
Above USD 5000	8	67.7	60	29.0
Total	144	44.4	2020	20.0

Note Out of total 2273 samples, 2164 gave effective reply on the relevant questions. *N* in the table stands for sample number in the category

groups had the highest level of foreign currency ratios, while the lowest groups had the lowest ratios, commonly in both Phnom Penh and in other regions. However, for the middle range of income groups, there was no clear positive relationship between the level of income and ratio. In all income level categories, the dollarization ratio in Phnom Penh was higher, almost double the corresponding levels in other regions. In all, we may well say that, when viewed that the individual household level, income dollarization was a phenomenon of the rich residing in Phnom Penh.

5.2 Expenditure

5.2.1 General View of Expenditure Dollarization

In our questionnaire, we asked not just the ratio of foreign-currency-denominated expenditure, but also the amount spent by individual households. It is possible to calculate the aggregated level of foreign-currency-denominated expenditure of the household sector as a whole. It is noted that some respondents replied that they did not purchase some of the items on the questionnaires during the designated period. Thus, the number of headcounts may differ by item.

Overall, the use of foreign currencies for expenditure was around 11%. This figure was far lower than the dollarization ratio measured using macro-data such as FCDs over M2. Depending on expenditure item, people used different currencies for purchase. For food and beverage, alcohol and tobacco, water and electricity, and health items including toiletries, KHR was used. Conversely, for housing (rent), communication, and furniture and appliances, foreign currency was frequently used. Depending on what was purchased, currency was differentiated. In general, durables like furniture and appliances, real estate, and related services were transacted in dollars, but others were in KHR. In other words, items that preserve their economic value for a certain period was regarded as savings in kind, and services derived from such goods were payable in dollars because they might be regarded as interest or dividend from the savings. KHR was used frequently for daily and repeated transactions. However, it should be noted that this choice of currency might not be decided at the sole discretion of buyers (household), and the result of interaction between sellers and buyers. Business practices or bargaining power between the seller and buyer, or competitiveness of the market might affect the choice of currency for transactions.

Generally, the level of income matters for expenditure dollarization. In all items, we could observe an increasing trend of foreign currency used for payment. The higher was the level of income, the higher was the ratios, that is, rich people used foreign currency frequently while the poor used it less. The ratio for food/beverage increased from 0.0 (lowest quintile of income group: q1) to 0.7% (highest quintile of income group: q5). For alcohol/tobacco, although the ratio remained relative low, it increased from 1.2 (q1) to 5.9% (q5). Expenditures for housing (rental), communications, or household items (furniture and appliances) had relatively high ratios in all categories of income level. For recreation/culture, clothing/footwear ratios were moderate, ranging from around 6–20%. Payments for restaurants, education, health including toiletries, and transportation had a low level of dollarization in all income groups. Expenditure dollarization was a clear phenomenon for the rich and for particular items.

5.2.2 Micro-Level Expenditure Dollarization

When we see the micro-level of expenditure dollarization of samples, again, there was a significant difference between those who are in Phnom Penh and in the rest of the country (Table 2).

In all items, except food, the ratios were higher in Phnom Penh than in other regions. Food expenditure showed the same level of foreign currency ratios in Phnom Penh and in other regions: both were quite low at around 2%. For expenditure of housing as well as furniture and appliance, ratios were similar, though in Phnom Penh it was slightly higher than in other regions. For such items, the richest group does not necessarily have the highest ratio. Rather, households in lower income groups also showed a rather high ratio of expenditure dollarization. For expenditures at restaurants, tobacco and alcoholic beverage, and clothing and footwear, there was a significant difference in the level of expenditure dollarization between Phnom Penh and other regions. For these items, the lowest income group in Phnom Penh nevertheless had rather high ratios. The remaining items had ratios that were twice as high in Phnom as those observed in other regions.

In all, we may well say that at the individual household level, expenditure dollarization was a phenomenon for the rich residing in Phnom Penh. There might well be a strong externality in the usage of foreign currency in Phnom Penh. However, it is noted that as for specific items, like food, housing, and furniture and appliances, the market practice or structure of the distribution channel might affect the choice of currency used, resulting in a similar level of expenditure dollarization ratios in both Phnom Penh and elsewhere.

5.3 Savings

5.3.1 Saving Dollarization

To investigate households' preference on the currency choice for assets, we study which currency they had in savings in the form of broad

Table 2 Expenditure dollarization

Phnom Penh												
Monthly Income Level	N	Food	Headcount	Tobacco and alcoholic beverage	N	Housing	N	Recreation and culture	N	Clothing and Footwear	N	Restaurant and eating out
		% of FC expenditure to total item expenditure		% of FC expenditure to total item expenditure		% of FC expenditure to total item expenditure		% of FC expenditure to total item expenditure		% of FC expenditure to total item expenditure		% of FC expenditure to total item expenditure
Below USD 300	17	0.6	2	40.0	0	na	2	50	8	55.6	7	51.4
Between USD 300 and 500	19	1.6	7	7.1	2	0.00	4	0.00	17	35.8	6	20.0
Between USD 500 and 1000	33	0	8	12.5	4	87.5	13	43.1	24	53.3	12	24.2
Between USD 1000 and 5000	72	2.4	21	14.3	8	81.3	19	45.8	50	59.2	23	31.7
Above USD 5000	8	8.8	3	66.7	3	100.0	3	60.0	8	75.0	5	56.0
Total	149	2.4	41	17.8	17	76.5	41	41.7	108	55.1	53	33.6

Phnom Penh										
Monthly Income	N	Communication	N	Education	N	Health inclu. Toiletry	N	Transportaion	N	Furniture & appliance
		% of FC expenditure to total item expenditure		% of FC expenditure to total item expenditure		% of FC expenditure to total item expenditure		% of FC expenditure to total item expenditure		% of FC expenditure to total item expenditure
Below USD 300	12	75.0	12	25.1	16	12.5	12	8.3	1	100.0
Between USD 300 and 500	19	65.7	13	12.0	18	16.1	19	0.0	3	53.3
	29	76.2	25	23.2	30	10.3	28	6.8	5	100.0

(continued)

Table 2 (continued)

Phnom Penh										
Monthly Income	N	Communication	N	Education	N	Health inclu. Toiletry	N	Transportaion	N	Furniture & appliance
		% of FC expenditure to total item expenditure		% of FC expenditure to total item expenditure		% of FC expenditure to total item expenditure		% of FC expenditure to total item expenditure		% of FC expenditure to total item expenditure
Between USD 500 and 1000										
Between USD 1000 and 5000	64	90.9	52	19.5	62	11.9	62	7.4	14	78.6
Above USD 5000	7	97.1	4	41.0	8	37.5	8	30.3	3	66.7
Total	131	82.9	106	20.[illegible]	134	13.7	129	7.7	26	79.2

Other regions												
Monthly Income	N	Food	N	Tobacco and alcoholic beverage	N	Housing	N	Recreation and culture	N	Clothing and Footwear	N	Restaurant and eating out
		% of FC expenditure to total item expenditure		% of FC expenditure to total item expenditure		% of FC expenditure to total item expenditure		% of FC expenditure to total item expenditure		% of FC expenditure to total item expenditure		% of FC expenditure to total item expenditure
Below USD 300	686	1.1	229	1.7	5	35.7	99	10.1	469	8.7	135	4.7
Between USD 300 and 500	349	3.2	112	4.6	3	35.0	60	17.9	256	13.4	75	6.7
Between USD 500 and 1000	465	2.9	168	5.4	7	50.0	105	18.3	342	21.0	114	11.2
Between USD 1000 and 5000	555	2.8	221	5.5	10	35.5	154	19.4	405	20.2	163	8.7

(continued)

Table 2 (continued)

Other regions

Monthly Income	N	Food	N	Tobacco and alcoholic beverage	N	Housing	N	Recreation and culture	N	Clothing and Footwear	N	Restaurant and eating out
		% of FC expenditure to total item expenditure		% of FC expenditure to total item expenditure		% of FC expenditure to total item expenditure		% of FC expenditure to total item expenditure		% of FC expenditure to total item expenditure		% of FC expenditure to total item expenditure
Above USD 5000	60	4.0	24	12.5	4	80.0	19	17.4	48	35.8	20	19.0
Total	2115	2.4	754	4.4	29	41.5	427	16.7	1520	16.2	507	8.3

Other regions

Monthly Income	N	Communication	N	Education	N	Health inclu. Toiletry	N	Transportaion	N	Furniture and appliance
		% of FC expenditure to total item expenditure		% of FC expenditure to total item expenditure		% of FC expenditure to total item expenditure		% of FC expenditure to total item expenditure		% of FC expenditure to total item expenditure
Below USD 300	594	22.3	403	3.9	635	3.4	567	2.2	59	39.8
Between USD 300 and 500	302	29.3	224	7.8	329	3.8	310	3.4	41	56.5
Between USD 500 and 1000	423	38.5	319	10.3	432	5.5	444	3.7	60	67.5
Between USD 1000 and 5000	511	52.1	379	11.8	511	6.1	522	4.6	100	55.9
Above USD 5000	54	51.8	44	18.0	54	17.7	57	5.1	13	61.5
Total	1884	36.0	1369	8.6	1961	5.0	1900	3.5	273	55.3

Notes The table shows the average level of foreign currency expenditure by item and by income level. *N* in the table stands for sample number in the category financial assets, in terms of cash held at home, bank deposits, and another form of saving schemes.

We find that about 60% of households in Cambodia had savings (in any form of financial assets), more specifically, out of 2237 households, 1351 households saved money. To assess currency preference in savings, we calculated the frequencies of households with KHR savings and USD savings. Surprisingly, those households with USD savings were likely to simultaneously have KHR savings, while there were also households who had savings in KHR only. Out of 2237 households with savings, 1157 households saved their money in KHR, of which 726 had only KHR savings, and 431 had both KHR and USD savings. Furthermore, out of 584 households with savings in USD, 153 had USD savings only, with the aforementioned 431 households having both KHR and USD savings. We find that Cambodian households were generally likely to save in KHR rather than USD, although USD savings were also widespread among Cambodian households.

We examine the amounts of savings by currencies. The results presented us a different picture of household's saving behaviors from what the views of households as discussed in the previous section. The sample size for the amounts of savings was reduced, since some households did not provide their amounts of savings. The mean value of amounts of saving in USD was larger than that in KHR, and about four times larger than that in KHR. Essentially, households were likely to save in KHR, and these amounts were generally small. However, it is necessary to interpret these results with caution. The amount of savings is generally related to the income level of the households. Normally, the higher is the income, the higher is the savings. There was the possibility that households with USD income tend to have a higher income than households with KHR income, and that the results then just represent the difference in income level between households with USD income or KHR income.

5.3.2 Deposits Dollarization

In terms of fund mobilization in Cambodia, formal bank deposits may play an important role and can be a key to de-dollarization as a monetary policy pathway[3]. To understand how many households have a deposit and in which currency they keep deposits, we analyze household behavior. Out of 2273 households, 459 households answered that they had more than one deposit account, which amounted to about 34% of households with savings, or 21% of the total households interviewed in the survey. The number of households having deposits seems still low despite the growing number of new entries of formal financial institutions in various forms, such as commercial banks and MFIs, suggesting that households were still intended to keep their money away from formal financial institutions.

We investigate the frequency of currency types of deposit accounts held by households. Among 459 households with deposits, 180 households answered that they had only KHR deposits, and 179 households answered that they had only USD deposits. Interestingly, more households than expected held KHR deposit accounts, and the frequency was as high as that for USD accounts. However, some of the households held two currency types of accounts at the same time. A total of 98 households answered that they had both KHR and USD deposit accounts, and two households answered that they had USD and another foreign currency accounts.

The data suggests that commercial banks were the most common option for Cambodian households for savings in formal financial institutions. In the survey, households were further asked about the type of institutions in which they had deposited. Out of 459 effective answers, we find that 324 households had an account only in commercial banks, and in total, there were 365 households and accounts in commercial banks. A total of 88 had an account only in MFI. A total of 35 households had more than one deposit and had accounts in both commercial banks and MFI simultaneous. Furthermore, we find that 12 households had an account in other informal institutions.[4] To investigate which currency was common in each institution, we calculate the frequencies of the currency type of deposits by institutions. There seems to be no clear difference in currency types between institutions, although the ratios of KHR deposits were slightly higher in commercial banks than in either MFI or other informal institutions.

5.3.3 Regional Difference in Currency Choice

We investigate whether there is any difference in foreign currency-saving behavior between regions, dividing the sample into Phnom Penh and the rest of the country. First, Table 3 shows the number of KHR/USD savings by regions. We find that households in Phnom Penh were more likely to have USD savings than households in the rest of the country. However, there is no clear difference in the popularity of KHR savings between Phnom Penh and the rest of the country. The percentages of having KHR savings both in Phnom Penh and the rest of the country were considerably high, 82 and 86%, respectively. This suggests that it was common for Cambodian households to save in KHR, and dollarization in Cambodia was not necessarily a consequence of household's reluctance to save in KHR.

Table 4 shows the number and percentages of households having KHR/USD deposits by regions. We find that there was no explicit difference in the deposit dollarization between regions, although the percentage of households with USD deposits to the total number of households with deposits in Phnom Penh was slightly higher than that in the rest of the country. The ratio of households having deposits as a percentage of total samples in Phnom Penh (0.27 = 41/150) was higher than that in the rest of the country (0.20 = 418/2123), reflecting the limited access to the financial system outside Phnom Penh.

Table 3 Households having KHR/USD savings

Area	KHR saving	USD saving	Having savings in any currencies	N
Phnom Penh	70 (82.4%)	59 (69.4%)	85 (100.0%)	150
Other regions	1087 (85.9%)	525 (41.5%)	1266 (100.0%)	2123
Total	1157 (85.6%)	584 (43.2%)	1351 (100.0%)	2273

Notes The table shows numbers of households having KHR savings, USD savings, and savings in any currency. Percentages of households having KHR/USD savings to the number of households having savings in any currency are shown in the parenthesis. Savings may include cash at home, deposits in financial institutions or other systems. Some households had both KHR and USD savings when interviewed. *N* in the table stands for sample number in the category

Table 4 Households having KHR/USD deposits

Area	KHR deposit	USD deposit	Having deposits in any currencies	N
Phnom Penh	26 (63.4%)	27 (65.9%)	41 (100.0%)	150
Other regions	252 (60.3%)	249 (59.6%)	418 (100.0%)	2123
Total	278 (60.6%)	276 (60.1%)	459 (100.0%)	2273

Notes The table shows numbers of households having KHR deposits, USD deposits, and deposits in any currency in financial institutions. Percentages of households having KHR/USD deposits to the number of households having deposits in any currency are shown in the parenthesis. Some households had both KHR and USD deposits when interviewed. *N* in the table stands for sample number in the category

5.4 Borrowings

In this section, we investigate the choice of currency in households' borrowing. Because Cambodia is generally categorized as low-income countries, it is more likely for households to borrow from a financial system rather than make deposits. As well as the commercial banking sector, the microfinance sector has been growing remarkably in recent years. Due to the development of MFIs, more households, even poor ones, have become more able to access funds when they need money or start a business. As of 2014, there are 39 registered MFIs and the networks of MFIs that provide loans are widely spread over the country (NBC 2015). In fact, we find that 545 households had loans from formal financial institutions such as commercial banks and MFIs at the time they were interviewed, which exceeded the number of households with deposits in formal financial institutions. This suggests that borrowing from formal financial institutions was more common than having deposits in them, although both numbers are low compared to other neighboring countries. With regard to de-dollarization policies, implementing measures on bank lending may be more effective to control dollarization than regulating deposits.

In the survey, the households were asked about their outstanding loans at the time they were interviewed and were asked about information such as lenders, currencies, and amounts of all loans they had. We found that 634 households, out of 2273 households, answered that they had loans at the time. Most of them (599 households) had just one loan, while 32 households had two loans from different lenders, and 3 households had 3 loans.

5.4.1 Breakdown of Loan Characteristics by Currencies and Lenders

We analyze characteristics of loans by currency and by lenders. For this analysis, when a household takes two loans, we regard them as two individual loans. Therefore, we count 674 loans borrowed by households at the time of the survey. It is noted that some households had more than one loan. We also found that about two-thirds of all loans (436 loans) were borrowed in USD, while about one-third of all loans (210 loans) were borrowed in KHR. Moreover, we found that 27 loans were in Thai baht, and one loan was borrowed in gold. According to the NBC, about 95% of loans provided by commercial banks are denominated in US dollars. Taking this fact into consideration, our data suggests that households might be less dependent on foreign currency loans than enterprises. As for lenders, 162 loans (24%) were granted by commercial banks, and 383 loans (57%) were provided by MFIs, while the rest of loans (19%) were from personal networks (relatives/friends), NGOs, or other informal lenders. We found that more than 80% of households relied on formal financial institutions when borrowing money.

We overviewed differences in loan characteristics (interest rates, amounts, and maturity) by currency. We found that both amounts granted and outstanding in KHR were smaller than those in other currencies on average. Interest rates in KHR loans were relatively higher than others, while interest rates on USD loans were the lowest (Table 5).

Loan characteristics might be partly a consequence of a lender's behavior. We found that there was, although small, a difference in currency denomination of loans between lenders. It may seem that formal lenders, especially commercial banks, had a tendency to provide loans in

Table 5 Loan characteristics by currency

Currency		Initial amount (USD)	Outstanding at the time of interview (USD)	Interest rate (%)	Maturity (month)
KHR	Mean	709.7	425.8	2.5	15.9
	Std. Errors	(723.84)	(505.47)	(0.56)	(7.19)
	N	207	163	82	166
USD	Mean	4795.4	2874.9	1.8	26.9
	Std. Errors	(7245.27)	(6280.01)	(0.46)	(13.85)
	N	431	310	276	375
Baht	Mean	13550.6	13336.5	2.3	18.0
	Std. Errors	(59248.67)	(60550.80)	(0.42)	(9.20)
	N	26	25	14	20
All Currencies	Mean	3864.5	2598.5	2.0	23.3
	Std. Errors	(13188.13)	(14458.52)	(0.56)	(13.13)
	N	664	498	372	561

Notes The table shows amount, interest rate, and maturity of loan by currency. *N* in the table stands for sample number in the category. Mean stands for mean value, and Std. Errors for standard error

foreign currencies, and this was consistent with commercial banks' balance sheet data from the NBC (Table 6).

5.4.2 Difference in Foreign Currency Borrowing Among Regions

We break down the sample and investigate the regional difference in tendencies of foreign currency and KHR borrowing behaviors. We find that the percentages of foreign currency loans were considerably high at 65% in the other regions, but that the percentage was 100% in Phnom Penh. In rural areas, not only were foreign currency loans prevalent when taken out by or when provided for Cambodian households, but KHR loans were also prevalent (Table 7).

Table 6 Loan characteristics by lender

Type of lender		Ratio of KHR loans to all loans	Ratio of USD loans to all loans	Initial amount (USD)	Outstanding at the time of interview (USD)	Interest rate (%)	Maturity (month)
Commercial Bank	Mean	0.2	0.8	5907.7	3441.3	1.8	28.7
	Std. Errors	(0.4)	(0.4)	(8551.5)	(7385.4)	(0.5)	(17.5)
	N	162	162	159	111	106	154
Microfinance	Mean	0.3	0.7	2765.3	1403.3	2.1	21.9
	Std. Errors	(0.5)	(0.5)	(3976.8)	(1696.4)	(0.6)	(10.1)
	N	383	383	379	263	253	376
Family, relatives, or friend	Mean	0.4	0.5	5185.3	5189.5	2.2	13.8
	Std. Errors	(0.5)	(0.5)	(30960.0)	(31275.4)	(0.6)	(8.5)
	N	102	102	101	99	6	19
NGO	Mean	0.4	0.6	3771.9	1362.5	1.7	16.8
	Std. Errors	(0.5)	(0.5)	(6840.9)	(1746.3)	(0.6)	(10.7)
	N	8	8	8	8	4	5
Infomal lender	Mean	0.5	0.3	603.6	603.6	2.2	6.0
	Std. Errors	(0.5)	(0.5)	(832.9)	(832.9)	(0.8)	(4.0)
	N	13	13	12	12	3	3

(continued)

Table 6 (continued)

Type of lender		Ratio of KHR loans to all loans	Ratio of USD loans to all loans	Initial amount (USD)	Outstanding at the time of interview (USD)	Interest rate (%)	Maturity (month)
Others	Mean	1.0	0.0	634.4	271.9	.	12.0
	Std. Errors	(0.0)	(0.0)	(915.9)	(333.3)	.	(0.0)
	N	4	4	4	4	0	3
All lenders	Mean	0.3	0.6	3847.7	2583.6	2.0	23.3
	Std. Errors	(0.5)	(0.5)	(13191.0)	(14469.3)	(0.6)	(13.1)
	N	672	672	663	497	372	560

Notes The table shows amount, interest rate, and maturity of loan by lender. *N* in the table stands for sample number in the category. Mean stands for mean value, and Std. Errors for standard error. Compared to Table 5, one sample did not reveal the lender

Table 7 Choice of loan currency

Area	USD loans holders	Households having loans in any currency	% of USD loan holders to households having loans in any currency
Phnom Penh	30	30	100.0
Other regions	395	604	65.4
Total	425	634	67.03

Notes The table shows numbers of households with USD loans and those with loans in any currency

6 Enterprise Survey

This section describes the widespread dollarization phenomenon from the perspective of enterprises in terms of several aspects, including revenue, expenditure, and financial activities. For the enterprise survey, we collected 856 samples from 25 provinces with reference to the Economic Census 2011 (covering 375,095 establishments).

6.1 Basic Structure of Survey

The survey on dollarization of enterprises in Cambodia was conducted in late 2014. The survey collected several pieces of financial data along with attributes of enterprises in all 25 provinces in Cambodia and investigated their currency usage. A total of 856 enterprises were surveyed and investigated regarding their financial and economic activities and currency. Enterprises were sampled at random from each stratum, classified according to asset sizes. Criteria for enterprise size were based on the definition of enterprises size from Ministry of Industry and Handicraft. The number of large enterprises was 204 out of the total 856 samples, and the number of medium-sized, small, and micro-enterprises was 183, 251, and 218, receptively. Compared with the size distribution from the Economic Census 2014, which is official survey data by the Cambodian government, our survey was slightly biased to the side of large enterprises, and to rural areas. Therefore, when we interpret the results of analyses, it is worth noting that the whole sample was subject to these biases.

Approximately 95% of the whole samples were owned fully or mainly by Cambodian citizens. Regarding industrial classification, in terms of the sample, the top three industries dominated more than 80% of the entire sample. The top industry in the sample was the wholesale and retail trade sector and its share in the whole sample was 42%. The second largest industry was the manufacturing sector (21%), and the third largest one was the information and communication sector (20%).

6.2 Sales

6.2.1 General View of Sales Dollarization

The dataset contained not only the ratio of foreign-currency-denominated sales, but also the total amount of sales of individual firms. It is possible to calculate the aggregated level of foreign-currency-denominated sales of the firms as a whole. Data from 25 provinces shows that around 78.3% of sales (business revenue) were received in foreign currencies. Among foreign currencies, USD was in highest usage, while Thai baht was also used to a comparable extent as that of KHR. Vietnamese dong was also used but in a more limited manner in the border area.

On an aggregate basis, in general, large firm's ratios were high while those of micro- and small firms were lower. Large firms might have direct access to international markets, allowing them to generate revenue in foreign currency, while small or micro-firms might export their products through a middleman and be paid in riels. Another possible explanation is that large firms were able to take initiative in determining the currency to receive for its sales or services. Frequently, we observe that a firm offers products both in USD and KHR. However, if a firm actually prefers to receive payments in USD, it might apply an exchange rate that disadvantages payment in KHR. For example, if the prevailing market rate is 3900KHR = 1 USD, the firm will instead use 4000KHR = 1 USD to calculate the price to be paid in KHR, pushing the buyer to voluntarily choose to pay in USD, the currency that the seller actually prefers.

It may be noted that employee number had a stronger positive correlation with sales dollarization ratio than simple asset-size-based firm classification, particularly for firms in the manufacturing sector. Such firms with more than 500 employees had almost 100% USD revenue. However, when the employee number decreases, the dollarization ratio of revenue also goes down. Firms with one to ten employees showed quite low dollarization ratio. We can see that large manufacturers might be directly involved in exports, allowing them to generate foreign currency revenue. In some cases, they might be involved in a network of an international value chain. However, for micro-, small-, or medium-sized manufacturers, direct access to the international market was limited. Thus, these firms were less dollarized in terms of revenue.

It should be noted that Vietnamese dong had some share in the sales of small firms. These firms had direct transactions with Vietnam, as they were located near the Vietnamese border. Small firms were actively engaged in cross-border trade with neighboring countries. Thai baht was also used, however, by large firms located near the Thai border.

6.2.2 Micro-Level Sales Dollarization

When we look into the individual level of sales dollarization, the story mentioned above changes slightly. If we divide the sample into Phnom Penh and the rest of the provinces, then, further classify firms by business types and size, we can observe that ratios of sales dollarization for micro/small firms in Phnom Penh have higher ratios than their peers in other regions in all categories of business types.

In the case of medium/large enterprises, though they have high ratios in general, the ratios in Phnom Penh are not always higher than those in other regions. Interestingly, manufacturing firms in other regions have rather low ratio of sales dollarization (Table 8).

Table 8 Sales dollarization

Area	Phnom Penh				Other regions			
Size	Micro and small		Medium and large		Micro and small		Medium and large	
	N	% of sales in FC to total sales	N	% of sales in FC to total sales	N	% of sales in FC to total sales	N	% of sales in FC to total sales
Type of Business								
Agriculture, forestry, and fishery related	0	na	0	na	2	15.0	3	57.3
Manufacturing	1	80.0	2	45.0	40	21.1	75	46.6
Wholesale/retail	21	60.2	4	75.0	175	39.8	53	58.0
Services	20	77.6	24	68.6	82	46.7	64	70.3
Total	42	69.0	30	67.9	299	39.0	195	57.7

Notes The table shows average level of sales in FC to total sales by type of business and by size of enterprise. N in the table stands for sample number in the category

6.3 Expenditure

Enterprises in Phnom Penh had a high ratio of expenditure dollarization. More than 90% of expenditure was spent in dollars, and more than 80% of firms in Phnom Penh had revenue in dollars. Thus, it is quite natural that firms conducted business-to-business transactions almost entirely in dollars, while business-to-consumer transactions were instead partly in KHR and in USD (Table 9).

In terms of dollarization of production input expenditure, if we divide the sample into Phnom Penh and other regions and then split by business type, we can observe that in Phnom Penh the ratios were higher than those in other regions in all respective groups of categories. Moreover, the ratios in Phnom Penh remained around 60–80% (except in one agriculture-related sample, micro/small), the ratios in other regions differed significantly ranging from 13–67%. Depending on the business type, the ratio differed significantly in other regions, but in Phnom Penh, the ratios stayed in a narrower range. We can infer that there were externalities even for the transactions of firms in Phnom Penh.

Table 9 Dollarization of expenditure (Production input/wage)

(A) Production Input								
Area	Phnom Penh				Other regions			
Size	Micro and small		Medium and large		Micro and small		Medium and large	
	N	% of expenditure in FC to total expenditure	N	% of expenditure in FC to total expenditure	N	% of expenditure in FC to total expenditure	N	% of expenditure in FC to total expenditure
Type of Business								
Agriculture, forestry, and fishery related	0	na	0	na	2	5.0	3	56.7
Manufacturing	1	99.0	5	82.0	42	31.1	97	53.1
Wholesale/retail	22	74.1	3	86.6	188	72.0	56	78.3
Other	30	70.5	21	64.7	89	47.8	71	58.9
Total	53	72.6	29	70.0	321	59.5	227	61.2
(B) Wage								
Area	Phnom Penh				Other regions			
Size	Micro and small		Medium and large		Micro and small		Medium and large	
	N	% of expenditure in FC to total expenditure	N	% of expenditure in FC to total expenditure	N	% of expenditure in FC to total expenditure	N	% of expenditure in FC to total expenditure
Type of Business								
Agriculture, forestry, and fishery related	0	na	0	na	3	33.3	4	20.0

(continued)

Table 9 (continued)

(B) Wage								
Area	Phnom Penh				Other regions			
Size	Micro and small		Medium and large		Micro and small		Medium and large	
	N	% of expenditure in FC to total expenditure	N	% of expenditure in FC to total expenditure	N	% of expenditure in FC to total expenditure	N	% of expenditure in FC to total expenditure
Manufacturing	1	0.0	12	79.1	38	13.1	114	15.9
Wholesale/retail	19	76.3	10	88.0	127	16.7	71	34.8
Other	36	85.9	33	84.1	82	51.8	83	67.3
Total	56	81.1	55	83.7	250	27.8	272	36.5

Notes The table shows average level of production input/wage expenditure in FC to total production input/wage expenditure by type of business and by size of enterprise. *N* in the table stands for sample number in the category

Dollarization ratios of personnel expenditure were around 60 to 70% in all firm size categories on an aggregate basis. The data from the firm survey showed consistent result with household survey. Wages and salaries were mainly paid in dollars. However, if we again divide the sample into Phnom Penh and other regions, and then split by business type, it is very clear that in Phnom Penh the ratios ranged from 76.3 to 88.0% in all type of businesses while in other provinces the ratios were comparatively low except for firms engaged in the service sector.

The dollarization of personnel expenses had a positive correlation with dollarization of revenue. It is necessary to examine the direction of causalities, but it is quite natural to interpret that those firms who were generating revenue in foreign currency tend to spend their personnel costs in foreign currency to alleviate risk associated with exchange rate fluctuation, particularly for those labor-intensive manufacturing enterprises hiring many workers, like the garment industries. However, such currency denomination of salary/wage might also be affected by worker preferences, including practices in the local labor market. It is necessary to examine the employee's demands as well as the labor market practices in a given industry to see what key is to determine the currency of payment.

The data suggests that sales and their expenditures were mixed with local and foreign currencies. A clear trend was not found in the relation between the ratio of expenditure in foreign currency and ratio of sales in foreign currency. Operations of some enterprises were completely dollarized, but those of others were completely in KHR. However, in some enterprises, sales were completely in foreign currencies, but expenditures were completely in KHR, and vice versa. The results suggest there is a huge dispersion of the extent and direction of currency mismatch among Cambodian enterprises, and that they are exposed to exchange rate risk.

In the survey, perception of exchange rate risk is examined. In the question asking about assessment of exchange rate risk, 411 of the 856 respondents answered that they perceived risk to some extent, while 434 said no risk. The results revealed that more than half of Cambodian enterprises did not think that their businesses were exposed to foreign exchange rate risk. Moreover, only 225 out of 856 responded to questions asking their views on the future exchange rate. This might imply that more than half of Cambodian enterprises were not conscious of exchange rate changes.

6.4 Dollarization of Financial Activities

We investigated the role of foreign currency and KHR in the financing behavior of enterprises. In the survey, managers of enterprises were interviewed about their outstanding loans. Specifically, they were asked about interest rates, maturity, and principal amounts, by currency and by lender.

We found that out of the 856 enterprises interviewed in the survey, 223 had a loan when interviewed. Because some enterprises had more than one loan, in total there are 237 loans in the dataset. To assess what kind of firms were dependent on external financing, we focused on questions asking firms about whether they had loans or not. We find that the manufacturing sector was more likely to take loans. However, the agricultural sector and wholesale/trade sector also tended to borrow money for financing. The data did not show any differences between large and small enterprises. Finally, we found that enterprises in Phnom Penh were less dependent on loans than those in other regions.

Surprisingly, almost all loans were denominated in USD. In particular, loans from formal financial institutions, such as commercial banks and MFIs, were all denominated in USD. We also assessed which currency that Cambodian enterprise taking foreign currency loans was using in its operation, and found that 60 enterprises (about 40% of enterprises with loans) were operating in KHR[5]. This reveals that Cambodian enterprises tended to borrow in foreign currency, although some of them were operating in KHR. Our findings indicate that when Cambodian enterprises financed their projects and operations, they almost always borrowed in USD, regardless of whether they mainly used KHR in operation. This suggests that there was the possibility that some Cambodian enterprises, particularly those that used KHR as the main currency in operation, could be exposed to the risk of currency mismatch between the currency in operation and loans (Table 10).

Table 10 Loan access and currency choice

(A) Access to loans				(B) Loan currency choice by lender			
	Having loans	N	% of enterprise having loans in category		KHR loan	USD loan	N
Type of Business				Commercial Bank	0	172	172
Agriculture, forestry, and fishery related	2	7	28.6	Microfinance	0	19	19
Manufacturing	69	178	38.8	Family, Relatives, or Friend	4	38	42
Wholesale/retail	113	359	31.5	Informal Lender	2	1	3
Other	39	312	12.5	Other	0	1	1
				Total	6	231	237
Size							
Micro and small	122	469	26.0				
Medium and large	101	387	26.1				
Area							
Phonm Penh	22	182	12.1				
Other regions	201	674	29.8				

Notes Panel (A) shows numbers of enterprise with loans by type of business, size, or area. Panel (B) shows currency choice of loans by lender. *N* in the table stands for sample number in the category

7 Conclusion

In this study, a survey on dollarization of households and firms in Cambodia was conducted by JICA-RI in collaboration with the NBC in late 2014. Micro-data gives us a different picture of dollarization from what we inferred from the extremely high ratio of dollarization measured using macro-data.

The results confirm that foreign currencies are widely used in every aspect of the transaction, by households as well as by enterprises. We can say that payment dollarization (means of payment) and real dollarization (unit of account) have developed alongside financial dollarization in

Cambodia, given its unique environment. However, the degree of dollarization may differ significantly by region, depending on the magnitude of network externalities, according to characteristics of households/enterprises, or by the type of transactions, depending on the specific business practice concerned.

Notes

1. Prakas is a regulation issued by a Minister, or by the Governor of the National Bank of Cambodia, concerning banking or financial issues. It must conform to the Constitution and to the law or sub-decree to which it refers (http://asianbondsonline.adb.org/regional/guides/definition.php?term=Prakas Accessed on 7 July, 2015).
2. According to the Cambodia Security Exchange, Phnom Penh Water Supply Authority (listed in April 2012), Grand Twins International Plc (listed in June 2014), and Phnom Penh Autonomous Port (listed in December 2015) are listed. (http://csx.com.kh/data/lstcom/listPosts.do?MNCD=5010; accessed on January 13, 2016).
3. The Cambodian security market is still immature, and there are only three firms listed. Thus, there are no alternative formal funding sources for the banking system.
4. This informal institution is called "WING" in Cambodia, and serves money transfer services all over the country.
5. We used the question "Which currency is your company usually using in operation?"

References

Basso, H.S., Calvo-Gonzales, O., and Jurgilas, M. 2011. Financial dollarization and the role of foreign owned banks and interest rates. *Journal of Banking & Finance* 35: 794–806.

Beckmann, E., and Stix, H. 2015. Foreign currency borrowing and knowledge about change rate risk. *Journal of Economic Behavior & Organization* 112: 1–16.0

Beer, C., Ongena, S., and Peter, M. 2010. Borrowing in foreign currency: Austrian households as carry traders. *Journal of Banking & Finance* 34(9): 2198–2211.

Brown, M., Ongena, S., and Yeşin, P. 2011. Foreign currency borrowing by small firms in the transition economies. *Journal of Financial Intermediation* 20(3): 285–302.

Csajbok, A., Hudecz, A., and Tamasi, B. 2010. *Foreign currency borrowing of households in new EU member states.* MNB Occasional Papers 87.2010. Magyar Nemzeti Bank.

De Zamaroczy, Mario and Soponha Sa. 2002. Macroeconomic adjustment in a highly dollarized economy: The case of Cambodia. IMF Working Paper WP/02/92, Washington, DC: International Monetary Fund.

Dodsworth, J.R., A. Chopra, C.D. Pham, and H. Shishido. 1996. Macroeconomic experiences of the transition economies in Indochina. IMF Working Paper WP/96/112, Washington, DC: International Monetary Fund.

Duma, Nombulelo. 2014. Asia's most dollarized economy: Causes and consequences. In *Cambodia entering a new phase of growth*, ed. Olaf Unteroberdoerster, 27–49. Washington, DC: International Monetary Fund.

Eichengreen, Barry, and Ricardo Hausmann (eds.). 2005. *Other people's money: Debt denomination and financial instability in emerging market economy.* Chicago: University of Chicago Press.

Fidrmuc, J., Hake, M., and Stix, H. 2013. Households' foreign currency borrowing in Central and Eastern Europe. *Journal of Banking & Finance* 37 (6):1880–1897

Ize, A., and Levy-Yeyati E. 2003. Financial dollarization. *Journal of International Economics* 59: 323–347.

Ize, A., 2005. Financial dollarization equilibria: A framework for policy analysis. IMF Working Papers 05/186, International Monetary Fund.

Khou, Vuthy. 2012. Functionality of the monetary plurality in Cambodia. PhD dissertation, Université Lumière Lyon 2 (In French).

Luca, A., and Petrova, I. 2008. What drives credit dollarization in transition economies? *Journal of Banking and Finance* 32: 858–869.

Menon, Jayant. 2008. Cambodia's persistent dollarization: Causes and policy options. Working Paper Series on Regional Economic Integration No. 19, Manila: Asian Development Bank.

National Bank of Cambodia (NBC). 2005. *Banking supervision annual report 2005.* http://www.nbc.org.kh/download_files/supervision/sup_an_rep_eng/Bsd_Annual_2005_En.pdf.

Okuda, Hidenobu. 2013. Dollarization and Banking in Cambodian Economy: An institutional analysis. Paper presented at Japan Association for Asian

Studies 2013 West Japan Meeting, November 9, 2013, Osaka City University (In Japanese).

Pellényi, G., and Bilek, P. 2009. *Foreign currency borrowing: The case of Hungary*. (No. 5.4). DIW Berlin, German Determinants of Foreign Currency Borrowing in the New Member States of the EU. Institute for Economic Research

Pum, Huot, and Khan Vanak. 2010. Cambodia: Coping with dollarization. In *Dealing with multiple currencies in transitional economies*, ed. Giovanni Capannelli and Jayant Menon, 51–97. Manila: Asian Development Bank.

Rosenberg, Christoph B., and Marcel Tirpák. 2008. Determinants of foreign currency borrowing in the new member states of the EU. No. 8-173. International Monetary Fund.

Rumbaugh, Thomas, Kotaro Ishi, Hong Liang, and Atsushi Masuda. 2000. Cambodia: Selected issues. IMF Staff Country Report. No. 00/135, Washington, DC: International Monetary Fund.

Samreth, Sovannroeun. 2011. An empirical study on the hysteresis of currency substitution in Cambodia. *Journal of Asian Economics* 22: 518–527.

Siregar, R. Y., and Chan, N. 2014. Factors behind foreign currency holding by household in Cambodia. CAMA Working Paper 58/2014, Australian National University

Steiner, K. 2011. *Households' Exposure to Foreign Currency Loans in CESEE EU Member States and Croatia*. Foucus on European Economic Integration Q1/11, Oesterreichische Nationalbank.

Valev, N. 2010. The hysteresis of currency substitution: Currency risk vs. network externalities. *Journal of International Money and Finance* 29 (2): 224–235.

Youdy, Bun. 2014. Chapter 10: Cambodia. In *Banking regulation review*, 5th ed, ed. Jan Putnis. London: Law and Business Research Ltd.

3

Asset Substitution and Currency Substitution behind Dollarization and De-dollarization Policy in the Lao PDR: Evidence from Bank-Level Data

Phetsathaphone Keovongvichith

1 Introduction

The Lao People's Democratic Republic (Lao PDR hereafter) has continued to make significant progress in promoting economic growth and financial development over the past decade. Its economy has performed well with annual Gross Domestic Product (GDP) growth rates averaging 7–8% in the period following economic reforms, though from a low base, marking the country as one of the highest economic performers in the international context. While the economic and financial reforms during the transition from a centrally planned to a market-based

The views expressed in this article are solely those of the author and do not necessarily represent the views of the Bank of the Lao PDR.

P. Keovongvichith (✉)
Bank of the Lao PDR, Vientiane, Lao PDR
e-mail: phetsakeobol@hotmail.com

K. Kubo (ed.), *Dollarization and De-dollarization in Transitional Economies of Southeast Asia*, IDE-JETRO Series, DOI 10.1007/978-3-319-57768-5_3

economy brought positive achievements for social and economic indicators, one of the most notable effects of the economic and financial liberalization in the country is the increased use of foreign currency (notably the US dollar and Thai baht) as a way of holding wealth and a means of transaction for goods and services by the domestic residents. This phenomenon (referred to in the literature as dollarization) has become one of the monetary problems that authorities face.

The dollarization phenomenon was neither sought nor encouraged by the monetary authorities. Rather, a main cause of the widespread use of foreign currency for domestic economic transactions was high inflation and sharp depreciation of the local currency, the kip, during the period of transition, coupled with a gradual relaxation of some restrictions on foreign currency deposits transformed unofficial holdings of foreign currency banknotes into formal foreign currency deposits (FCDs).

To illustrate the magnitude of dollarization in the Lao PDR, it is useful to present the ratio of FCDs in proportion to broad money, which is a conventional indicator of dollarization. The dollarization ratio of this country had been almost 40% as early as 1988 and reached a peak of almost 80% in 1999. The dollarization process has begun to reverse following successful economic stabilization, falling to 58.2% in 2006, and to 42.4% in 2013 (See Fig. 1(B) in Chap. 1).

This paper examines the trend of dollarization in the Lao PDR. The unique feature of this study is an examination of financial dollarization using bank-level data originally obtained from selected state-owned commercial banks (SOCBs), which are key players in the Laotian banking sector. The disaggregated data on deposits allows us to examine how the composition of depositors and their behavior evolved in response to macroeconomic and banking environment. Unlike previous studies on dollarization in the Lao PDR (Pani 2002; Menon 2007, 2008; Kyophilavong 2010) which examine only macro-level data, this paper offers a deeper look into the trend of financial dollarization.

Another merit of this paper is the consolidated review of de-dollarization policy measures taken by the Bank of Lao PDR (BOL), the monetary authorities of the country, which contribute significantly to containing the growth of dollarization in the country.

The rest of this paper is organized as follows. Section 2 presents a brief overview of economic and monetary developments in the Lao PDR. Section 3 analyzes the levels and trends of dollarization with macro- and bank-level data. A thorough review of de-dollarization policy is made in Sect. 4. Section 5 contains concluding remarks.

2 An Overview of Economic and Monetary Developments

The process of dollarization in the Lao PDR is closely linked with numerous economic and monetary events that took place over the past two and a half decades (Box 1).

Box 1: Chronology of policy changes surrounding Laotian economic and financial developments during 1986–2014

1. November 1986: Lao PDR begins to move from centrally planned economy to market-oriented economy under auspice of "New Economic Mechanism" during the IV Congress of the Lao People's Revolutionary Party.
2. March 1988: Council of Ministers issues Resolution No. II/PSL to transform a mono-bank system into a two-tier banking system.
3. October 1988: Actual implementation of the banking system reform.
4. September 1988: Law on Foreign Investment Promotion and Management enacted by the National Assembly, paving the way for foreign banks to open business in the Lao PDR.
5. July 1989: First Nationwide Banking Conference convenes under chairmanship of the late Chairman of Council of Ministers (Mr. Kaysone Phomvihane) and Council of Ministers' Decree on Commercial Banks Activities issued.

6. October 1989: A joint venture–foreign bank (JDB) entry permitted to operate for the first time in Vientiane Capital, and allowed to mobilize FCDs and lend in foreign currencies.
7. September 1990: Decree on Foreign Currency Management and Precious Metals (No. 53/CM) issued.
8. June 1993: Prime Minister's Decree on the Organization and Activity of the Bank of the Lao PDR No. 95/PM issued.
9. October 1995: Law on Bank of the Lao PDR No. 05/95/NA passed by the National Assembly.
10. September 1995: Fixed exchange rate removed and adoption of a "managed floating".
11. June 1995: Maximum lending rates lifted for commercial banks, and subsequently minimum deposit rates removed in January 1996.
12. July 1997: Asian financial crisis erupts.
13. July 1998: Consolidation and restructuring of state-owned commercial banks.
14. October 1999: Law on Bank of the Lao PDR No. 05/95/NA revised and amended.
15. March 2000: Council of Ministers' Decree on Commercial Banks upgraded into Presidential Decree on Commercial Banks (No. 02/PR).
16. August 2002: Presidential Decree on Foreign Currency Management and Precious Metals No. 01/PR issued.
17. December 2006: Presidential Decree on Commercial Banks replaced by Law on Commercial Banks No. 03/NA as passed by the National Assembly.
18. May 2007: Decree on Foreign Currency Management and Promotion of the Use of kip for Domestic Transactions No. 150/PM issued.
19. March 2008: Presidential Decree on Foreign Currency Management and Precious Metals No. 01/P amended.
20. September 2009: Decree on the Implementation of Commercial Bank Law No. 275/PM issued.

21. January 2011: Lao Securities Exchanges launched for initial public offering (IPO) trading.
22. December 2012: Law on Securities (No. 21/NA) enacted.
23. December 2014: Law on Foreign Currency Management (No. 55/NA) enacted.

In the pre-reform period, the Lao PDR had a centrally planned economy and a mono-bank system where there was no separation between the functions of the central bank and commercial banks and the government-owned and administratively controlled all banking operations and foreign exchange. Under this tightly controlled regime, a complex system of exchange rate control was practiced. Foreign currency holdings by domestic residents were strictly prohibited (though tolerated) and foreign exchange for international transactions was centrally allocated through a state-owned bank, Banque Pour Le Commerce Exterieur Lao (often referred to BCEL as "foreign trade bank"). Export proceeds had to be surrendered and residents were not permitted to hold FCDs.

Nonetheless, private foreign exchange transactions were conducted in the parallel exchange market. Multiple official exchange rates were used for official transactions, and exchange rates between the official and parallel markets varied widely from 1985 to 1987 (Lathouly 1995).

The government of the Lao PDR launched its economic and financial reforms under the auspices of the "New Economic Mechanism" in 1986. Banking and monetary reforms were touted as key components of market-oriented economic reforms which included (1) deregulation of the banking sector, (2) liberalization of the foreign exchange regime, and (3) promotion of foreign direct investments. In the early stages of economic reforms, the Lao PDR experienced high inflation and an unstable exchange rate. Liberalization of the foreign exchange regime also resulted in massive devaluation of official exchange rates (See Fig. 2 of Chap. 1).

In March 1988, the government unified the various official rates and adopted a single exchange rate system. Under the new system, the BOL set the buying and selling rates for the kip/US dollar. The unified official rate was set close to the prevailing parallel market rate. As a result, the official rate was devalued from 95 kip per US dollar to 350 and later 450, reflecting a steep depreciation of the kip in the parallel market. The government also managed to keep the gap between the official and parallel market exchange rates under 10% throughout the period of 1989–1993, as required by the concessional loan conditionality jointly imposed by the International Monetary Fund (IMF) and the World Bank (Lathouly 1995).

In September 1990, the government issued a Decree on the Management of Foreign Exchange and Precious Metals (No. 53/PM), setting a legal basis for all commercial banks to accept FCDs from the public for the first time. Restrictions on foreign currency holdings were lifted. Residents and enterprises were allowed to maintain FCDs in local commercial banks. Commercial banks were authorized to extend credit in foreign currency to domestic enterprises.

In September 1995, the BOL decided to abolish the official exchange rate and formally adopted a "managed float" exchange system. Under this system, small and regular adjustments of the official/commercial bank exchange rate were made in line with parallel market developments. As a result, the commercial exchange rate depreciated to around 930 kip per US dollar. The measures taken by the BOL temporarily helped to restore the stability of the foreign exchange market, and the spread between the commercial bank and parallel market rates remained below 2.5% until August 1996.

The Laotian economy was severely affected by the 1997 Asian financial crisis originating in Thailand, and accommodative monetary and fiscal policies aggravated the severity of the situation. To cope with the economic downturn due to the Asian financial crisis, in 1998 the BOL removed bank-by-bank credit ceilings, leading to credit growth and a growth in broad money of 94 and 113%, respectively (IMF 2000). The country experienced high inflation, with the annual inflation rate reaching a peak of 129% in 1998–1999. The value of the kip against the US dollar also depreciated by more than 80%.

By 2006 macroeconomic stability was fully restored as the country embarked on an exchange rate-centered monetary policy by targeting an exchange rate within a band of 5% per annum. When necessary, the BOL would intervene in the foreign exchange market to maintain the stability of the nominal exchange rate. In August 2008, the BOL also introduced a daily reference rate for commercial banks. This policy has enhanced the capacity of the BOL to manage the exchange rate with more flexibility for both the kip/Thai baht and kip/US dollar exchange rates. As a result, yearly inflation rates were gradually brought under control, declining from 127% in 1999 to a low of 6.8% in 2006. This trend has continued ever since. Since then the Lao PDR has continued to maintain macroeconomic stability with a low and one digit inflation rate.

In addition, large capital flows raised a boom during this period, resulting in an appreciation of the kip against the US dollar. As a result, public confidence in local currency holding has returned. From the perspective of broad money (M2) in proportion to GDP (Fig. 3 of Chap. 1), the ratio of M2 to GDP has increased rapidly in recent years since local currency deposits as a component of M2 have grown much faster than FCDs, demonstrating increased public confidence in Lao kip deposits. This also helps to enhance development in the underdeveloped financial sector in the Lao PDR.

3 The Laotian Experience of Dollarization from 1988 to 2013

This section presents empirical evidence on dollarization in the Lao PDR from 1988 to 2013. The analysis is divided into two parts; the first part uses aggregate data for the dollarization ratio, while the second employs disaggregated bank-level data.

3.1 Analysis on the Trends of Dollarization

In the Lao PDR, it has been a common practice for businesses and households to use foreign currency as a medium of exchange and unit of account instead of the kip. The use of the US dollar and the Thai baht is seen all over the country, with large transactions commonly taking place in urban areas. The use of foreign currency can also be found outside of the major cities as well, such as in those provinces with long borders where border trade activities and smuggling are common. In places like hotels, restaurants, and shops foreign currency has been frequently used by vendors and tourists. These tendencies are more prevalent in parts of the urban service sector including the real estate sector and private schools, companies and to a less extent in the retail sector—primarily in high-value imported consumer goods such as computers and automobiles.

In the local market, prices are quoted in Thai baht and US dollars and shops stand ready to accept either foreign or local currency, but when accepting kip, the exchange rate quoted is typically significantly undervalued, encouraging the buyers of such services to pay in Thai baht or US dollars. Despite its significance, however, it is difficult to analyze the extent of the use of foreign currency cash for payments as there is no reliable estimate of foreign currency cash in circulation.

We examine the trend of financial dollarization using the FCD to broad money ratio (Fig. 1). The dollarization ratio was as high as 40% at the beginning of the economic transition in 1988 and remained broadly the same until 1996. In 1998, dollarization rose to 68% and reached a

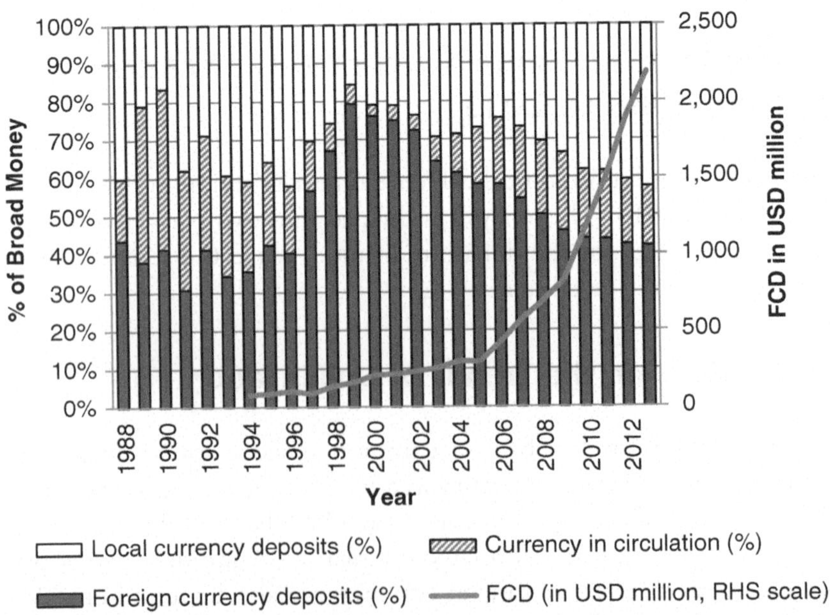

Fig. 1 Composition of broad money and FCDs in US dollar, Lao PDR, 1988–2013. *Source* Otani and Pham (1996); *IMF Country Report* (various issues)

peak of almost 80% in 1999 (in part due to the effects of devaluation). In the subsequent years, the dollarization ratio dropped continuously from its peak and in 2013 was stable at 42, a level similar to that seen in the 1990s.

There are two factors that explain this trend of deposit dollarization: (1) the removal of restrictions on foreign currency holdings, and (2) macroeconomic instability resulting from the 1997 Asian financial crisis. First, restrictions on foreign currency holdings were lifted and commercial banks were initially allowed to accept FCD accounts for both residents and nonresidents in 1988. The ratio of FCDs to M2 in the banking sector immediately reached about 40% in 1988 and remained roughly the same until 1996. The regulatory changes to FCDs might have allowed banks to absorb the foreign currency cash circulating domestically outside the banking system.

Second, macroeconomic instability in the late 1990s is closely linked to increased deposit dollarization. A large depreciation produces a rise in FCDs in local currency terms due to the valuation effect, which mostly explains the trend of dollarization ratio in 1998–1999. In addition, macroeconomic stabilization beginning in 2000 was associated with a downward trend in the dollarization ratio. As shown in macroeconomic data in Chap. 1, the inflation and exchange rates have generally remained low and stable since 2001, even as the dollarization ratio has been falling.

However, a record of low inflation and a stable exchange rate over the past decade did not bring down the dollarization ratio below the pre-shock level of 1996. This could partly be explained by hysteresis, or ratchet effect, a concept which describes a situation in which dollarization persists despite disinflation and exchange rate stabilization.

We present the composition of foreign and local currency deposits of the entire banking sector. Figure 2 shows a decomposition of deposits by currency and by three types of deposits, namely demand deposits, savings deposits, and time deposits. The figure shows that the ratio of FCDs to total deposits was 70.6% in 2006, and it declined to 48.7% in 2014. First, a large portion of FCDs are demand and savings deposits. Until 2008, the sum of demand and savings FCDs accounted for more than 50% of the total deposits of the entire banking sector, and it still accounts for 34.7% as of 2014. A portion of demand and savings FCDs

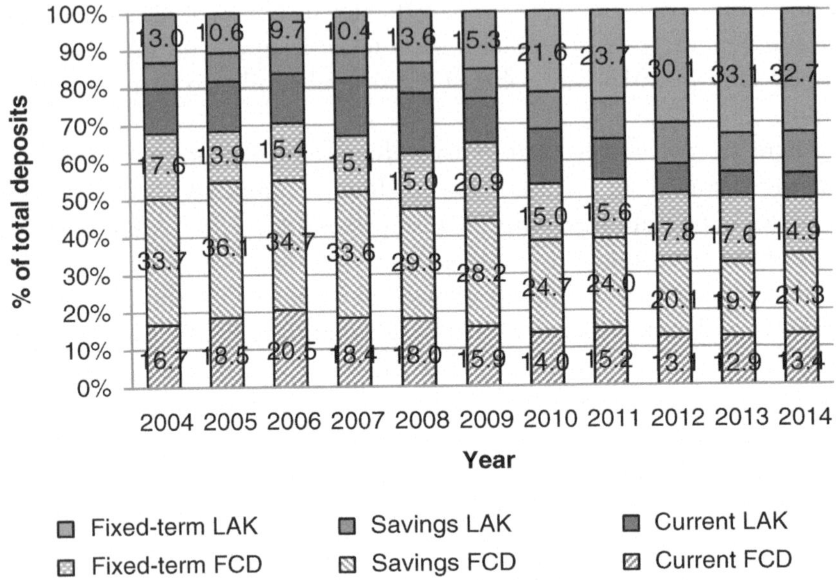

Fig. 2 Composition of deposits by currency and by type of deposits, Lao PDR, 2004–2014. *Source Quarterly Reviews of Monetary Statistics*, Bank of the Lao PDR (various issues) *Note* LAK stands for Lao Kip

is possibly held for transaction purposes, such as international and domestic payments.

Second, when we examine local currency deposits we find that fixed-term kip deposits have been growing faster than other deposits in recent years, resulting in a notable increase in its share in total deposits, which rose from 9.7% in 2006 to 32.7% in 2014. This is a stark contrast with the fixed-term FCDs whose share remains stable at around 15%. The robust growth in local currency fixed-term deposits strongly suggests that asset substitution has phased out.

3.2 Analysis with Bank-Level Data

In addition to an analysis of the general trend of the dollarization ratio, this paper further examines bank-level data. The banking system in the

Lao PDR has been dominated by state-owned commercial banks (SOCBs) . As of October 2014, the banking system consists of the central bank, (BOL) and four SOCBs[1], three joint venture banks, seven private banks, and 21 branches or subsidiaries of foreign banks. Collectively, these banks operate through a service network of 87 branches, 415 service units, 113 exchange bureaus, and 826 automated teller machines (ATMs) throughout the country. In terms of market share, SOCBs account for almost 60% of total bank assets. SOCBs also clearly dominate in terms of total loans and total deposits, at shares of 66.5 and 62.2%, respectively, during 2009–2013.

SOCBs include BCEL, Lao Development Bank (LDB), and Agriculture Promotion Bank (APB). While these three banks do not necessarily represent the banking sector, their high shares in the banking sector allow us to infer the trends of the whole banking sector. BCEL[2] is a foreign trade bank and the biggest bank in the country, dealing with international banking business and mainly operating in urban areas with 19 branches and 64 service units throughout the country. LDB[3] focuses its banking business on small and medium enterprises (SME), operating mainly in urban areas with 18 branches and 69 service units as of June 2014. APB[4] was formerly known as a policy-based bank before its transformation into a commercial bank in October 2006. Its banking business is centered on promoting financial access for farmers and households in rural areas. Due to its specific nature, APB is the only bank that has a wider service network in rural areas, with 17 branches and 82 service units throughout the country.

Table 1 summarizes the structure of loans and deposits by currencies during 2000–2013 for BCEL, LDB, and APB. First, with Table 1, we perform a cross-sectional comparison among these three banks. We consider that BCEL represents depositors of urban areas, and APB represents depositors of rural areas. We find that the extent of deposit dollarization in rural areas is much lower than that found in urban areas. As of 2013, the ratio of FCDs to total deposits is 54.9% for BCEL, and 14.7% for APB.

Second, in BCEL and LDB we also observe a declining share of the US dollar on both fixed and savings deposits, and an increasing share of kip in both fixed and savings deposits. At BCEL, the share of US dollar

Table 1 Types of deposits and loans of selected commercial banks, Lao PDR, 2000–2013

(A) Composition of deposits by currency, BCEL

	Current deposits						Savings deposits						Term deposits						Total
	LAK		USD		THB		LAK		USD		THB		LAK		USD		THB		
	Kip, bil.	%	Kip, bil.	%	Kip, bil.	%	Kip, bil.	%	Kip, bil.	%	Kip, bil.	%	Kip, bil.	%	Kip, bil.	%	Kip, bil.	%	Kip, bil.
2002	111	8.3	397	29.7	11	0.8	22	1.6	405	30.3	79	5.9	17	1.2	243	18.2	51	3.8	1336
2003	90	5.8	414	26.8	15	1.0	29	1.9	422	27.4	109	7.1	66	4.3	331	21.4	66	4.3	1542
2004	139	7.8	509	28.7	14	0.8	39	2.2	546	30.8	113	6.4	78	4.4	268	15.1	67	3.8	1773
2005	235	10.2	620	26.9	39	1.7	87	3.8	650	28.2	219	9.5	114	5.0	259	11.2	79	3.4	2302
2006	242	9.0	772	28.7	52	1.9	103	3.8	780	29.0	221	8.2	120	4.5	316	11.8	85	3.2	2692
2007	316	9.6	839	25.6	65	2.0	155	4.7	933	28.4	321	9.8	164	5.0	370	11.3	118	3.6	3282
2008	450	10.9	1063	25.7	51	1.2	260	6.3	978	23.7	373	9.0	302	7.3	510	12.3	145	3.5	4132
2009	655	12.0	988	18.1	112	2.1	515	9.4	1298	23.8	513	9.4	592	10.8	584	10.7	202	3.7	5458
2010	1561	20.5	926	12.1	123	1.6	728	9.5	1592	20.9	754	9.9	975	12.8	680	8.9	282	3.7	7621
2011	1140	11.0	1752	17.0	177	1.7	1100	10.6	1938	18.8	1136	11.0	1939	18.8	779	7.5	369	3.6	10,330
2012	1019	8.2	1678	13.5	179	1.4	1685	13.5	2367	19.0	1342	10.8	2791	22.4	885	7.1	499	4.0	12,446
2013	972	6.9	1686	12.0	218	1.5	1923	13.6	2629	18.7	1572	11.2	3458	24.5	1091	7.7	545	3.9	14,093

Source Author's calculation based on data compiled from commercial banks

Notes Percentage refers to the share of a deposit in total deposits. LAK, USD, and THB stand for Lao kip, US dollar, and Thai baht, respectively

Table 1 (Continued)

(B) Loan-to-deposit ratio by currency, BCEL				
Year	Loan-to-deposit ratio by currency			
	Total (in LAK) %	THB (in LAK) %	USD (in LAK) %	LAK %
2002	67.3	39.6	74.3	44.5
2003	53.1	16.4	62.7	30.1
2004	46.6	16.6	55.2	24.7
2005	50.3	10.1	66.9	23.1
2006	26.5	13.7	28.2	29.7
2007	26.4	10.9	27.5	35.2
2008	33.8	20.5	35.6	36.6
2009	36.0	31.3	40.3	31.3
2010	37.5	31.0	46.2	31.4
2011	49.8	31.3	64.0	42.0
2012	56.7	62.6	61.0	50.8
2013	67.4	57.7	73.7	65.6

Source Author's calculation based on data compiled from commercial banks

Table 1 (Continued)

	(C) Composition of deposits by currency, LDB																		
	Current deposits						Savings deposits						Term deposits						Total
	LAK		USD		THB		LAK		USD		THB		LAK		USD		THB		
	Kip, bil.	%	Kip, bil.	%	Kip, bil.	%	Kip, bil.	%	Kip, bil.	%	Kip, bil.	%	Kip, bil.	%	Kip, bil.	%	Kip, bil.	%	Kip, bil.
2003	170	21.0	38	4.7	5	0.7	106	13.1	132	16.3	115	14.2	27	3.4	127	15.6	90	11.1	810
2004	190	22.2	57	6.7	11	1.3	111	13.0	149	17.4	143	16.8	27	3.2	94	11.0	73	8.6	855
2005	187	21.5	65	7.4	17	1.9	130	15.0	164	18.8	173	19.9	17	1.9	56	6.5	62	7.1	871
2006	276	25.2	108	9.8	20	1.8	141	12.8	220	20.0	172	15.7	21	1.9	66	6.1	75	6.8	1098
2007	406	27.9	172	11.8	33	2.3	192	13.2	250	17.2	236	16.2	32	2.2	61	4.2	74	5.1	1457
2008	501	33.1	91	6.0	29	2.0	236	15.6	232	15.4	212	14.0	45	3.0	79	5.3	87	5.7	1512
2009	572	30.0	160	8.4	51	2.7	309	16.2	246	12.9	247	13.0	83	4.3	110	5.7	131	6.9	1909
2010	413	19.4	119	5.6	34	1.6	452	21.3	372	17.5	305	14.4	133	6.3	121	5.7	175	8.2	2123
2011	494	20.3	187	7.7	46	1.9	476	19.5	347	14.2	326	13.4	190	7.8	175	7.2	196	8.0	2438
2012	468	16.9	218	7.9	39	1.4	614	22.2	308	11.1	357	12.9	301	10.9	218	7.9	243	8.8	2767
2013	413	12.9	129	4.0	57	1.8	765	23.9	451	14.1	489	15.3	387	12.1	227	7.1	279	8.7	3195

Source Author's calculation based on data compiled from commercial banks
Notes Percentage refers to the share of a deposit in total deposits. LAK, USD, and THB stand for Lao kip, US dollar, and Thai baht, respectively

Table 1 (Continued)

(D) Composition of deposits by currency, APB																			
	Current deposits						Savings deposits						Term deposits						Total
	LAK		USD		THB		LAK		USD		THB		LAK		USD		THB		
	Kip, bil.	%	Kip, bil.	%	Kip, bil.	%	Kip, bil.	%	Kip, bil.	%	Kip, bil.	%	Kip, bil.	%	Kip, bil.	%	Kip, bil.	%	Kip, bil.
2000	48	59.8	0	0.5	0	0.1	19	23.7	1	1.0	2	2.6	9	11.1	0	0.5	1	0.6	81
2001	52	49.6	2	1.9	0	0.0	26	25.2	2	1.9	3	2.9	17	15.9	1	1.3	1	1.2	105
2002	46	36.7	0	0.4	0	0.0	37	29.6	2	1.9	4	3.6	30	24.3	2	1.7	2	1.8	125
2003	78	38.8	2	0.8	0	0.0	45	22.4	4	1.9	5	2.7	62	30.8	2	1.2	3	1.4	201
2004	97	33.9	2	0.6	1	0.4	48	16.8	9	3.1	9	3.3	115	40.4	1	0.5	3	0.9	285
2005	103	31.4	5	1.5	1	0.2	61	18.7	10	3.1	15	4.5	127	38.8	2	0.7	4	1.1	328
2006	172	42.7	5	1.3	1	0.2	68	16.9	10	2.4	14	3.4	121	30.1	5	1.2	7	1.9	403
2007	333	51.1	2	0.4	2	0.4	86	13.2	16	2.4	26	3.9	160	24.5	9	1.3	18	2.7	651
2008	326	43.0	5	0.7	3	0.4	93	12.3	23	3.0	29	3.8	247	32.6	10	1.4	21	2.8	757
2009	336	35.4	7	0.8	4	0.4	136	14.4	30	3.1	48	5.0	351	37.0	9	0.9	28	2.9	949
2010	299	23.8	5	0.4	2	0.2	195	15.5	30	2.4	65	5.1	600	47.8	15	1.2	46	3.6	1257
2011	354	20.9	12	0.7	3	0.2	289	17.1	49	2.9	100	5.9	799	47.3	25	1.5	60	3.5	1691
2012	366	16.2	10	0.5	6	0.3	408	18.1	53	2.4	125	5.5	1192	52.8	28	1.2	68	3.0	2258
2013	381	13.4	74	2.6	5	0.2	505	17.9	67	2.4	158	5.6	1527	54.0	32	1.1	81	2.9	2830

Source Author's calculation based on data compiled from commercial banks
Notes Percentage refers to the share of a deposit in total deposits. LAK, USD, and THB stand for Lao kip, US dollar, and Thai baht, respectively

Table 2 Components of deposit accounts by type of account holder of selected commercial banks, Lao PDR, 2002–2014

Bank	Year	Type of account holder	Demand deposits			Saving deposits			Fixed deposits			Total
			LAK	THB	USD	LAK	THB	USD	LAK	THB	USD	
Unit: Kip, billion												
BCEL	2002	Individuals	2	0	27	18	65	259	15	49	224	659
		Corporate	109	2	370	4	14	146	1	3	19	667
	2014	Individuals	161	11	175	2536	1782	2591	4691	669	1291	13,905
		Corporate	1173	26	2524	277	49	486	157	0	106	4798
LDB	2004	Individual/Corporate	190	2	57	111	21	149	271	73	94	967
	2014		661	5	175	1011	73	412	5273	304	226	8140
APB	2002	Individual	7	0	0	37	4	2	30	2	2	86
		Corporate	39	0	0	0	n.a.	n.a.	n.a.	n.a.	n.a.	39
	2014	Individual	76	3	3	654	198	71	1964	91	33	3094
		Corporate	501	4	9	n.a.	n.a.	n.a.	n.a.	n.a.	n.a.	513

Source Author's calculation based on data compiled from commercial banks
Notes Deposit amounts are compiled by currency and by type of account holder. LAK, THB, and USD stand for Lao kip, Thai baht, and US dollar, respectively. There are some discrepancies in figures between Tables 1 and 2

fixed-term deposits to its total deposits declined from 21.4% in 2003 to 7.7% in 2013, while the share of local currency fixed-term deposits rose from 1.2% in 2002 to 24.5% in 2013. Similarly, at LDB, the share of US dollar fixed-term deposits declined from 15.6% in 2003 to 7.1% in 2013, whereas the share of local currency fixed-term deposit rose from 3.4 to 12.1% in the same period. This implies an unwinding of asset substitution.

Finally, when we examine LDB, whose main depositors are SMEs, we find that the share of deposits by currency shows that depositors tend to keep deposits in US dollars and Thai baht proportionally for saving accounts and for fixed deposits. Interestingly, its demand deposits are largely in local currency, which implies that settlements of SMEs are largely in local currency.

Table 2 presents the composition of deposits by type of account holder and by type of deposits for three SOCBs (BCEL, LDB, and APB). Account holders are classified into corporations and individuals. Among these three banks, LDB does not differentiate between individuals and corporations, probably due to its focus on SMEs.

Several observations can be made from Table 2. First, the weight of corporate accounts has declined in both BCEL and APB. In BCEL, the shares of corporate and individual accounts were nearly the same in 2002. However, the deposits of individual accounts have grown much faster than those of corporate accounts. In 2014, the latter is almost three times larger than the former. There was a similar change in APB.

Second, fixed deposits have been more favored by individuals whereas demand deposits have been more favored by corporations, regardless of currency type. This apparent preference of corporations for more liquid deposits suggests that their demand deposits are held to facilitate transactions rather than as an investment or store of value instrument, while individual/households keep deposits as a financial portfolio. Saving deposits have been held by both individuals and corporations, but the former overwhelms the latter. Rises in fixed deposits at BCEL and APB are attributable to changes in the composition of depositors, with an increasing weight of individual accounts.

Third, we can see that for fixed deposits of individual accounts, there has been a notable shift from US dollar deposits to kip deposits. In contrast, when we look at the demand deposits of corporate accounts, we find that US dollar deposits continue to account for more than a half of the total demand deposits of corporate accounts.

In summary, observation of bank-level data leads us to conclude that the decline in the dollarization ratio (FCDs to M2) is attributable to a change in the composition of depositors from corporations to individuals and to the preference of individuals to save in local currency fixed deposits held for asset portfolios. In contrast, the corporate sector tends to hold demand deposits for transaction purposes, and the large part of their demand deposits is FCDs. Households' savings deposits would be also used for transaction purposes. For demand deposits and saving deposits, the weights of FCDs remain high, implying that FCDs for transaction purpose are more persistent than FCDs for asset substitution.

4 Evaluation of De-dollarization Policy in Lao PDR

4.1 Evaluation of De-dollarization Policy

The Laotian de-dollarization policy has evolved through different arrangements over the past 2 decades (Box 2). This section attempts to provide an empirical assessment of de-dollarization policy. The methods of policy evaluation definitely have some limitations. There are many ways that a policy can influence the market behavior, and it is often quite difficult to establish a causal connection between a policy and an actual outcome.

Box 2: Chronology of major regulatory and policy changes in Lao PDR, 1988–2015

Year	
October 1988	Commercial banks allowed to accept foreign currency deposits

September 1990	Decree on Foreign Currency Management and Precious Metals (No. 53/PM)
September 1995	Fixed exchange rate regime replaced by a managed float exchange rate regime
October 1996	Decree on Cheque Payment (No. 175/PM)
June 2002	Regulation on reserve requirement ratio comprising kip and foreign currency issued and later amended in May 2006
August 2002	Decree on Foreign Currency Management and Precious Metals upgraded to Presidential Decree (No. 01/PR)
September 2006	Commercial banks first promote the use of ATM cards and utility payment (bills for water and electricity) through banking system
May 2007	Decree on Foreign Currency Management and Promotion of the Use of the kip for Domestic Transaction (No. 150/PM)
September 2007	Nationwide campaign on the use of national currency through media, commercial advertisement, posters, etc.
March 2008	Presidential Decree on Foreign Currency Management and Precious Metals revised
March 2008	BOL Circular on foreign exchange allowing commercial banks and their exchange bureaus to sell foreign exchange to public equivalent to 20 million kip per person per day (equivalent to US$2500) with only ID card or passport (No. 57/BOL)
August 2008	BOL Circular on reference rate: kip/US dollar determination for commercial banks
September2009	Decree on the Implementation of Commercial Bank Law (No. 273/PM)
February 2010	Inter-ministry Committee on Law Enforcement and kip Promotion with the role of conducting

	regular inspections on shops and markets, and corrective action on shops that make payments and quote prices in foreign currencies
September 2013	BOL Circular to commercial banks (No. 792/BOL) to lend in foreign currency only to companies with foreign exchange incomes
October 2014	Decree on Cheque Payment (No. 386/PM) revised
December 2015	ATM Pool Switch for commercial banks launched

In addition to macroeconomic stabilization, Laotian authorities employed other measures, including convertibility of local currency, restrictions on foreign currency loans, promotion of the use of local currency for domestic transactions, and improvements to the domestic payment system and usability of the local currency.

4.1.1 Restoring Macroeconomic Stability

Perhaps the most striking measure that led to a decline in the use of foreign currency was successful macroeconomic stabilization. By learning from the painful experience of the Asian financial crisis and the subsequent high inflation, severe devaluation, and slow economic growth, the BOL took substantial measures to address the long-standing roots of economic instability. A monetary policy framework included implementation of tight monetary policy, reduced credit growth, and exchange rate flexibility, with the exchange rate as the principal tool. Over the past 10 years, the monetary authorities were able to maintain a single-digit inflation rate and a stable exchange rate. The significant improvement in macroeconomic stability has resulted in substantial de-dollarization in the Lao PDR (IMF 2013).

In terms of asset substitution, since the ratio of foreign to local-currency-denominated deposits is considered to positively relate to

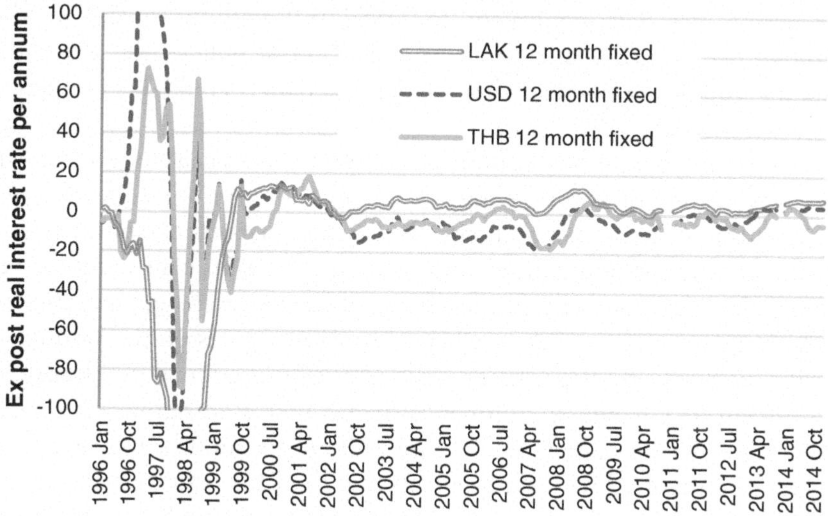

Fig. 3 *Ex post* real interest rates on local and foreign currency fixed deposits, Lao PDR, January 1996–December 2014. *Sources International Financial Statistics*, IMF; Bank of Lao PDR website: http://www.bol.gov.la/english/interrate1.html *Notes* LAK, USD, and THB stand for Lao kip, US dollar, and Thai baht, respectively

the gap in real returns, a fall in inflation (i.e., a rise in real return of local-currency-denominated deposits) should lower the demand for FCDs relative to local currency deposits. Figure 3 shows real interest rates on local currency deposits and foreign currency deposits. The fall in the dollarization ratio that began in 2003 coincides with a switch from a highly negative real interest rate on local currency deposits to a positive return; since then, the real return of local currency deposits has exceeded those of FCDs for most of the times.

4.1.2 Convertibility of Local Currency

In August 2013, the BOL issued a newly revised circular on foreign exchange (No. 243/BOL). To avoid public concerns and restore confidence in the capacity of the supply of foreign exchange by the banking sector, the BOL allowed commercial banks and their exchange bureaus to sell foreign exchange to the general public equivalent to 20 million kip per person per day (equivalent to US$2500) without specifying the purpose or requiring a complex process. This policy was aimed at building public confidence that foreign exchange could be purchased whenever needed.

Another important implication of this policy is that it helps the BOL to contain the foreign exchange black market. As a result, the gap between the black market and official exchange markets narrowed. Many agents, companies, individuals, and tourists turned to banks and formal money changers, not only for purchases of foreign exchange but also for sales of foreign exchange. According to available figures on the volume of foreign exchange trading, the amount of foreign currency purchased by the Bureau de Change of commercial banks increased significantly from US$10.5 million to about US$18–20 million per month. However, the biggest cost involved with this policy is that the BOL spends a substantial amount of foreign reserves on market intervention aimed at maintaining the stability of currency, thus limiting the level of foreign reserves.

4.1.3 Restrictions on Foreign Currency Loans

In September 2013, the BOL issued a regulation on commercial banks (No. 792/BOL) designed to restrict lending in foreign currencies only to companies with foreign exchange incomes. The main objective was to mitigate credit risk associated with unhedged borrowers. This regulation was introduced amid a high amount of nonperforming loans that resulted from lending to borrowers without a source of foreign currency earning. The regulation was supportive of the campaign for the use of local currency for domestic payment.

4.1.4 Improvement of Domestic Payments System and Usability of Local Currency

Underdevelopment of domestic payment systems is also one of the factors that cause the use of foreign currency because cash payment in local currency is inconvenient for large payments, since a large sum of cash is needed to buy high-value products. The main domestic payment instruments are cash, and to a lesser extent, checks, as the latter are cumbersome to use.

Starting in the early 2000s the BOL encouraged commercial banks to develop a modern payment system. BCEL has taken the leading role in developing a modernization scheme for payment system and became the first bank to introduce the core banking system which can support an online system of branches in the form of real-time automated telling machine (ATM) service within the country.

Payment is now available for high-value transactions through banks or other modes of payments. At present, modern and electronic payments system such as debit cards, credit cards and inter-linkage of ATMs in the commercial banking system, in particular, has become a part of people's lives in the country. Under the BOL's Master Plan of modernization of payment system (2011–2015), Real-Time Gross Settlement (RTGS) and an Automatic Clearing House application have already been implemented, and ATM Pool and e-Payment Gateway systems are now underway. For example, BCEL stands ready to install an Electronic Data Capture (EDC) machine to facilitate debit/credit cards payment for shops that need this type of service and provide a special discount from 10–20% for their clients when they buy products from designated shops. There was a good response from customers. ATM cards are increasingly used by the public, and people can withdraw cash from ATMs only in local currency with lower service charge even though their accounts are in foreign currency.

As for the usability of the local currency, its small denomination incentivizes the use of foreign currency because cash payment in local currency is inconvenient for large payments. Prior to 2000, the highest denomination banknote was 5000 kip, which was first issued in 1997. It had a monetary value equivalent to about US$3 initially but its value fell to less than US$1 in 2001 due to the depreciation of the kip.

The BOL introduced the higher denomination of 10,000 and 20,000 kip banknotes in 2002, the 50,000 kip banknote in 2006, and the 100,000 kip banknote in 2011. The 50,000 kip banknote and the 100,000 kip banknote, for example, had a monetary value equivalent to US$5.2 and US$12.5 at the time of introduction of these banknotes. The BOL also improved the quality of banknotes and distribution.

The amount of local currency in circulation has been growing and the kip is increasingly used for numerous purposes. As shown in the financial statistics in Chap. 1, the amount of cash in circulation in the proportion of GDP has significantly increased from 0.5% in 2000 to about 8% in 2013.

4.1.5 Promotion of the Use of Local Currency for Domestic Transactions

The Decree on Foreign Currency Management and Promotion of the Use of the Kip for Domestic Payment (No. 150/PM), issued in May 2007, aimed to increase awareness among all agents, companies, and individuals around the country and encourage them to use only local currency for domestic payments, regardless of the size of the transaction. This decree provides a legal basis for the BOL's mandates and for relevant authorities to provide cooperation in instructing respective bodies under their supervision to comply with the legal requirements for tax payment and remuneration in local currency. The decree also gives the BOL a mandate to collaborate with authorities to conduct regular inspections of business units, companies, and shops to determine whether they are making payments and quoting prices in local currency. The Decree permits the BOL and competent authorities to award prizes to those who provide support and cooperation and to take action against those who violate the regulations. According to a report available from the Monetary Policy Department (BOL 2014), the BOL has issued letters of appreciation to 24 business entities, letters of warning to 193 entities, and imposed a penalty to 11 entities during 2007–2014.

In March 2008, the BOL amended and upgraded the Prime Minister's Decree on foreign exchange management to a Presidential Decree (No. 01/P) and issued implementation instructions in April 2010 incorporating more provisions on effective legal action against those violating the regulations in both minor and severe cases. Provisions and models for good conduct were set. Because of this upgrade to a higher legal status, the regulation could be more stringently enforced. The BOL also created a steering committee for law enforcement and kip promotion consisting of members from key agencies such as the Ministry of Justice, the Court and prosecutors, the Economic Police, the Industry and Trade Department of Vientiane Prefecture, and so on, with the role of implementation, coordination, and monitoring of market conduct. This committee conducted regular inspections to monitor the price quotation of goods and services in the markets, shops, companies, and trade fairs or exhibitions.

The authorities have carried out active promotion campaigns nationwide to encourage the use of local currency. These aimed to persuade the public to change their behavior and rebuild public confidence in the kip. These campaigns included dissemination seminars on the regulatory framework from the central to provincial levels in public offices, schools, universities, and companies. The purpose of the seminars was to persuade the public to strictly comply with the existing legal framework. Furthermore, authorities used public media to promote the use of local currency through radio, television, promotional ads, songs, and posters (Box 3).

Box 3: Example of song title composed by Laotian national artists to promote the use of Kip. *Source* Bank of Lao PDR's Website http://www.bol.gov.la/MPD_2012/index.html

1. Let's join hand to use Kip nationwide
2. Lao people must love to use Lao Kip
3. Lao Kip is a symbol and dignity of our nation
4. Lao Kip is a symbol of our sovereignty
5. The Value of the Lao Kip
6. Lao Kip, Lao Society
7. Our Nation, Our Lao Kip
8. Money and Gold
9. Lao National, Lao Kip
10. Kind hearted merchants
11. Lao currency, Lao Kip
12. Let's maintain the value of Kip

While it is difficult to quantify how much this policy contributed to the de-dollarization of the economy, from eyewitness reports and observation in the field, there have been some positive outcomes. Many shops now increasingly quote prices and accept payment for goods and services in local currency. Public behavior has generally changed to cooperate with the BOL to enforce the implementation of the Law. According to a preliminary report based on a market survey conducted by the committee for foreign currency law enforcement and kip promotion, more than 200 out of 500 business entities, companies, and shops were cooperating with the BOL and quoting prices and accepting payment in local currency.

The Lao authorities consider that in the context of the country, reliance on only market incentives/economic measures is not sufficient to persuade people to use local currency for domestic payment (Pansivongsay 2008). Thus, the authorities emphasize other measures to boost confidence in the kip, including promotion of the use of kip through the media. It is expected that the BOL will continue both the kip promotion campaign and the legal measures until people are proactive and accept only kip for domestic transactions (Phouthonesy 2008).

4.2 Policy Options for De-dollarization

In pursuing the ultimate goal of minimizing the use of foreign currency in the economy, what are the possible policy options for the monetary authorities? The remainder of this section sheds some light on the policy options suitable for the Lao PDR.

Maintaining a sound macroeconomic environment by keeping inflation low and maintain a stable exchange rate is the most critical component of a de-dollarization strategy. This view is also echoed in a speech by the former BOL Governor that "devaluation of the kip would lead to a lack confidence in the national currency and would cause people to convert the kip into foreign currencies to protect their savings."[5] Besides, a policy specifically aimed at reducing dollarization to increase the domestic monetary base through regulations and legal restrictions should be carefully implemented, as it may lead to capital flight and underground transactions. Instead, promotion of the use of the kip through incentives rather than regulations should be pursued.

4.2.1 Development of a Domestic Financial Market

Although the problem of asset substitutions has improved as shown by in the decline in the proportion of foreign currency fixed deposits to total deposits, further effort is required to develop deep and liquid domestic financial markets that can provide alternative investment opportunities to FCDs and reduce the motivation for financial dollarization. Issuance of medium to long-term government bonds in local currency provides a vehicle for domestic investment and can serve as a benchmark for the interest rate.

Similarly, the development of a well-functioning foreign exchange market backed by high levels of foreign reserves would ensure easy market access to foreign exchange, limiting the demand for foreign currency for precautionary reasons. High foreign reserves also play an important role in a dollarized economy as they serve as the first line of defense in the case of a bank run and help to ensure public confidence in the exchange rate.

Although there has been an attempt to develop a domestic financial market in recent years by the authorities, it is still in an early stage of development. The Lao Stock Exchange (LSX) was established in October 2010, and only four companies have been listed in the market during the past 5 years. The domestic bond market is also shallow, and at present the government securities denominated in local currency are only short-term securities, such as the Treasury bills and long-term bonds issued in 2015 for 570 billion kip with maturities of less than 1 year and interest rates of 4–5% per annum. The scope of the market remains restricted and market participants are mostly banks.

4.2.2 Prudential Regulation of the Financial System

Prudential measures might also be effective for dealing with asset substitution. These measures can make foreign currency loans and deposits less attractive, internalizing the real cost of doing business in foreign currency. Prudential measures include narrow open foreign currency position limits, higher liquidity requirements on FCDs, a higher risk premium on dollar deposits in deposit insurance scheme, and higher capital and provisioning requirements on foreign currency loans, especially for borrowers without foreign exchange revenues. They also include stronger collateral and valuation rules for foreign-currency-denominated loans.

Since January 2001 the BOL has set different ratios for local currency deposits and FCDs for reserve requirements. The reserve requirement ratio is 5% for local currency and 10% for foreign currency. These reserve requirement ratios have been kept unchanged since May 2006.

For the open position of foreign currency, a BOL regulation on foreign currency exposure (No. 818/BOL) issued in October 2010 requires commercial banks to maintain a net open position for a single foreign currency for short and a long position not more than 20% of tier-one capital, and a net foreign currency position for all currencies for short and long position not exceeding 25% of tier-one capital.

Third, general loan loss provisions regulations do not distinguish between foreign currency loans and local currency loans. According to a BOL decision issued in April 2010, there is a unified rate for commercial banks to make provisions for nonperforming loans in the range of 0.5–1% of total loans (BOL Decision No. 242/BOL). Similarly, there is also one unified premium rate in the deposit insurance scheme that the commercial banks in Lao PDR shall contribute by 0.1% of total deposits to the Lao Depositor Protection Fund (BOL regulation No. 283/BOL issued in August 1999).

4.2.3 Measures on Currency Substitution

In parallel with policy measures to deal with asset substitution, complementary measures should be considered to control currency substitution or holdings of foreign currency for domestic transaction purposes. For example, policies that promote the use of local currency for payments through convenient and lower cost services than those for foreign currency could be pursued. Similarly, another policy option is control on domestic account transfers of FCDs since demand deposit FCDs are held for domestic transactions as well as for the settlement of international trade. Instead of an immediate ban on domestic account transfers of

FCDs, one option is to impose higher service fees or taxes. When firms encounter higher costs associated with fund transfers, they may shift to transactions using local currency deposits. However, controls on domestic account transfers of FCDs may backfire; transactions may go underground, using foreign currency cash instead of local currency deposits. The policy change may cause a massive withdrawal of demand deposit FCDs. Therefore, the policy must be carefully designed with advance notice given to depositors and safeguards for banks put in place.

Furthermore, public agencies should take a leading role in conducting operations in local currency as much as possible. Increased promotion of tax payments in local currency can support an increase in demand for local currency, as can public payment for wages, goods, and services in local currency.

5 Conclusions

With the implementation of market-oriented reforms in the Lao PDR during the late 1980s, the banking sector was reformed and restrictions on foreign currency holdings were largely removed. Subsequently, a lack of experience in macroeconomic management in dealing with the 1997 Asian financial crisis led to high inflation and a sharp depreciation of exchange rate. As a result, the Lao PDR has experienced high dollarization. The ratio of FCDs to broad money increased from 43.8% in 1988 and reached a peak of almost 80% after the 1997 Asian financial crisis, and remained around 40% following economic stabilization in the latter half of 2000s.

We examine the situation of deposit dollarization using the bank-level data. Major findings could be concluded as follows. First, changes in FCD holding of individuals for asset substitution (fixed deposits) coincided more closely to macroeconomic stabilization, and its growth decelerated more sharply than that of FCD holding of corporations for transaction motives (demand and savings deposits). FCD for transaction purposes might be more difficult to contain when compared with FCDs for asset substitution. Second, FCDs are more prevalent in urban areas than in rural areas.

The authorities have introduced a series of de-dollarization policy measures. These include maintaining macroeconomic stability, improvement and strict enforcement of regulations on foreign exchange management, improvement of domestic payment system and usability of local currency, and nationwide promotion of the use of local currency for domestic transactions. A sharp increase in local currency in circulation from 0.5% of GDP in 2000 to 7.8% in 2013 and 9.2% in 2014, respectively, suggests a remarkable achievement of the de-dollarization policies.

Dollarization is a multifaceted problem due to the mixture of asset substitution, currency substitution, and precautionary demand for foreign exchange in the face of underdeveloped financial system. For successful de-dollarization, each purpose of foreign-currency-denominated assets must be addressed by a composite of de-dollarization strategies; one strategy does not fit all components of dollarization. Thus, there is a spectrum of policy options that Laotian authorities could consider pursuing to contain the use of foreign currency in the domestic economy. The guiding principle here is that policy measures should generally include the maintenance of long-term macroeconomic stability and enhancement of the attractiveness of local currency.

Notes

1. One of these SOCBs is Noyoby Bank, which is classified as a specialized and public bank, set up by the government in September 2006 to provide loans for rural development in areas designated by the government. It does not accept deposits from the public and its source of funding is the government budget allocation, as stated in its charter.
2. BCEL was established as a SOCB in November 1989, succeeding branches of the central bank.
3. LDB was established in April 2003 as a result of the merger of two SOCBs, namely Lane Xang Bank and Lao May Bank.
4. APB was established in June 1993, originally as specialized policy bank for supporting the agriculture sector.
5. Khamphouvong (2010).

References

Bank of Lao PDR (BOL). 2014. Progress report on the implementation of foreign currency management and Kip promotion. Monetary Policy Department, Bank of the Lao PDR (in Lao).

International Monetary Fund (IMF). 2000. Lao People's Democratic Republic: Recent economic developments. IMF Staff Country Report No. 00/03, Washington, DC: International Monetary Fund.

IMF. 2013. Lao People's Democratic Republic: Staff report for the 2013 article IV consultation. IMF Country Report No. 13/369, Washington, DC: International Monetary Fund.

Khamphouvong, P. 2010. Central Bank to keep kip stable. *Vientiane Times*, Jan 4.

Kyophilavong, P. 2010. Lao People's Democratic Republic: Dealing with multiple currencies. In *Dealing with multiple currencies in transitional economies: The scope for regional cooperation in Cambodia, the Lao People's Democratic Republic, and Vietnam*, ed. G. Capannelli, and J. Menon. Manila: Asian Development Bank.

Menon, J. 2007. Dollarization and the multiple currency phenomenon in Lao PDR: Costs, benefits and policy options. ADB Institute Discussion Paper No. 58, Tokyo: Asian Development Bank Institute.

Menon, J. 2008. Dealing with multiple currencies: What options for the transitional economies of Southeast Asia? *Journal of the Asia Pacific Economy* 13 (2): 131–146.

Lathouly, P. 1995. *Macroeconomic policies and institutions in the Lao PDR. UNESCAP Country Report*. Bangkok: United Nations Economic and Social Commission for Asia and the Pacific.

Otani, I., and C.D. Pham. 1996. The Lao People's Democratic Republic: Systemic transformation and adjustment. IMF Occasional Paper 137, Washington, DC: International Monetary Fund.

Pani, M. 2002. Dollarization in the Lao PDR, in IMF Country Report No. 02/61. Washington, DC: International Monetary Fund.

Pansivongsay, M. 2008. Central Bank urges greater use of Kip. *Vientiane Times*, Sept 2.

Phouthonesy, E. 2008. Central Bank Governor campaigns on the use of kip. *Vientiane Times*, Oct 6.

4

Dollarization in Myanmar?

Koji Kubo and Set Aung

1 Introduction

Myanmar has seldom been analyzed in the literature on dollarization. Menon (2008) documents the state of dollarization in the transitional economies of Southeast Asia but excludes Myanmar. In the 1990s, the country faced high inflation and chronic depreciation of the kyat, its legal tender, which potentially stimulated asset substitution just as in the other transitional economies in Southeast Asia.

The views expressed in this paper are those of the authors, and not necessarily those of the organizations with which they are affiliated.

K. Kubo (✉)
Institute of Developing Economies, Japan External Trade Organization (IDE-JETRO), Chiba, Japan
e-mail: Koji_Kubo@ide.go.jp

Set Aung
Central Bank of Myanmar, Naypyitaw, Myanmar
e-mail: Winston.set@cbmnet.co

K. Kubo (ed.), *Dollarization and De-dollarization in Transitional Economies of Southeast Asia*, IDE-JETRO Series, DOI 10.1007/978-3-319-57768-5_4

In June 2015, dollarization arose as renewed concern in Myanmar. Banks in the country faced a sharp rise in the withdrawal of foreign currency deposits (FCDs) and some banks ran out of US dollar notes. The Central Bank of Myanmar imposed a ceiling of US$5000 on withdrawals of FCDs in US dollar notes.[1] At the same time, the Central Bank reminded the public that domestic transactions must be carried out in the local currency.

Newly available data on FCDs show that the proportion of FCDs to total deposits peaked at 45.5% in 2002. Likewise, the proportion of FCDs to broad money reached a high of 24.5% in 2001. These figures imply that the country once faced a significant level of deposit dollarization.

While the indices suggest a high degree of dollarization, we argue that, different from the other transitional economies of Southeast Asia, the demand for foreign exchange has been shaped by administrative controls in Myanmar. First, drawing on financial statistics, we illustrate that asset substitution and currency substitution have been less relevant in Myanmar than in the peers. Second, we analyze how administrative controls encouraged exporters to maintain their export earnings as FCDs for international trade settlements and currency conversion.

The discussion in this chapter contributes to the formulation of de-dollarization strategies in Myanmar, the country in an early stage of dollarization. Identifying how the demand for foreign exchange is formed is an indispensable step for formulation of de-dollarization strategies.

The remainder of the chapter is organized as follows. In Sect. 2, we depict financial statistics and illustrate the trends of dollarization index focusing on changes in components of broad money. We find that the high dollarization indices of the country were largely due to a low level of local currency deposits. In Sect. 3, we discuss how administrative controls shaped demand for foreign exchange. Here, we classify foreign exchange into FCDs, cross-border deposits, and foreign currency banknotes, and illustrate differences in the demand for each type of foreign-currency-denominated assets. In Sect. 4, we review recent reforms that may have implications on dollarization. In Sect. 5, we examine impacts of dollarization on the economy and discuss measures for de-dollarization. In Sect. 6, we present our concluding remarks.

2 Asset Substitution and Currency Substitution in Myanmar?

2.1 Macroeconomic Background

Myanmar has an economic environment that potentially favors dollarization. There have been three episodes of demonetization, in which the government revoked the country's legal tender without respecting its conversion to other currencies.[2] Furthermore, Myanmar faced chronic inflation in the 1990s, with an average annual inflation rate of 25.3% (See Fig. 2c of Chap. 1). The year-on-year inflation rate exceeded 60% for several months during this period. Inflation was attributable to the chronic monetization of fiscal deficits. High inflation accompanied a gross disparity between the official and parallel market rates; as of September 2007, the official exchange rate of the Myanmar kyat vis-à-vis the US dollar was K5.6303, whereas prevailing parallel rates were over K1300.

The parallel foreign exchange market originated in the incomplete economic reforms in the late 1980s. In September 1988, Myanmar (then Burma) initiated a transition from "the Burmese way to Socialism"—a variant of a planned economy—to a market-based economy. During the previous regime, foreign trade had been monopolized by the government, and foreign exchange was centrally administered at a fixed official exchange rate. Since 1989, the private sector has been permitted to engage in foreign trade, though under restrictive administrative controls (Myat Thein 2004).

The reform was incomplete in a sense that the government maintained the central administration of foreign exchange at the fixed official exchange rate within the state sector, while tolerating the parallel market for foreign exchange in the private sector (Kubo 2013). Private exporters were tacitly tolerated to sell their export proceeds directly to importers at the rates that they set themselves. Since then, the parallel market has been setting multiple market exchange rates for the buying and selling of foreign exchange. These rates were not officially recognized but were generally accepted by the public. The prevalent parallel market for foreign exchange in the private sector signified decentralized holding of foreign exchange among those who traded them.

Has US dollar offered a means of inflation hedge in Myanmar? Figure 1–2(C) of Chap. 1 shows US dollar sometimes depreciated in the parallel market despite inflation. Depreciation of US dollar was observed in 1999, 2003, and for a sustained period of 2006–2011. The Myanmar kyat appreciated not only in nominal terms but also in real terms during 2006–2011. This indicates that US dollar does not always offer a means of inflation hedge.

2.2 Underdeveloped Financial System

The financial sector in Myanmar has been underdeveloped, with settlements of transactions largely cash-based. Figure 1 summarizes Myanmar's monetary aggregates. The bars indicate three components of money as a percentage of gross domestic product (GDP): currency outside of banks, local currency (Myanmar kyat) deposits, and FCDs.

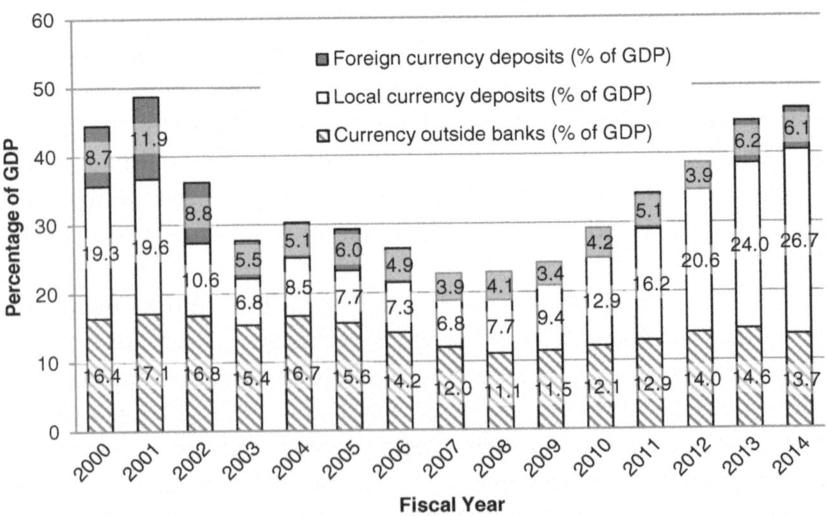

Fig. 1 Monetary survey, Myanmar, fiscal years 2000–2014. *Source* Central Bank of Myanmar. *Notes* Figures are as of the end of each fiscal year. *FCD* foreign currency deposit

The local currency in circulation outside the banking system as a percentage of GDP has been high in Myanmar when compared with the dollarized economies of its peers, Cambodia and Lao PDR. This is consistent with our perception that the economy is cash-based. Furthermore, assuming that local currency cash and foreign currency banknotes are close substitutes in these countries, a larger stock of local currency in circulation in Myanmar implies a smaller stock of foreign currency banknotes outside the banking system.

In contrast, local currency deposits fluctuated tremendously; there was a sharp fall during the period 2002–2004 and the subsequent stagnation that lasted until 2007. As a backdrop to the fluctuations in local currency deposits, there were contagious bank runs at major private banks in February 2003.[3] These bank runs resulted in a sharp decline in local currency deposits—from 19.6% of GDP in the end of fiscal year 2001 (March 2002) to 10.6% in 2003 (March 2004) and 6.8% in 2004 (March 2005).[4]

The recovery of local currency deposits was constrained by the strict regulation implemented after the bank runs. The financial authorities introduced a prudential regulation—the deposit-to-capital ratio control—to limit the total amount of deposits that a bank could accept to seven times its paid-up capital.[5] Those banks which were not able to increase paid-up capital were not allowed to expand deposits. Despite the strict control, there have been frequent rumors of bank runs and massive withdrawal of deposits until recently. Examples of abortive bank runs include the case of Kanbawza Bank—the country's largest private bank—in October 2012, and that of United Amara Bank in November 2014.

Local currency deposits have recovered in recent years. In July 2010, new banking licenses were granted for the first time since May 1997 to four private banks.[6] Three of these newly licensed banks were listed in the top 10 largest private banks in Myanmar in March 2012, accounting for 13% of the private banks' total deposits.[7] Furthermore, the deposit-to-capital ratio control was lifted by 2011. These two changes are associated with a recovery of local currency deposits.

As for local currency deposits, time deposits exhibit a faster growth than demand deposits. Figure 2 shows the decomposition of deposits into FCDs, local currency demand deposits, and local currency time

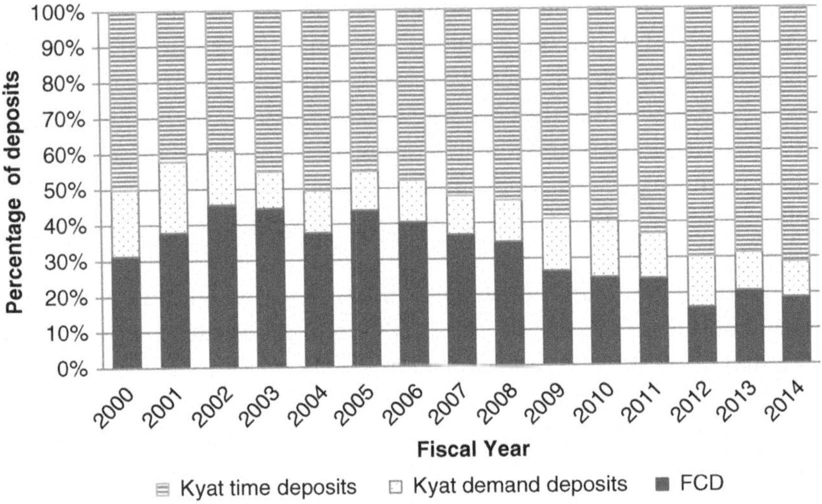

Fig. 2 Composition of deposits in Myanmar, 2000–2014. *Source* Central Bank of Myanmar. *Note* FCD: foreign currency deposit

deposits. As in Lao PDR (Chap. 3 of this volume), savings mobilization proceeded with a rise in local currency time deposits. The proportion of local currency time deposits to total local currency deposits increased from 67.9% in 2001 to 87.7% in 2014.

2.3 Financial Dollarization in Myanmar?

We evaluate the state of dollarization in Myanmar with financial statistics. Figure 3 depicts two indices of deposit dollarization: the ratios of FCDs to total deposits and to broad money. In the financial statistics reported by the Myanmar authorities to the International Monetary Fund (IMF), FCDs are not counted in broad money. The figures here, however, count FCDs as broad money. Figure 3 also shows FCDs in terms of US dollar.

Although the ratios of FCDs to total deposits and to broad money were high especially in the early 2000s, with levels similar to those in Vietnam, we must be cautious when interpreting these as a symptom of

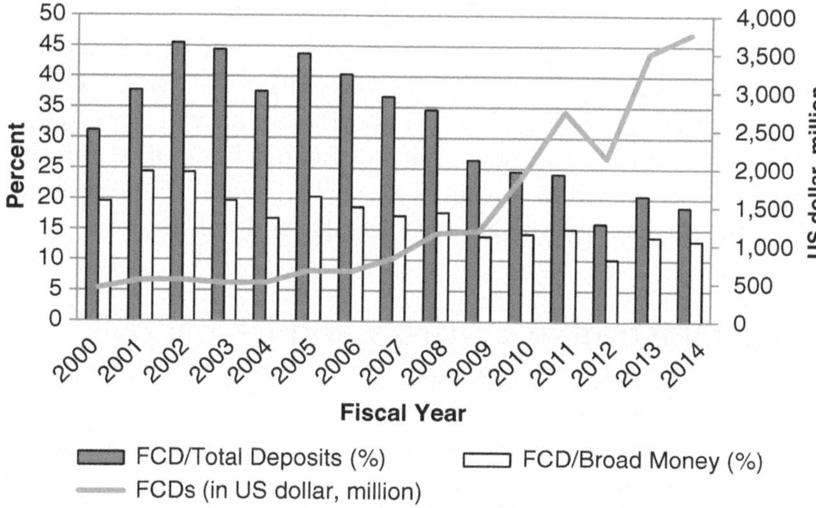

Fig. 3 Deposit dollarization in Myanmar, 2000–2014. *Source* Central Bank of Myanmar. *Note* FCD: foreign currency deposit

asset substitution. The high ratios were largely due to low levels of local currency deposits. The proportion of FCD to total deposits fell by more than 50% in a decade, which is again mainly attributed to changes in local currency deposits. Local currency deposits as a percentage of GDP expanded nearly fourfold, from 6.8% in 2007 to 26.7% in 2014 (Fig. 1). Another important factor is the sharp appreciation of the Myanmar kyat vis-à-vis the US dollar during the period 2007–2012: from K1276 per US dollar in March 2007 to K813 in March 2012 in the parallel market (Fig. 1–2(C) of Chap. 1). This sharp appreciation dampened the weight of FCDs in the monetary aggregate regardless of its growth in US dollar terms.

In addition, FCDs were mostly demand deposits, and time deposits were marginal.[8] During the period when state banks monopolized international banking services until August 2012, these banks offered two types of FCDs: current deposits in foreign currencies[9] with no interest and 6-month time deposits in US dollars with 1% interest per annum. The fact that private firms favored current deposits implies that FCDs were held more for transaction purposes rather than for asset portfolios.

Turning to the asset side of the banks' balance sheet, it is also notable that as of the end of fiscal year 2014 both private and state banks had not made foreign currency loans (FCLs). The banks hold foreign currency assets, with the majority deposited in nostro accounts with foreign banks abroad, while some are deposited in the Central Bank of Myanmar or domestic banks or held in foreign currency banknotes.[10] The absence of FCLs in turn contained the growth of FCDs and dollarization.

3 Administrative Controls and Demand for Foreign Exchange

We examine relationship between the administrative controls and the demand for three types of foreign exchange, namely FCD, cross-border deposits, and foreign currency banknotes.

3.1 Administrative Controls and Foreign Currency Deposits

The administrative controls on foreign exchange and trade were considered to have shaped the demand for FCDs. Such administrative controls differed substantially between the state sector, including the state economic enterprises (SEEs) and the private sector.

In the state sector, as mentioned above, the allocation of foreign exchange was centrally controlled and foreign exchange revenues were accumulated as FCDs of the Union Government at least until 2012 (Kubo 2013). Exporting SEEs surrendered all their export revenues to the state budget. The Union Government maintained this foreign exchange as FCDs at the Myanma Foreign Trade Bank (MFTB), one of three state banks[11] that handled foreign exchange. The Union Government then allocated the foreign exchange budget from its FCD account to importing SEEs. In this system, any foreign exchange surplus of the state sector led to an increase in FCDs at the MFTB rather than an accumulation of foreign reserves at the central bank. It was a characteristic of Myanmar's foreign exchange management that the government maintained foreign exchange as FCDs instead of transferring it to foreign reserves of the central bank, which became a subject of reform later.

The private sector, on the other hand, faced three notable controls that incentivized firms to hold FCDs. First, in contrast to the state sector, there was, in principle, no surrender requirement for the export earnings of private export firms.[12] Instead, firms were required to deposit their export earnings as FCDs at state banks.

Second, until the policy reform of April 2012, there was no formal facility for private export firms to convert foreign exchange to local currency, which necessitated private exporters and importers to trade FCDs themselves. The state banks did not buy or sell foreign exchange with private firms. FCDs could therefore not be withdrawn in Myanmar kyat.[13] Moreover, FCDs could not be withdrawn in foreign currency banknotes because of the Foreign Exchange Regulation Act of 1947, which prohibited residents from holding foreign currency. However, the financial authorities tolerated domestic account transfers of FCDs at the state banks. By transferring their FCDs to private importers' accounts, private exporters sold FCDs to importers at free market prices. As a result of such trading, either the exporters or the importers always had to maintain a part of their working capital as FCDs.

Third, the government imposed regulations to influence the sources and uses of foreign exchange. As part of a policy known as "export-first and import-second," the government issued import licenses subject to conditions such as the importers submitting formal export earnings (FCDs) that fully covered the cost of the imports. Banks maintained records on the source of all FCDs. As a result, foreign exchange from other sources such as revenues from smuggling exports could not be deposited as FCDs or used for formal imports. In the segmented foreign exchange market, importers' demand for export earning FCDs grew, which gave rise to the parallel market trading between exporters and importers.

The data on FCD suggest the link between FCD and administrative controls. First, there were large transfers of foreign assets from the MFTB to the central bank during fiscal year 2012 (IMF 2013), which was accompanied by a decline in FCDs. A portion of the government's FCDs at the state bank was transferred to the central bank to strengthen its international reserves. As a result, the foreign assets of the central bank increased from US$0.54 billion at the end of fiscal year 2011 to US$2.86 billion in 2012, corresponding with a sharp drop in FCDs of the banking sector as shown in Fig. 3.[14]

Second, natural gas exports by a SEE contributed to the trade surplus of the state sector and thus an increase in FCDs. Table 1 summarizes the trade balance by the state and private sectors.[15] Natural gas exports increased from an average of US$0.71 billion in 2001–2003 to US$4.05 billion in 2012–2014. The average annual trade surplus for the state sector was US$3.68 billion in 2012–2014, while the private sector experienced trade deficits averaging up to US$5.93 billion. While there are no FCD data disaggregated into state and private sectors, the coincidence of the rise in FCDs in terms of US dollars with the growth in the trade surplus of the state sector in the latter half of the 2000s suggests that a large portion of FCDs may belong to the state budget.

Table 1 Trade balance by state and private sectors, Myanmar, fiscal years 2001–2014

Fiscal year	Government			Private sector		
	Exports	Imports	Trade balance	Exports	Imports	Trade balance
	Unit: USD million					
2001	1216	958	259	1333	1777	−444
2002	1422	511	911	1653	1786	−133
2003	1048	703	345	1308	1532	−224
2004	1653	626	1027	1262	1354	−92
2005	1951	614	1337	1603	1368	235
2006	3155	1125	2031	2068	1804	264
2007	4028	910	3119	2373	2444	−70
2008	4310	1954	2357	2469	2590	−121
2009	4496	1270	3225	3091	2911	180
2010	5362	1788	3574	3499	4624	−1126
2011	5064	2426	2638	4072	6609	−2538
2012	4566	1518	3048	4411	7551	−3139
2013	6104	2538	3566	5100	11,222	−6122
2014	7170	2754	4415	5354	13,879	−8525

Source Selected monthly economic indicators, Central Statistical Organization (CSO), Myanmar

Nonetheless, we have at least two special considerations when analyzing the relationship between FCDs and trade balance. On the one hand, in the state sector a considerable portion of natural gas export revenues has been paid to foreign stakeholders. In the Balance of Payment Statistics, the transfer of income to foreign countries sharply increased after the rise in natural gas exports, which averaged to US$1.66 billion per annum during 2005–2011.[16] A rise in natural gas export revenues does not fully translate into a rise in FCDs. On the other hand, in the private sector imports through formal channels necessitated FCDs at state banks. The increase in private sector imports should therefore also require a rise in private sector FCDs.

In summary, administrative controls shaped the demand for FCDs in both the state and private sectors. In the state sector, the government maintained foreign exchange as FCDs instead of transferring it to foreign reserves of the central bank. In the private sector, firms maintained FCDs to adapt to administrative controls on foreign exchange and trade, not necessarily from the motivation of asset substitution.

3.2 Controls on Trade and Cross-Border Deposits

It is thought that cross-border deposits and offshore accounts were made more attractive by the restrictive controls on foreign exchange and trade. In terms of exports, Myanmar Customs did not allow export goods to clear customs unless there was evidence of advance payments from foreign buyers. For imports, the banks were instructed not to allow advance payments by importers to foreign suppliers, requiring them to make payments after the arrival of goods or with letters of credit (L/Cs).[17] While these controls might protect Myanmar's private firms from breach of contract by foreign trade partners, compliance with the controls would narrow their trade opportunities.

Cross-border deposits facilitated private firms to circumvent these controls. Both exporters and importers set up shell companies in a third country, such as Singapore, and maintained offshore accounts. When foreign buyers did not agree on advance payments, Myanmar's exporters transferred dummy payments from their shell company accounts in a third country to their own bank accounts in Myanmar for the sake of customs clearance. They later received payments from foreign buyers in their shell company accounts. Likewise, when the foreign suppliers did not agree to deferred payments or L/Cs, Myanmar's importers made advance payments from their shell company accounts in a third country to their foreign suppliers and later replenished the funds in these accounts through a money transfer from Myanmar after the delivery of the goods to Myanmar. In these cases, the shell companies appeared as foreign buyers/suppliers in the trade documents. Consequently, private exporters and importers tended to maintain a part of their working capital as cross-border deposits.

The controls on the prices of imported and exported goods also encouraged importers and exporters to make transactions using cross-border deposits. The government levied a tax on both exports and imports, and some businesses tended to set very low prices in order to evade tax payment (under-invoicing). To address the opportunistic behavior of importers, trade authorities would, for example, set a minimum import price for some products below which import licenses would not be issued. This led to problems especially when the prices set by trade authorities were sticky while international prices were changing on daily basis. Consequently, even *bona fide* importers had no choice but to mention the price set by trade authorities in the invoices (over-invoicing) using a shell company. In such a case, shell companies in a third country and cross-border deposits were also still needed for proper settlements with their foreign suppliers.

Also, balance in offshore accounts was accumulated and used for settlements of smuggling as banks did not accommodate international money transfers of illegal transactions. Cross-border deposits were traded among exporters and importers in Myanmar's parallel foreign exchange market.

Furthermore, the economic sanctions imposed by the United States on the grounds of Myanmar's human rights abuse and public corruption stimulated the use of cross-border deposits. In October 2007, US sanction increased the difficulty of all cross-border financial transactions in US dollars from/to Myanmar. As a result, most private importers/exporters opened offshore accounts informally and maintained revenues in a third country, with which they made international payments/settlements as a way to circumvent US sanctions.

3.3 Foreign Currency Banknotes

The holding of foreign currency banknotes by domestic residents was prohibited by the Foreign Exchange Regulation Act of August 1947. In February 1993, the government introduced foreign exchange certificates (FECs) to reconcile the prohibition of the use of foreign currency banknotes with the needs of foreign tourists and investors in the country. FECs were equivalent to US dollars, but they were often traded at a discounted price in the parallel market since the administrative controls limited the uses of FECs.[18] There was also a period when foreigners were forced to buy a certain amount of FECs before entering the country. As of December 2012, FECs in circulation amounted to 30.92 million units (1 FEC unit is equivalent to US$1 in face value).[19] This was equivalent to just 0.45% of the local currency in circulation outside the banking sector if valued at a prevailing parallel rate.

The usage of foreign currency banknotes was limited when compared with FCDs. The source of FCDs was, in principle, restricted to formal export revenues. As banks distinguished the sources of foreign exchange, only the foreign exchange earned from formal export revenue could be deposited as FCDs and used for formal imports. Foreign currency banknotes from informal sources such as smuggling exports could not be deposited as FCDs. This marks a stark contrast with the practices in the peer (Cambodia, Lao PDR, and Vietnam), where foreign currency from any source can be deposited as FCDs and used for any current account transactions.

Furthermore, while smuggling and mis-invoicing of international trade have been pervasive in Myanmar, they may not be necessarily associated with inflows of foreign currency banknotes. The country has a sophisticated system of informal cross-border money transfers, known as "*hundi*", which developed under the tight administrative controls on foreign exchange and trade (Set Aung 2009). The *hundi* money transfer operators employ account offsetting, saving the labor of physically transporting currency across borders. For example, informal money transfer operators offset inward remittances from Myanmar migrant workers with the outward money transfers of smuggling importers' payments to their foreign suppliers; operators complete money transfers by channeling migrant workers' offshore foreign exchange balance to importers' offshore accounts, and importers' kyat balance to accounts of migrant workers' families in Myanmar. Therefore, remittances from migrant workers do not always mean a net inflow of foreign currency banknotes into Myanmar. The developed *hundi* system may have contained the circulation of foreign currency banknotes in the country.[20]

While no quantitative data are available, these as a whole imply that foreign currency banknotes in circulation have been limited in Myanmar. If this was the case, we can further infer that payment dollarization was limited on the ground that payment dollarization would coincide with a large stock of *foreign* currency banknotes in circulation.[21] A large stock of *local* currency in circulation is consistent with our inference.

4 Reforms Since 2011 and Dollarization

Since 2011, the government has implemented bold reforms in foreign exchange management and controls on international trade, including (1) exchange rate unification and abolition of the restrictions on currency convertibility, and (2) entry of foreign banks and introduction of FCLs. We consider the implications of these reforms on dollarization.

4.1 Convertibility of Myanmar Kyat

We can summarize the major reforms on foreign exchange as below. First, in April 2012, the central bank abolished the official peg and moved to a managed float. In the state sector, however, the central administration of foreign exchange at the administrative exchange rate has remained, though it was devalued to a level close to the market rate.

Second, the government liberalized foreign exchange controls. The Foreign Exchange Management Law and the Foreign Exchange

Management Regulation were enacted in August 2012 and September 2014, respectively, superseding the Foreign Exchange Regulation Act of 1947. Under the new law, residents are allowed to hold foreign currency regardless of whether the source is domestic or foreign. The new regulation states that legally earned foreign currencies not exceeding an amount equivalent to US$10,000 may be held by residents for a period of 6 months, and that residents who wish to hold foreign currency banknotes totaling more than US$10,000 or to hold any amount for more than 6 months may sell them to moneychanger license holders or deposit them as FCDs at authorized dealer banks. Under the law, FCDs can be withdrawn in foreign currency banknotes instead of in FECs. Furthermore, in March 2013, the central bank announced the abolition of FECs with a 90-day exchange period beginning April 1, 2013.

Third, the government abolished the restrictions on the uses and sources of foreign exchange. In April 2012, the government lifted "export-first and import-second" policy that caused segmentation in the foreign exchange market. The Foreign Exchange Management Law of August 2012 clearly states that no restriction shall be imposed on either inward or outward current international transactions. As per the Foreign Exchange Management Regulation of September 2014, outward current international transactions of individual residents related to travel, medical, educational, or conference purposes up to an amount equivalent to US$10,000 do not require approval from the central bank. The outward current international transactions in foreign exchange (of any amount) of a company do not require the central bank's approval. Accordingly, since the enactment of the regulation, evidence of the receipt of goods has been no longer a requirement when Myanmar's importers order international money transfers at banks. Finally, in June 2015, Myanmar Customs abolished the advance payment condition for customs clearance for Myanmar's exporters.

The authorities complemented these reforms with regulatory changes to establish formal foreign exchange market. In November 2011, the central bank granted moneychanger licenses to private banks, who began foreign exchange trading with private exporters and importers. In August 2012, the central bank granted authorized dealer licenses to some private banks, allowing them to conduct international banking services and accept FCDs. This terminated the state banks' monopoly of international banking. The amount of FCDs in these banks accounts for 22% of total FCDs as of July 2015.

The entry into the foreign exchange market by private banks has offered a formal facility for the private sector to convert foreign exchange.[22] During the previous regime, the state banks did not buy and sell foreign exchange with the private sector; banks' FCD liabilities were fully covered by foreign-currency-denominated liquidities. This required private exporters and importers to maintain FCDs at least temporarily for currency conversion. With the reforms, private exporters and importers no longer need to maintain FCDs for currency conversion.

However, trading of FCDs among private exporters and importers persists even after the reforms. For fiscal year 2014 (April 2014 through March 2015), the monthly average customer dealing[23] of foreign exchange at banks was US$114 million, whereas the monthly average private exports were US$446 million. This indicates that majority of currency conversion in the private sector was conducted outside banks. Trading of FCDs outside banks has history over two decades, and it may still take some time for exporters and importers to abandon the acquired practice and move to the formal foreign exchange market.

Also, there remain some benefits for firms to maintain cross-border deposits. The controls on the prices of imported and exported goods still exist. Furthermore, using shell companies in a third country, firms can make use of trade financing services of banks abroad. The reforms may not provide enough incentives for private firms to replace their cross-border deposits with domestic assets.

4.2 Entry of Foreign Banks and Foreign Currency Loans

Along with the entry of foreign banks, foreign currency loans (FCLs) were started in Myanmar. In October 2014, nine foreign banks were granted provisional licenses to open branches that could lend in permitted foreign currencies (mainly the US dollar) and local currency, but to only foreign corporations and local banks. They can take deposits in local or foreign currency, but again from only foreign corporations and local banks. They cannot take deposits from local corporations and households. They may lend to local corporations only in partnership with local banks in any forms, including syndicated loans. In April 2015, foreign banks that had met all the requirements to open a branch were granted branch licenses and they began operations in Myanmar, making the country's first FCLs to foreign corporations.

As foreign banks' branches still do not have sufficient local currency deposits, and do not want to take a currency position by selling their US dollar capital, they are interested in lending mostly in US dollars. Monetary authorities have indicated that the reserve requirement ratio on FCDs could be raised in order to encourage banking operations in local currency and to avoid possible dollarization in the future.[24] When the currency exchange market is developed,[25] these foreign banks' branches will be able to obtain local currency from local banks without needing to sell their foreign currency capital and will then be able to lend more in local currency.

FCLs can grow further among local banks. The Foreign Exchange Management Law of 2012 allows local banks that are authorized dealer license holders to provide FCLs to residents even though the Central Bank of Myanmar still restricts the FCLs provided by them. However, since foreign bank branches have been allowed to make FCLs, it is likely that local banks are also allowed to do the same if they present sound risk management policies.

5 Does Dollarization Matter in Myanmar?

5.1 Does Dollarization Matter?

Based on our observation that the private sector holds foreign-currency-denominated assets largely for the purposes of international trade settlements, we conclude that it does not necessarily affect the domestic price level directly or interfere with the functions of monetary policy. This is because their foreign-currency-denominated assets are not necessarily close substitutes for local currency in terms of financial assets and means of payment.

Furthermore, since local banks still do not make FCLs, we see that dollarization is not yet a direct threat to the stability of the financial system in Myanmar. In the balance sheet of both state and private banks, the FCDs of residents account for 94.7% of total foreign currency liabilities, which are almost fully covered by foreign currency liquidities. FCDs in Myanmar are therefore not directly imposing exchange rate risk and liquidity risk on the banking sector.[26] The problem is rather that FCDs are not intermediated by the banking sector. FCLs are, however, a double-edged sword; while they might add to credit creation, they also create exchange rate and liquidity risk in the banking sector.

A more practical problem associated with dollarization in Myanmar is the instability of parallel exchange rates. Dollarization, or the decentralized holding and trading of foreign exchange among residents, is highly compatible with the parallel foreign exchange market, which is prone to hoarding, resulting in unstable parallel market rates. Although the Central Bank of Myanmar has moved to a managed float, its daily reference rate has been more or less following the parallel market rates, rather than guiding them. Figure 4 shows the trends in the official daily reference rate and the parallel market rate of US dollar banknotes. It is clear that the parallel rate is more volatile than the official rate. Dollarization imposes a challenge for the financial authorities to stabilize exchange rate.

Apart from exchange rate instability, a rise in demand for US dollar banknotes caused a disturbance in June and July of 2015. Withdrawals of FCDs in US dollar banknotes from the banks increased and some banks ran out of stock. The Central Bank of Myanmar issued an instruction in June 2015 imposing a ceiling on US dollar banknote withdrawals of US $5000 per day, half the previous amount of US$10,000, and later further restricted withdrawals by introducing a limit on the frequency of withdrawals to twice a week per account. Although the instruction was not applied to foreign investors, international organizations, and local and international non-governmental organizations, banks still restricted their cash withdrawals due to limited stock of US dollar banknotes.

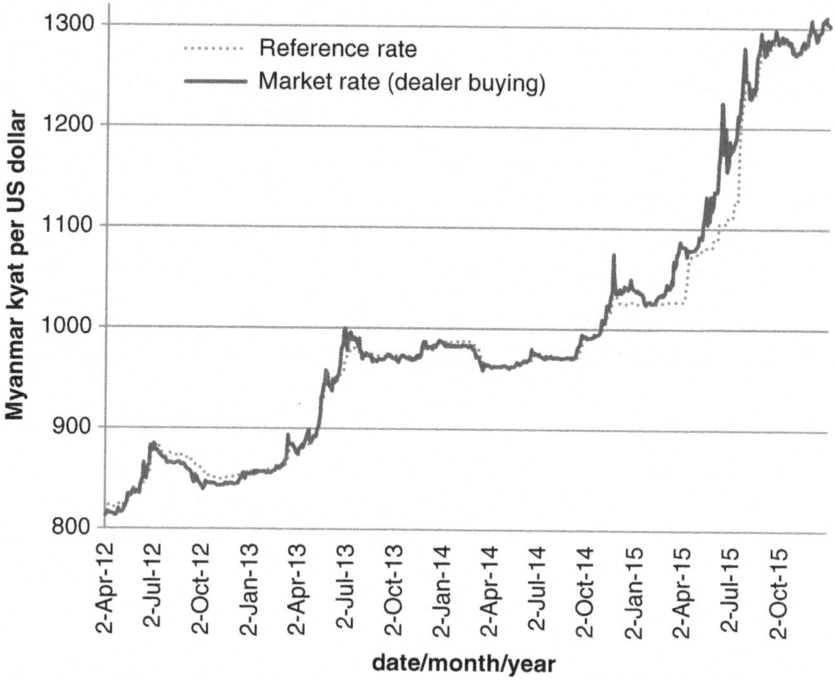

Fig. 4 Daily official and parallel market exchange rates, Myanmar, April 2012–December 2015. *Sources* Central Bank of Myanmar website; E-trade Myanmar database

This incident, however, could be attributed more to policy distortions and arbitrage by residents. While the official reference rate has been set along with the parallel market rate since the start of the managed float in April 2012, it overvalued the Myanmar kyat more than 10% over the parallel rate during depreciation of the Myanmar kyat in June 2015 (Fig. 4). As official moneychangers including banks set their buy rate of the US dollar in accordance with the official reference rate,[27] the official buy price of US dollar and the informal dealer buy price of US dollar notes diverged as well. It was natural that those who needed to convert their FCDs to the kyat withdrew FCDs in US dollar banknotes and sold them to informal moneychangers.[28] This could partially explain the increased demand for US dollar banknotes in June and July 2015.

Nevertheless, concerns are prevalent among residents over dollarization. In June 2015, the central bank sent a reminder to governmental organizations that payments of domestic transactions must be carried out in the local currency. In October 2015, the central bank announced the revocation of the foreign exchange acceptor and holder licenses of domestic businesses such as hotels and restaurants.[29] While these measures were not necessarily targeted at dollarization, domestic residents associated them with dollarization.[30]

5.2 De-dollarization in Myanmar

We find that FCDs of the state sector and those of the private sector have been held for different purposes. Thus, measures to contain FCDs are different in two sectors. As for FCDs of the state sector, they are more or less equivalent to the foreign reserves of the country. Whether they are held as FCDs of the state sector or the foreign reserves at the Central Bank is a matter of the state budget administration. This problem is not substantive.

As for FCDs of the private sector, private exporters and importers hold them to facilitate currency conversion. Compared with the sophisticated parallel market that developed during the restrictive controls on foreign exchange and trade in the past, the newly established formal market built around the authorized dealer banks may not be so convenient for private exporters and importers. Especially when the reference exchange rate set by the Central Bank diverges from the prevalent market rate, uncompetitive exchange rates that authorized money changers and banks have to advertise would distract firms from the formal market.

To contain dollarization or the decentralized holding of foreign exchange and to absorb the parallel market into the formal market built around the authorized dealer banks, the authorities must address any motives of residents for the holding of foreign exchange. In Myanmar, the motives may root in the need to facilitate international trade settlements and currency conversion in the face of the strict controls on foreign exchange and trade in the past.

Eliminating such controls is the first step to let residents abandon their acquired practices of foreign exchange holding and informal transactions. As for FCDs, the reforms have eliminated obstacles to the conversion of FCDs to local currency. However, this has not provided sufficient incentives for residents to move to the formal market.

One policy measure to encourage private exporters and importers to convert FCDs at banks instead of in the parallel market is to raise the cost of FCD domestic account transfers. Banks can be instructed to raise the fees for domestic account transfers of FCDs, which are currently as low as US$2–3. A higher fee would discourage bilateral trading of FCDs among exporters and importers using account transfers, and replace them with trading with banks. A potential side effect of such a policy is that banks extract monopolistic rents from currency trading, leading to a flight from FCDs to cross-border deposits. A too much high cost of conversion of FCD would lead firms to shift from formal exports/imports using FCDs to smuggling exports/imports. To avoid this, a proper environment must be created to restrain banks from taking excessive margins in foreign exchange trading.

Finally, as for cross-border deposits, the inconvenience associated with international trade settlements necessitate exporters and importers to hold them. Establishing convenient formal channels for international trade settlements would therefore be an effective step in containing cross-border deposits. This includes a provision for trade financing.

6 Conclusion

Newly available data on FCDs reveal that Myanmar once experienced a high level of deposit dollarization. The ratio of FCDs to total deposits reached 45.5% in 2002, though it declined to 18.7% in 2014. The ratio of FCDs to broad money was as high as 24.5% in 2001, and it came down to 13.2% in 2014.

However, one must be cautious when interpreting these figures as a reflection of high dollarization in the country. We show that the demand for foreign exchange has been shaped by administrative controls on foreign exchange and trade. On the one hand, a considerable portion of FCDs might belong to the state budget. This is a legacy of the central administration of foreign exchange allocation in the old planned economy regime. On the other hand, in the private sector, foreign exchange regulations limited the sources of FCDs to formal export earnings, and exporters and importers held FCDs for use in international trade and currency conversion.

In terms of payment dollarization, Myanmar appears to remain in a nascent stage as the circulation of foreign currency banknotes appears to be limited by three factors. First, the government had prohibited the holding and use of foreign currency banknotes with the Foreign Exchange Regulation Act of 1947 while introducing FECs to contain the circulation of foreign currency banknotes. Second, the local currency in circulation outside banks, which would be substitute for foreign currency banknotes, has been high. Third, the informal cross-border money transfer system, *hundi*, was developed, replacing the physical carriage of foreign currency with account offsetting. With the *hundi* system, the country's foreign assets are accumulated as cross-border deposits in foreign countries such as Singapore, rather than in the form of foreign currency notes domestically.

We conclude that dollarization has not yet imposed significant risk on Myanmar's banking system as it does in the other CLMV countries. As long as local banks do not make FCLs and they almost fully cover their foreign currency liabilities with liquid foreign currency assets, both exchange rate risk and liquidity risk are mitigated.

Dollarization or the decentralized holding of foreign exchange by residents is attributable, at least partially, to the acquired practices of foreign trade settlement procedures which have evolved during the period of the strict administrative controls on foreign exchange and trade. As long as the acquired practices remain preferred by private businesses, dollarization will persist in Myanmar. In this regard, de-dollarization policy in Myanmar should incorporate the establishment of convenient formal channels for international trade settlements, providing incentives for private firms to abandon the acquired practices.

Notes

1. Although the ceiling was set, it was not applicable for foreign investors, international organizations, and local and international non-governmental organizations.
2. The government demonetized large denomination notes in May 1964, November 1985, and September 1987.
3. Turnell (2003) provides a detailed account of the 2003 Bank Run.
4. Myanmar's fiscal year runs from April 1 to March 31 of the next calendar year.
5. The ratio was relaxed to ten times, but the timing of this change is not certain.
6. Before the entry of these four newly licensed banks, there were 20 private banks.
7. The figure is calculated from the data in the 2011–2012 annual report of the central bank.
8. Based on interviews by one of the authors with state banks in July 2014. One reason is that the interest rate was lower than those of the local currency deposits. Another was that the fixed FCDs did not count toward the margin when importers open L/Cs at the state banks; these banks usually required 100% margin with current account FCDs for opening L/Cs.
9. US dollar, Euro, and Singapore dollar.
10. As of March 2015, commercial banks' foreign currency assets are broken down as follows: 69.1% in foreign banks abroad, 21.7% in cash holdings, 6.4% in domestic banks, and 1.4% in the Central bank and others in the sundry accounts.
11. These were the MFTB, the Myanma Investment and Commercial Bank (MICB), and the Myanma Economic Bank (MEB).
12. There were several exceptional cases where the government ordered the private exporters to sell their export earnings at the unfavorable overvalued exchange rates.
13. This is one of the characteristics of the de facto multiple exchange rate regimes in Myanmar before the reforms in April 2012. See Kubo (2014) for details of these multiple exchange rate regimes.
14. The central bank also started two-way foreign exchange auctions with the domestic banks that may have helped the accumulation of foreign reserves.

15. The trade figures in this paragraph are retrieved from the *Selected Monthly Economic Indicators* of the Central Statistical Organization, Myanmar.
16. The figure is from the *Balance of Payments Statistics* of the IMF.
17. The legal basis of the instruction was the Foreign Exchange Regulation Act of 1947. Furthermore, the banks imposed a 100% margin on FCDs for importers opening L/Cs; that is, without a sufficient amount of FCDs at the state banks, importers could not pay with L/Cs.
18. FEC could hardly be used for formal imports by 2001 after the gradual tightening of administrative controls.
19. The figure is quoted in Xinhua News, "Myanmar announces period for exchanging abolished FEC with foreign currencies" (2013).
20. As another effect of the *hundi* system, while inflows of foreign currency cash were limited, the foreign assets of corporations and individuals would accumulate in foreign countries, especially Singapore, as cross-border deposits.
21. In Myanmar, moneychangers accept only spotless US dollar notes. Notes with tears or stains are at least discounted. This behavior implies that US dollar notes have been rarely circulated for transaction settlements among domestic residents, but have been held as a means of savings.
22. While liberalizing the trading of foreign exchange, the Foreign Exchange Management Regulation of 2014 introduced a limit on the foreign exchange net open position of banks to 30% of their Tier I capital.
23. Customer dealing refers to banks' sales and purchase of foreign exchange with firms and households.
24. As of December 2015, the reserve requirement ratio for local currency deposits was 5%, while no reserve requirement ratio was set on FCDs.
25. The Central Bank of Myanmar is preparing the framework to foster foreign exchange swap among banks.
26. While the state banks used to require 100% margin with FCD to open L/Cs, some private banks reduce the margin for importers opening L/Cs. As a result, these private banks are subject to exchange-rate-induced credit risk.
27. Moneychanger licenses have been granted not only to banks, but also to private nonfinancial institutions. A moneychanger license permits the holder to buy and sell foreign currency notes at rates that are in the band of plus or minus 0.8% of the Central Bank's daily reference rates.
28. The demand for US dollar notes rose so high that the trading price of US dollar notes in the parallel market exceeded the trading price of

FCDs. Usually, US dollar notes are traded at a lower price than FCDs because of cash handling costs. The higher price of US dollar notes in the parallel market aggravated the situation, stimulating not only individual but also corporate depositors to withdraw FCDs in US dollar notes for currency conversion in the parallel market.
29. The foreign exchange acceptor and holder license only allows businesses to accept payments in foreign currency. Licensed businesses include airlines, freight forwarders, hotels, restaurants, and travel agencies.
30. Reuters, "Myanmar revokes for ex licenses to control 'dollarization.'" (2015).

References

International Monetary Fund (IMF). 2013. Myanmar: 2013 Article IV consultation and first review under the staff-monitored program. IMF Country Report No. 13/250. Washington, DC: International Monetary Fund.

Kubo, K. 2013. Myanmar's two decades of partial transition to a market economy: A negative legacy for the new government. *Post-Communist Economies* 25 (3): 357–370.

Kubo, K. 2014. Foreign exchange market reform in Myanmar: Achievements and challenges. *Journal of Southeast Asian Economies* 31 (2): 210–224.

Menon, J. 2008. Dealing with multiple currencies: What options for the transitional economies of Southeast Asia? *Journal of the Asia Pacific Economy* 13 (2): 131–146.

Myanmar announces period for exchanging abolished FEC with foreign currencies. 2013, March 22. *Xinhua News*. http://news.xinhuanet.com/english/business/2013-03/22/c_132254083.htm. Accessed 7 Jan 2016.

Myanmar revokes forex licences to control 'dollarization.' 2015, October 18. *Reuters*. http://www.reuters.com/article/myanmar-forex-idUSL3N12I04K20151018. Accessed 7 Jan 2016.

Set Aung, W. 2009. *The role of informal cross-border trade in Myanmar*. Asia paper. Stockholm: Institute for Security and Development Policy.

Thein, Myat. 2004. *Economic development of Myanmar*. Singapore: Institute of Southeast Asian Studies.

Turnell, S. 2003. Myanmar's banking crisis. *ASEAN Economic Bulletin* 20 (3): 272–282.

5

Dollarization and De-dollarization Policies: The Case of Vietnam

Thi Hoang Anh Pham

1 Introduction

This chapter analyzes dollarization and the de-dollarization policy measures implemented in Vietnam during 1990–2015. Dollarization, which is the circulation and use of US dollars, has a long history in Vietnam and has attracted interest from a number of researchers such as Dodsworth et al. (1996), Phan (1995), Nguyen, T.H. (2002, 2011), Hauskrecht and Nguyen (2004), State Bank of Vietnam (SBV) (2007, 2013), and Pham et al. (2014). Most studies focused on analyzing and evaluating the degree of dollarization as a whole based on the conventional theory of dollarization that includes (i) asset substitution in the form of foreign-currency-denominated assets and (ii) currency substitution (i.e., the use of foreign currency as a method of payment and foreign currency quotation for goods and services). Unlike them, Nguyen, T.H. (2002, 2011) evaluated

T.H.A. Pham (✉)
Banking Academy of Vietnam, The State Bank of Vietnam,
Hanoi, Vietnam
e-mail: anhpth@hvnh.edu.vn

K. Kubo (ed.), *Dollarization and De-dollarization in Transitional Economies of Southeast Asia*, IDE-JETRO Series, DOI 10.1007/978-3-319-57768-5_5

the degree of dollarization in different economic sectors including households, enterprises, and banks from both sides of the balance sheet. Utilizing a dataset collected in Vietnam during 1990–2000, this study found that individuals and households were heavily dollarized in terms of bank deposits and foreign currency cash in circulation.

Hauskrecht and Nguyen (2004) indicated that the main causes of dollarization in Vietnam were high inflation and the depreciation of the Vietnamese dong (VND), the legal tender of the country. These findings are similar to those of Pham et al. (2014) and the SBV (2007, 2013). In addition, increasing dollarization in Vietnam resulted partly from its greater integration with international trade and finance since 1986 as well as the poor coordination between the exchange rate and interest rate policies that led to a shift from dong to dollar assets (Nguyen 2002). In assessing dollarization's impacts on the economy, Hauskrecht and Nguyen (2004) found that dollarization had a negative impact on investment activities and the effectiveness of monetary policy implementation in addition to intensifying local currency depreciation. These findings are consistent with those of the SBV (2007, 2013) and Pham et al. (2014). Nguyen, T.H. (2002, 2011) argued that with an increasing degree of dollarization, the banking system might face foreign exchange exposure if it held net open foreign exchange transactions.

This study contributes to the extant literature in several unique ways. First, a thorough review of foreign exchange regulations provides evidence that these regulations are closely linked to both dollarization and de-dollarization in Vietnam. Some regulations could be associated with a higher degree of dollarization and others with de-dollarizing the economy. Second, the interest rate differential is found to be an important factor that could reduce dollarization in Vietnam by creating incentives that motivate residents to keep dong assets instead of foreign currency deposits (FCD). Third, as Vietnam is a less-monetized economy, foreign currency in circulation has been taken into account to measure dollarization status, and the volume of foreign currency in circulation has been estimated using net private transfers extracted from Balance of Payments statistics. Fourth, due to the interconnectedness between dollarization and goldization,[1] this study argues that de-goldization (e.g., imposing regulations on gold trading, regulations on net open positions in gold assets and liabilities, etc.) was used as a de-dollarization measure in Vietnam.

The remainder of this chapter is divided into five parts. Section 2 reviews the macroeconomic background and exchange rate policy development since the economic reorganization in 1986. In Sect. 3, the study provides an overview of the dollarization trend in Vietnam from 1990 to 2015. Next, Sect. 4 analyzes the main causes of dollarization in Vietnam before an evaluation of the de-dollarization measures implemented by the SBV in Sect. 5. Finally, Sect. 6 summarizes the analysis and concludes the study.

2 Macroeconomic Background and Exchange Rate Policy Development

2.1 Macroeconomic Background

Much like in other communist countries, Vietnam implemented an internal-oriented and closed economic policy in which goods and commodities could only be exchanged in a socialist system, and trading activities were conducted in the ruble at soft prices. For years, the ex-Soviet Union had been Vietnam's main trading partner. Since both countries had non-convertible currencies, compensation trade was dominant. Vietnam relied heavily on the Soviet Union for many of its strategic imports, such as oil, fertilizer, steel, and cotton (Brahm and Le 1993). At that time, the Vietnamese economy was centrally planned with government intervention in all macro and microeconomic policies. This model was effective and efficient during wartime; however, in the long run it distorted supply–demand principles in addition to causing many serious economic consequences.

One of the most remarkable policy measures implemented by the Vietnamese government was the comprehensive "Price-Wage-Money" program launched on September 14, 1985. The government also issued a new dong note with a denomination 10 times the value of the old dong (Decision 01-HĐBT-TĐ, dated September 13, 1985). This action, however, caused panic in the markets as people rushed to dump VND in favor of purchasing commodities and staples. From 1985 to 1988, we can see that while GDP growth was low at around 4% year, the inflation rate topped 700% in 1985. Along with hyperinflation, the deposit interest rate climbed from 7% (in 1985) to 20% per month (in 1988)[2]; however, the real interest rates remained negative.

To overcome these economic difficulties, Vietnam carried out an economic reform known as DOI MOI in Vietnamese in December 1986, which transformed the country from a centrally planned economy into a socialist-oriented market economy. As a part of these reforms, Vietnam reconfigured the financial and banking sector by establishing a two-tier banking system in 1988 under which four state-owned commercial banks were separated from the SBV (the central bank). This provided a legal framework for the SBV to focus on the issue of price stability (Rosengard and Huynh 2008; Nguyen 2012). Inflation rates decreased sharply from 67/68% (in 1990, 1991, respectively) to single digit in 1993 (Fig. 1), while GDP growth peaked at 9.54% in 1995.

The country achieved both price stability and output growth from 1995 to 2007, apart from a period of lower growth in 1998–1999 after the Asian financial crisis. Figure 1 shows the downward trend in

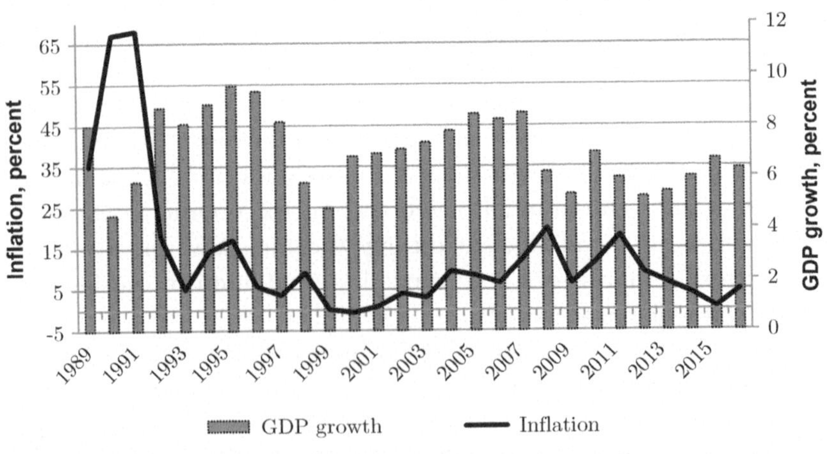

Fig. 1 Macroeconomic indicators in Vietnam, 1989–2016. *Sources ADB key indicators* (period 1989–1990); *general statistics office* (period 1991–2015) and expectation for 2016

economic growth from 9.5% in 1995 to 4.8% in 1999 before recovering to 6.9% in 2001. Moreover, inflation rates became negative at −0.6% in 2000, and turned to a positive number of 0.8% in 2001.

However, the global financial crisis of 2008–2009 affected Vietnam's economy in the following ways:

i. Economic growth fell to 5.3% in 2009 and then recovered to 6.9% in 2010
ii. The year-on-year inflation rate exceeded 28% in August 2008, its highest in 17 years[3]
iii. Stock and real estate prices tumbled, declining by nearly 70% and 50%, respectively, from January to December 2008
iv. Market interest rates rose substantially from 7.5% in January 2008 to 19% in July 2008 for 3-month deposits
v. The trade balance recorded a deficit of US$14.21 billion in the first 6 months of 2008.

In 2009, in response to the global financial crisis in general and the domestic economic turbulence in particular, the Vietnamese government launched a stimulus package[4] aimed at supporting economic growth, ensuring social security, and accelerating poverty reduction. However, this package was not particularly beneficial to the country. Rapid credit expansion caused by the stimulus package led to a high nonperforming loan ratio of 17.2% in 2012 (To et al. 2013; Pham et al. 2014). In addition, internal weaknesses of the economy (e.g., the economic structure model, corruption, and asset bubbles) and the banking system led to a recession in 2011 with a low economic growth rate of roughly 5% and inflation of 6%, compared with an average rate of 7.3 and 7.1%, respectively, in the period of 2000–2010.[5]

2.2 Exchange Rate Policy Development

Before 1988, Vietnam followed a multiple exchange rate regime that consisted of an official or trade exchange rate, a non-trade exchange rate, an internal exchange rate, and a beside parallel market rate. The official rates overvalued the VND. With the long-term goal of achieving freely convertible VND, the SBV established Foreign Exchange Transaction Centers in Ho Chi Minh City and Hanoi in 1991 followed by the formation of an interbank foreign exchange market in 1994. By doing so, the SBV created an organized official market so that demand for and supply of foreign currencies (mostly the US dollar) were matched. Through this market, the SBV was also able to monitor the supply and demand of foreign exchange and formulate policies with regard to the management of monetary policy as well as foreign exchange reserves.

Since 1992, the SBV has attempted to maintain the stability of the USD/VND exchange rate in order to stabilize the macro-economy. This action continued especially during the Asian financial crisis in 1997 when most currencies in Asia (such as the Thai baht, the Indonesian rupiah, the Malaysian ringgit, etc.) suffered large devaluations against the US dollar. This led to an overvaluation of VND against the US dollar and harmed the competitiveness of Vietnamese goods and services, which led to severe trade deficits from 1994 to 1997.

In August 1998, the SBV approved Decree 63/1998/ND-CP on foreign exchange management, replacing Decree 161/HDBT/1988, which focused on the rights of residents and nonresidents to possess and use foreign currency (FC) and open FC accounts at commercial banks for current and capital transactions. Decree 63 was considered an improvement in the management and control of foreign exchange in line with international standards. It aimed to enhance the convertibility of the dong. In addition, Vietnam implemented a "cautious" exchange rate policy that allowed for the gradual devaluation of the VND by increasing the official exchange rate four times within one year (from February 1998 to February 1999) and combined this with strict exchange controls. This was known as an adjustable (or effective) pegged exchange rate regime that, according to Ohno (1999), could help the country stabilize the real effective exchange rate. Indeed, in 1999 this regime proved its effectiveness because Vietnam's trade balances became positive for the first time ever.

With its next intervention in February 1999, the SBV approved Decision No. 64/1999/QD-NHNN7 and Decision No. 65/1999/QD-NHNN7, declaring that an official exchange rate of VND vis-à-vis the US dollar would be announced every working day. In addition, a trading band on both sides based on the average actual exchange rates of the preceding days in the interbank market was implemented. Formally, the trading rate at commercial banks could be determined freely among the licensed banks subject to the requirement that buying and selling rates remained within established ceilings and floors, with the margin around the official rate set at +0.1%. The trading band was later widened to ±0.25% (effective July 1, 2002). While Vietnam officially announced that it would follow a managed floating exchange rate system,[6] in reality, the exchange rate system functioned as a form of the conventional pegged arrangement against US dollar (2005–2007).[7] In addition, since 2004, the Governor of the SBV has announced an annual target for exchange rate change at the beginning of every year. This implies that the SBV used the exchange rate as a nominal anchor when implementing its monetary policy, limiting the functioning of the crawling peg. Against the stable official exchange rate, the parallel market premium has been positive most of the time (Fig. 2).

Rather than allowing the exchange rate to be determined by trading in the market, the SBV intermittently devalued the official exchange rate.

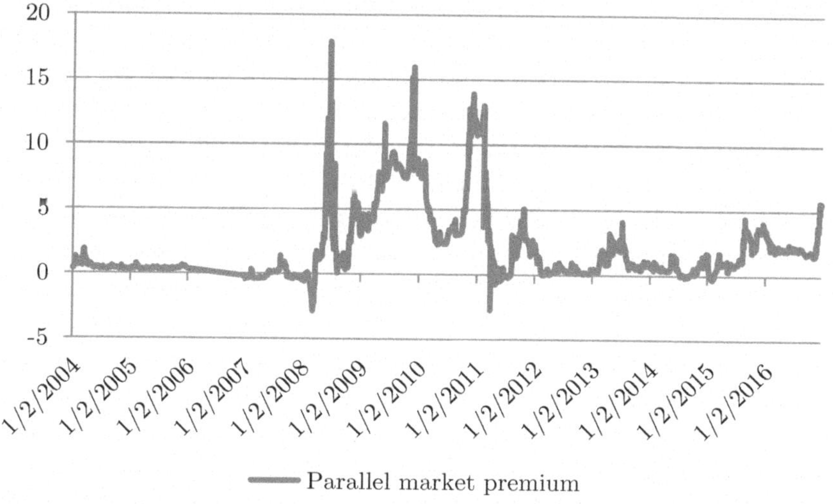

Fig. 2 Development of the parallel market premium in Vietnam, 2004–2016 (in percent). *Source* Author's calculations based on data from SBV's website and www.vangsaigon.com.vn

The SBV also occasionally adjusted the width of the trading band. All this indicates that the official exchange rate has been heavily managed. In order to absorb unexpected external shocks from the largest economy, the SBV made an official announcement regarding a new exchange rate mechanism as of January 4, 2016. Under the new mechanism, the official rate was replaced by a central rate that will be determined by three factors: (i) weighted average of US dollar–dong rate in the interbank market of the previous trading day, (ii) changes in rates of eight major foreign currencies,[8] and (iii) specific macroeconomic targets.

3 Dollarization Trends in Vietnam

Vietnam has a long history of using the US dollar. In fact, use of the US dollar has occurred in parallel with local currency use since the 1960s. During the Vietnam War (1955–1975), US dollars were widely used and stored by residents in the South where the US army bases were located. In contrast, foreign currency was banned in the North (Decree 102/CP, dated July 6, 1963). After the reunification of Vietnam in 1975, the socialist model was applied throughout the country. Vietcombank (Bank for Foreign Trade of Vietnam) was the only bank that could provide international banking services and enable foreign exchange transactions.

Given the economic difficulties before 1988, it can be said that the Vietnamese government's efforts to reform the local currency were a failure. During that period, the inconvertibility of the VND and the loss of public confidence in VND's value led to a public preference for gold and foreign currencies (mostly the US dollar) as financial assets and means of payments. Prices of most durable goods such as motorbikes, radios, televisions, refrigerators, real estate, etc. were quoted in gold and US dollars (Pham and Vuong 2010: 268–269). Rationing of foreign exchange stimulated the parallel market that supplied foreign currencies to both individuals and firms. Therefore, it could be said that Vietnam experienced both dollarization and goldization, where foreign currency notes and gold performed medium-of-exchange and store-of-value functions but were not deposited with the banking system (Pham et al. 2014).

To measure dollarization, FC liabilities and assets in the banking system were utilized. Figure 3 shows a downward but unsustainable trend in the ratio of FCD to M2. The ratio increased sharply and reached a peak of 41.2% in 1991. After that, it decreased to 30.3% in 1992, 23.0% in 1993, and 20.3% in 1996. A reversal of the ratio occurred following the Asian financial crisis; the ratio increased to 23.6% in 1997, 24.6% in 1998, and further to 31.7% in 2001. This movement might be associated with (i) a large depreciation of the VND during the Asian financial crisis and (ii) an increase in the USD interest rates in international money markets to a peak of 6.5% in 2000 (Hauskrecht and Nguyen 2004) leading to an increase in the USD interest rate in Vietnam as well. Since 2002, the FCD to M2 ratio has largely exhibited a declining trend including over the period of the global financial crisis, reaching 11% in 2014.

In addition to the FCD to M2 ratio, we also present the ratio of FC loans to total loans (local currency and FC loans), which is an index of loan dollarization. As shown in Fig. 4, the loan dollarization index exhibits a fluctuating but downward trend. From a peak of 38.6% in 1994, loan dollarization decreased to 19.3% in 2001. After a slight increase from 2002 to 2005, it declined gradually to 10.08% in February, 2016.

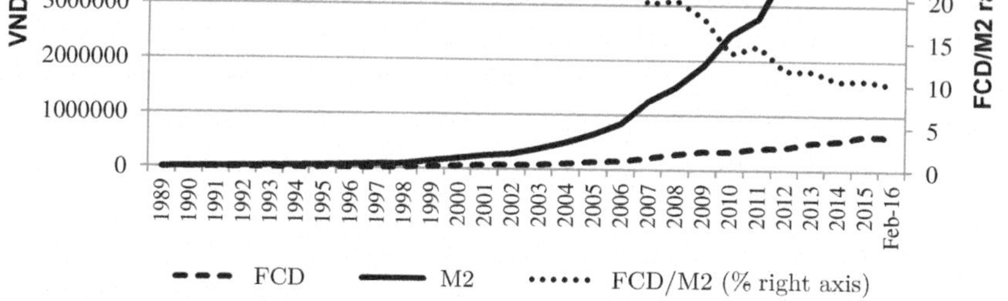

Fig. 3 FCD, M2, and FCD/M2 ratio in Vietnam, 1989–Feb, 2016. *Sources* IMF's international financial statistics and SBV's website. *Note* Foreign currency and money supply of dong (in billions)—left axis; FCD/M2 ratio in percent—right axis

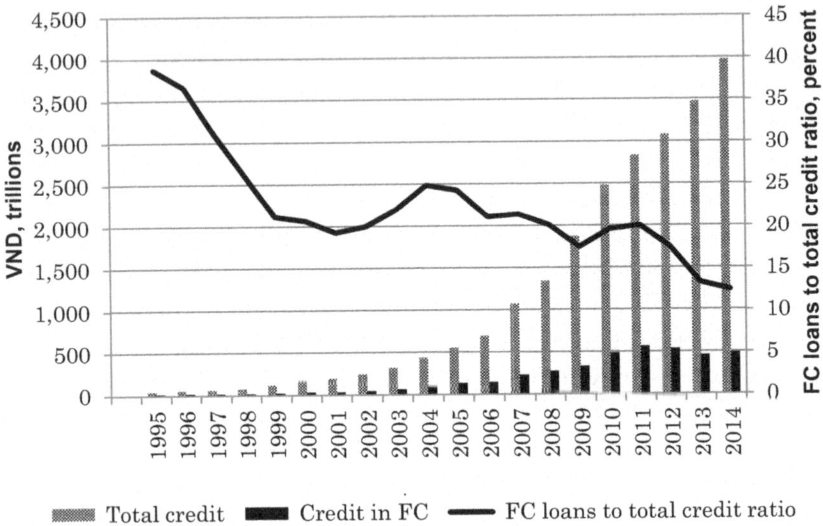

Fig. 4 FC loans, total credit, and FCL/total credit ratio in Vietnam, 1994–2014. *Sources* IMF's International Financial Statistics and SBV's website. *Note* FC loans and total credit (in trillions) of dong-left axis; FCL/total credit ratio in percent-right axis

In summary, financial dollarization decreased in Vietnam from 1989 to 2014, dropping to a low of 10–12%. According to the IMF's dollarization criteria (Balino et al. 1999), Vietnam can be classified as moderately dollarized. However, the FCD to M2 ratio and FCL to total credit ratio may not reflect all aspects of the dollarization status because of the exclusion of foreign currency cash outside the banking system and foreign currency borrowings from foreign entities. Moreover, we realize that absolute levels of the US dollar, FCD, and FCL have continued to increase and have remained high from 2009 to the present.

In less-monetized countries similar to Vietnam, for an accurate evaluation of the state of dollarization, we take into account the foreign currency in circulation. Using Nguyen T.H.'s (2002) method, the amount of foreign currency cash in circulation in the Vietnamese economy was estimated on the assumption that net private transfers are its main source. Based on foreign currency cash in circulation data calculated in Chap. 1, Fig. 5 presents this alternative dollarization index. We calculate the ratio of FC cash in circulation to the sum of the money

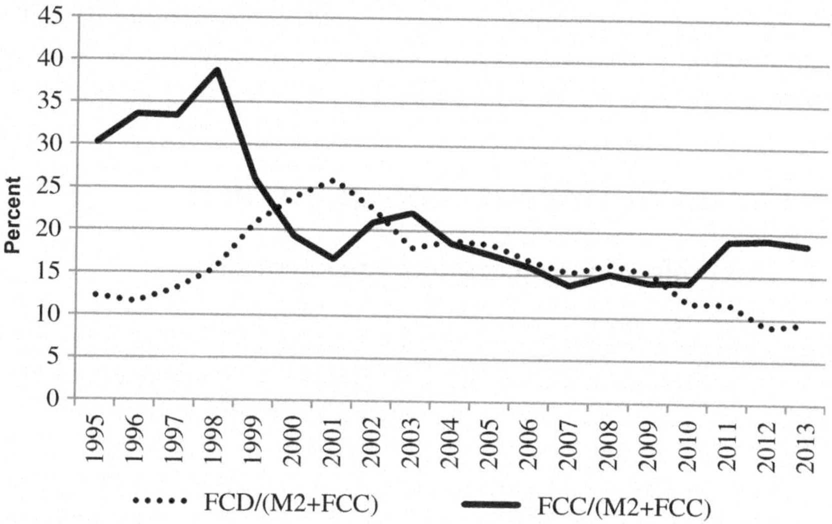

Fig. 5 Development of deposit dollarization and cash dollarization in Vietnam, 1995–2013. *Sources* IMF's International Financial Statistics and data from Chap. 1's calculations

supply (M2) and FC cash. The figure shows that a reduction in deposit dollarization was accompanied by an increase in FC cash in circulation except for the period of 2004–2009. This means that deposit or loan dollarization indices may not reflect the accurate state of dollarization, and FC cash in circulation warrants more attention.

While automated telling machine in the form of FCD as a percentage of M2 became notable in 1991, the USD had been used as a medium of exchange and a unit of account in the country since the Vietnam War in the 1960s.[9] Foreign currencies (the US dollar in most cases) were used in quotations for goods and services. For example, before 2010, prices of most durable goods (such as automobiles,[10] motorbikes, radios, televisions, refrigerators, laptops, real estate, etc.) and services (such as hotel rooms, spa services,[11] etc.) were quoted in US dollars. Even tuition fees at some universities[12] and English-training centers were quoted in US dollars. Due to the expected depreciation of the dong, even when residents lent money in dong, they still converted their money into an equivalent amount of US dollar or gold and asked borrowers to repay with an equivalent amount in dollars or gold at the maturity date. The parallel exchange rate was applied. This was generally seen in lending–borrowing transactions between individuals and in urban areas.

4 Causes of Dollarization in Vietnam

4.1 Unstable Macroeconomic Background

Macroeconomic instability is considered to be one of the factors that resulted in high dollarization in many countries (Reinhart et al. 2003; Galindo and Leiderman 2005; Herrera and Valdés 2005; Kokenyne et al. 2010). In this section, we explore the inflation and depreciation of the VND that could be the factors underlying dollarization. Similar to other countries, dollarization in Vietnam could be correlated with high inflation (Hauskrecht and Nguyen 2004; Nguyen, T.H. 2002, 2011). As shown in Sect. 2.1, the country experienced high inflation in the 1980s and early 1990s. Indeed, Vietnam has experienced a higher rate of inflation than most Asian economies (Jongwanich and Park 2009). Corresponding to high inflation rates of 67 and 68% in 1990 and 1991, respectively, the FCD to M2 ratio reached a peak of 41.5% in 1991. A sharp decline in the inflation rate since 1992 has been accompanied by a downward trend in deposit dollarization, in which the ratio remained around 20% from 1992 to 2008. However, high inflation from 2008 to 2011 was not accompanied by a rise in dollarization.

In addition, lower economic growth and a high trade deficit resulted in devaluation pressure on the VND, which could underpin dollarization. Inconvertibility of the VND and subjective factors such as residents' ingrained habits of favoring gold and foreign currencies (mostly the US dollar) could promote demand for FC deposit and cash.

4.2 Foreign Exchange Regulations

Another notable factor explaining deposit and loan dollarization was the regulatory framework related to foreign exchange as well as a banking system that created incentives for residents to hold foreign-currency-denominated assets.

First, regulations allowed residents to keep deposits in FC at commercial banks. Decree 161 on "Regulations on foreign exchange management," dated October 18, 1988, replaced Decree 102/CP of 1963. One of the significant changes in the new Decree was that individuals and institutions were required to deposit FC revenues in commercial banks (surrender requirements). In addition, it allowed commercial banks to conduct foreign exchange transactions as well as international banking and broke Vietcombank's monopoly (Nguyen 2012). Changes in foreign exchange regulations aimed to attract foreign currency from any source[13] circulated and traded in parallel markets into the banking system.

On October 25, 1991, the Vietnamese Council of Committee approved Decision 337-HĐBT on foreign exchange management in which all FC must be deposited at commercial banks licensed for foreign exchange transactions. This regulation was introduced for some "positive" purposes such as preventing parallel foreign exchange activities and reducing the amount of FC cash in circulation and creating "commodities" for Foreign Exchange Transaction Centers in Ho Chi Minh City and Hanoi. This regulation, however, would also contribute to a rise in FCD since 1991.

In February 1995, Decision No. 48-QD/NH7 was approved, which implemented regulatory changes on money transfers from Vietnamese citizens residing overseas. According to this, residents were allowed to withdraw their money from FCD accounts in FC or local currencies as per requirement. In addition, overseas Vietnamese could open FC saving accounts at Vietnamese commercial banks licensed for foreign exchange and repatriate their money. The government waived income tax upon receipt of remittances from overseas Vietnamese.[14] These measures created incentives for overseas Vietnamese to transfer their money to Vietnam, especially through the banking system. This kind of fund has been a vital source of capital and contributed greatly to Vietnam's economic development (Do et al. 2014; Dang 2014). This would, however, be a cause for the high deposit dollarization in the country.

Second, the SBV approved Decision 28/QĐ-NH8, dated March 1, 1993, which allowed commercial banks to provide loans in FC. This regulation would benefit both banks and borrowers. Commercial banks can provide loans using FCD, achieve target credit growth,[15] and earn profits, while borrowers have access to cheaper sources of funds for their businesses because of the large differential between VND and USD lending interest rates. However, this adds to dollarization.

Finally, less-effective and overly restrictive regulations on foreign exchange stimulated a parallel market for foreign exchange (Nguyen 2012). Sometimes residents could not buy foreign currencies in the official exchange market (e.g., in 2009)[16] even if they fulfilled legitimate requirements set by the SBV for current account transactions; this was especially during periods of turbulence in the market. The existence of, and inconsistent controls over, the parallel market could be another factor relevant to understanding dollarization. For example, according to the Ordinance on Foreign Exchange (2006), residents are allowed to buy FC from commercial banks only if they submit the required documents such as import contracts or other documents proving their needs are legitimate. In contrast, documentation requirements were absent in the parallel market.

In addition, during a period of macroeconomic and exchange rate instability, the government may impose strict administrative controls over the parallel market.[17] These restrictions may have a negative psychological impact on residents, causing them to favor FC and gold. They may believe that if the SBV has to impose such strict controls, then it must be short of foreign exchange. In this case, residents would hoard their FC assets, leading to an increase in the demand for FC and gold.

4.3 Interest Rate Differentials

Large interest rate differentials were considered another notable factor in explaining dollarization (To et al. 2013; Le et al. 2013). We calculate the interest rate differential by subtracting the return to FCDs, which is the sum of nominal FCD interest rate and change in exchange rate, from the nominal VND interest rate. A larger interest rate differential indicates a higher return to VND deposits relative to FCDs. Figure 6 shows an inverse relationship between interest rate differentials and deposit dollarization (Appendix 1). Specifically, a decrease in interest rate differentials from 12% in 1994 to a negative number in 1997–2001[18] was accompanied by an increase in the deposit dollarization ratio from 20% in 1994 to 31.7% in 2001 (Fig. 3). Analogously, since August 2011, the SBV has maintained positive interest rate differentials through administrative controls, which coincided with a decline in the deposit dollarization ratio (Figs. 6, 7). The relationship between interest rate differentials and the deposit dollarization index could be interpreted as showing that a larger interest rate differential makes VND deposits more attractive compared with FCDs, which prompts depositors' portfolio rebalancing between FCD and VND deposits.

However, in terms of loan dollarization, lower USD loan rates in comparison with VND loan rates could encourage borrowers to take USD loans. For example, during 1994–1997, FC loan rates were between 8.5 and 9%,[19] while rates for VND loans were at 20.4%. In these cases,[20] institutions preferred taking FC loans, and the regulations accommodated such behavior.

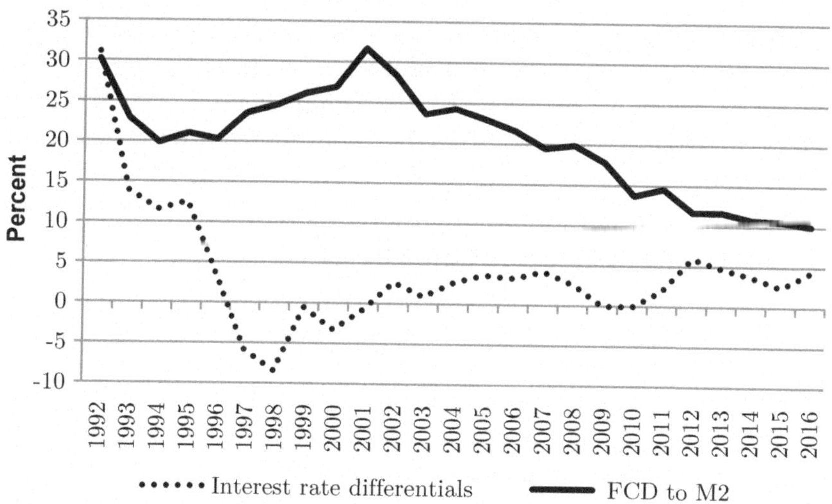

Fig. 6 Interest rate differentials between Dong- and Dollar-denominated deposits and deposit dollarization in Vietnam, 1989–2016.[30] *Sources* Author's calculations based on data collected from the IMF, SBV

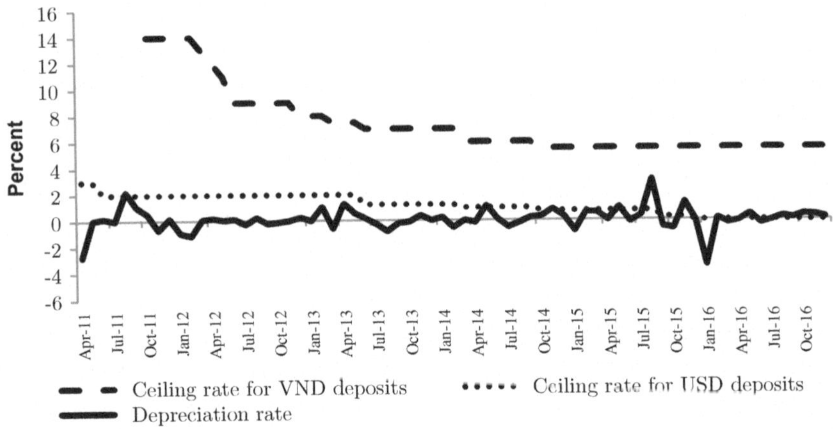

Fig. 7 Ceiling rate for dong deposits, ceiling rate for US dollar deposits, and depreciation rate in Vietnam, 2011–2016. *Source* Author's compilation from the SBV's website

5 De-dollarization Policies

Stabilizing the macroeconomic environment, especially maintaining price stability, is an important step in de-dollarization. In addition to macroeconomic stabilization, we describe the comprehensive de-dollarization strategy undertaken by the SBV that contributed to the decline in dollarization.

5.1 Foreign Exchange Regulations

As noted in Sect. 4, there was a close link between foreign exchange regulations and dollarization status. Some regulations could increase dollarization, while others were conducive to de-dollarization. This section reviews the foreign exchange policy measures taken by the SBV during 1988–2015 to de-dollarize the economy.

First is convertibility of VND. The government realized that if the convertibility of the dong could be improved, residents could buy foreign currency whenever they needed it, which might reduce the hoarding of foreign exchange. Therefore, enhancing convertibility of VND would reduce dollarization. To enhance convertibility, the government took the following steps:

i. Liberalizing current accounts by approving the Ordinance on Foreign Exchange and Decree 160/2006/NĐ-CP on Guidelines of the Ordinance (dated December 28, 2006). The Ordinance clearly states that demand for FC in all current transactions will be satisfied by authorized commercial banks (current account liberalization). In addition, the Ordinance prohibited quotation of prices and payments in FC within Vietnam. It also imposed administrative sanctions on violations related to foreign exchange.
ii. Gradually liberalizing capital account transactions by giving incentives to attract foreign direct investment (FDI) and foreign portfolio investment (FPI) inflows as well as allowing FDI and FPI outflows (Pham et al. 2014).

The enhanced convertibility of the dong has contributed to (i) the reduction in parallel foreign exchange transactions and (ii) compliance with IMF Article VIII. However, in practice, the SBV at times did not accommodate the demand for foreign exchange even though the demand was for current account transactions, especially in periods of excess demand for foreign currencies.

The second measure entails controls on a foreign exchange such as foreign exchange position to equity ratio of banks, surrender requirements, and other administrative measures in the parallel market (Table 1). These were imposed to (i) prevent speculation in foreign currencies, (ii) increase the supply of foreign currency so as to stabilize the market, and (iii) reduce devaluation pressure on the VND. With this movement, public confidence would increase, leading to a greater use of the dong and a reduction in dollarization.

During 2010–2011, due to large interest rate differentials between the dong (around 20% for loans) and the dollar (4–5% for deposits) and SBV's commitment to stabilizing the VND exchange rate, Vietnam's commercial banks operated carry trading activities. Banks attempted to mobilize US dollars, convert (sell) the dollar to buy dong, and then make loans in dong. To maximize profits through carry trading activities,

Table 1 Foreign exchange controls in Vietnam, 1988–2016. *Source* The author compiles from legal documents approved by the State Bank of Vietnam

Policy measures	Details
Foreign exchange position to equity ratio	SBV imposed limits on foreign exchange position to not exceed 30% of a commercial bank's equity in both long and short sides (September 1998). This ratio decreased to 20% in March 2012.
Foreign exchange surrender requirements	In August 1998, SBV imposed foreign exchange surrender requirements of up to 80% of available balances (Decision 173/QD-TTg), reduced to 50% (August 1999), and fully relaxed them in May 2003. In November 2009, surrender requirements wesssre applied to seven state-owned corporations and extended to all state-owned corporations in 2011.
Administrative measures on the parallel market	The government used police and other authorities to stop parallel market operations. They imposed very strict punishments on illegal activities in the foreign exchange and gold markets.

Vietnam's commercial banks (e.g., small commercial banks) held the largest short foreign exchange position (−30% in terms of equity), resulting in devaluation pressure at the loans' maturity dates and turbulence in Vietnamese foreign exchange markets. To militate against this, the SBV cut the maximum open foreign exchange position from 30% of a commercial bank's equity on either side (implemented in September 1998) to 20% on March 20, 2012 (Circular 07/TT-NHNN). By limiting foreign currency position, the SBV aimed to reduce speculative activities of commercial banks.

In addition, the government approved Decree 202/2004/NĐ-CP on "Sanctioning of administrative violations in monetary and banking activities" and Decree 95/2011/NĐ-CP (Amendments on Decree 202/2004/NĐ-CP), which prescribed punishments for illegal activities in the foreign exchange and gold markets.[21] The police confiscated FC and VND used for illegal transactions. For example, on December 6, 2011, the police uncovered an illegal foreign exchange transaction of US $500,000 between the Minh Phuc Company and the Kim Mai Gold

Company.[22] Another strict administrative control on foreign exchange involved police and market surveillance teams sent to control the parallel market, especially during the period of exchange rate instability. However, the effectiveness of these measures on dollarization and the foreign exchange market is still questionable for several reasons. For example, during that time, the observable parallel market was almost closed, but illegal foreign exchange transactions may still have occurred in unobservable contexts. In addition, the parallel market could not be shut for a long time because of the illiquidity of the official foreign exchange market.

5.2 Interest Rate Policies

Interest rates were found to be the most flexible and effective channels in the transmission mechanism of monetary policy, especially for stabilizing the exchange rate in Vietnam (Le et al. 2013). Therefore, the Vietnamese authorities exercised various controls on interest rates in response to exchange rate developments, especially during periods of exchange rate instability. In what follows, a chronology of interest rate regulations is delineated for both the dong and the US dollar as part of wider de-dollarization interventions (Table 2). Specifically, three periods can be identified.

July 1991–July 2000: Interest rate controls. To maintain credit targets and money supply growth, beginning in 1990, the SBV imposed a ceiling on lending rates for loans in different currencies (the dong and the dollar) and in different economic sectors. In 1992, the SBV directed and linked nominal interest rates to the inflation rate for the first time to ensure positive real interest rates. In addition, the establishment of the interbank money market in 1993 was a turning point toward the modern central bank function of implementing monetary policy. However, there were some limitations of the interbank money market such as the small amount of intermediary funds, the lack of a clearing system, and the legal framework on interest rates (Nguyen 2003).

August 2000–March 2011: Interest rate liberalization. The SBV approved a new interest rate mechanism that allowed commercial banks

Table 2 Chronology of interest rate ceiling in Vietnam, 1991–2016. *Source* The author compiles from legal documents approved by the State Bank of Vietnam

Effective date	USD deposit rate ceiling,%	VND deposit rate ceiling, %	Ceiling on lending, %
July 11, 1991		24	72
Dec 6, 1993			7.5 (for US dollar)
Mar 25 1994			8.5 (for US dollar)
April 28, 1994			25.2 (for dong short-term loans); 20.4 (for dong long-term loans)
Oct 19, 1994			9.0 (for US dollar)
Jan 1, 1996			21 (for dong short-term loans); 20.4 (for dong long-term loans)
July 16, 1996			19.2 (for dong short-term loans); 20.4 (for dong long-term loans)
Sep 1, 1996			18 (for dong short-term loans); 18.6 (for dong long-term loans)
Oct 1, 1996			15 (for dong short-term loans); 18 (for dong long-term loans)
June,28 1997			12 (for dong short-term loans); 13.2 (for dong long-term loans); 8.5 (for USD)
August 2000– April 8, 2011: Interest rate liberalization			
April 9, 2011	3		
June 2, 2011	2		
Oct 6, 2011		14	
Mar 12, 2012		13	
Apr 11, 2012		12	
May 8, 2012			15
May 25, 2012		11	

(continued)

Table 2 (continued)

Effective date	USD deposit rate ceiling,%	VND deposit rate ceiling, %	Ceiling on lending, %
June 8, 2012		9	13
Dec 21, 2012		8	12
Mar 25, 2013		7.5	11
May 10, 2013			10
June 28, 2013	1.25	7	9
Mar 18, 2014	1	6	8
Oct 29, 2014	0.75 for individual and 0.25 for institution	5.5	7
Sep 29, 2015	0.25 for individual and 0 for institution		
Dec 17, 2015	0 for both individual and institution		

dong-denominated lending rates reliant on the benchmark base interest rate announced officially by the SBV. However, Nguyen, X.T. (2003) argued that this was not too different from the ceiling mechanism in that lending rates were set within a base rate and band. In November 2001, control of the lending rates was abolished, and interest rates were fully liberalized in June 2002. In other words, interest rates were determined based on the bank's appraisal as well as through bank–customer negotiations. By liberalizing the interest rate, the SBV aimed to enhance the convertibility of the dong.

April 2011–Present: Interest rate re-controls: To overcome the negative effects of the global financial crisis, the SBV re-imposed the interest rate ceiling on foreign currency and the dong-denominated deposit rate in April 2011 and October 2011, respectively. The maximum rate also applied to loans in the five priority areas of agriculture, supporting industries, export, medium-sized companies, and high-tech industries. Moreover, the monetary authority adjusted the interest rate ceiling based on specific macroeconomic circumstances (Table 2).

Since April 2011, the SBV has sought to maintain higher returns on the dong-denominated deposit rate in comparison with foreign currency deposits by imposing a ceiling rate on foreign currency deposits (US dollar in this case) at a rate lower than the market rate[23] and by announcing its commitment to a maximum rate of dong devaluation. By doing so, the SBV made domestic assets more attractive than foreign ones. Moreover, every time the SBV reduces the ceiling rate for dong deposits, it also reduces the US dollar deposit rate so that the attractiveness of dong deposits is maintained (Figs. 6, 7). In other words, the SBV gives the residents incentives to move from foreign assets to domestic alternatives in order to reduce dollarization in Vietnam.

The SBV also made it a goal to prevent interest rate races (namely interest rate wars) among commercial banks in Vietnam.[24] During periods of illiquidity, Vietnam's small commercial banks have to increase deposit rates to attract an inflow of funds to meet the liquidity ratios imposed by the SBV. In this case, residents tend to move money from banks offering lower rates and deposit it in banks with higher rates. Larger banks have no way of doing this other than through higher deposit rates. In turn, small banks also increase their rates leading to an interest rate race and instability in the money market.

5.3 Restrictions on Loans in Foreign Currencies

Aware that an increase in foreign currency loans could lead to greater pressure on the VND exchange rate at a loan's contract date, especially during the period from 2000 to 2010, the SBV applied the following policy measures in April 2011 aimed at reducing the amount of FC loans:

i. Restrictions on institutional entities that could take foreign-currency-denominated loans from banks. According to the regulations, only companies with foreign currency revenues are allowed to borrow in foreign currency;
ii. Reserve requirement ratio for foreign currency deposits at commercial banks was raised from 4 to 6%, and then 7% in 2011. This measure would raise the cost of mobilizing foreign currency from individuals and institutions for commercial banks;
iii. Limits on the amount of foreign currency available to import goods that could be produced by Vietnamese companies (Document No. 4186/NHNN-CSTT on June 04, 2010 approved by the SBV).

However, loan dollarization could still continue in 2015, and then 2016 and 2017 because the SBV extended the expiry date of the temporary exceptional provision for commercial banks in providing short term dollar loans to specific economic entities.[25] The expiry date was moved to December 31, 2015 instead of the end of 2014 (Circular 43/2014/TT-NHNN, dated December 25, 2014), then March 31, 2016 (Circular 24/2015/TT-NHNN, dated December 8, 2015), December 31, 2016 (Circular 07/2016/TT-NHNN, dated May 27, 2016), December 31, 2017 (Circular 31/2016/TT-NHNN, dated November 15, 2016). Why did the SBV do this? One reason could be the credit crunch[26] that has gripped Vietnam since 2012. By allowing commercial banks to provide short-term dollar loans, the SBV could achieve its targets of credit growth that promote economic growth.[27] However, as mentioned above, this could hamper reductions in foreign-currency-denominated loans.

5.4 Goldization and De-goldization

"Goldization" refers to the use of gold as a medium of exchange and store of value. In Vietnam, gold has been a close substitute for US dollar-denominated assets as a store of value, and it has sometimes been used as a means of exchange. In the context of macroeconomic instability, dollarization and goldization interacted with each other, each intensifying the effects of the other (Nguyen et al. 2013; Pham and Nguyen 2013; Pham 2014). In addition, goldization adds to dollarization when there is a surge in the world gold price. In such contexts, residents prefer to hold gold as a store of value, which leads to a large gap between gold prices in the international and Vietnamese markets because of excess demand. If this occurs, gold shops would engage in arbitrage activities where they would buy gold in the global market and sell it domestically. However, according to regulations imposed by the government, only authorized gold trading companies (before Decree 24, dated April 03, 2012) and the SBV (after Decree 24) were officially allowed to import gold from foreign countries. In order to earn profit, gold shops or unauthorized gold traders would import illegally, leading to excess demand for FC in the parallel foreign exchange market. These activities would lead to a depreciation pressure on the value of the dong and create incentives for residents to keep FC. Therefore, by launching the following policy measures aimed at de-goldization, the government could break down these links, stabilize the VND exchange rate, and pursue de-dollarizing the economy.

First, to prevent turbulence in the gold market caused by too many gold bar brands, the SBV decided to establish a national brand. This would be the official brand of gold bars in Vietnam. It was expected to address problems of quality and price in the Vietnamese gold market. The national brand, however, was controversial because of conflicts between the SBV and jewelry companies in Vietnam. Two conflicting views prevail in both the academic and nonacademic worlds. One view argued that a national brand for gold bullion was not legal and was in fact exceptional in the world. They disagreed with the new policy because the SBV is a monetary authority and should not be a gold manufacturer or trader in the market. This view believed that the SBV's monopoly over the gold supply would be unfair to other market participants. The other side supported the SBV's policy. They argued that the establishment of a national brand for gold bars could be the best way to stabilize the gold market. Moreover, by doing so, the Vietnamese government could control gold smuggling activities and therefore stabilize domestic gold prices and goldization.

Second, similar to de-dollarization measures, in June 2012, the SBV set regulations stipulating that commercial banks not be allowed to borrow or lend in gold. In addition, it also imposed a daily net open position in gold assets and liabilities to bank's equity ratio of 2% (Circular 38/2012/TT-NHNN, dated December 28, 2012). All of these measures are aimed at reducing speculative activities around the gold bar and stabilizing the gold market, at least in terms of prices and the parallel premium on gold.[28]

Third, instead of paying interest, the government required commercial banks to charge fees for gold deposits at all maturities.

Fourth, the government approved Decree 24/2012/ND-CP (April 2012), which was stricter than ever before regarding gold trading management. Due to many entities and less-effective regulations on the gold trading businesses, the Vietnamese gold market suffered from instability. To stabilize the gold market, the government imposed the following regulations:

i. The use of the gold bar as a medium of exchange is illegal and strictly prohibited by the government.
ii. Gold trading is under a license system.

The following are the requirements for obtaining the license on gold bar trading: (i) being established and operating according to legal provisions; (ii) having charter capital of at least 100 billion VND (equivalent to $4.5 million); (iii) having at least 2 years of experience in gold trading; (iv) having paid tax on gold business of at least 500 million VND/year (equivalent to US$22,700) during the past 2 years (upon verification by the tax authority); and (iv) having branches and sale offices in three or more provinces and centrally affiliated cities in Vietnam.[29] By doing this, the SBV expected to eliminate inadequate and small gold businesses, reduce the number of participants, and stabilize the gold market.

6 Conclusion

This chapter has analyzed the state of dollarization and the de-dollarization policy measures implemented in Vietnam between 1990 and 2015. A downward trend in deposit and loan dollarization in Vietnam was observed. However, for a less-monetized economy such as Vietnam, these conventional indices do not reflect the full story of dollarization. Thus, it is also necessary to look at foreign currency in circulation. Interestingly, this chapter suggests that while deposit and loan dollarization decreased significantly, since 2009, foreign currency in circulation increased sharply. This finding implies that along with reducing deposit dollarization, foreign currency in circulation deserves closer attention.

In addition, the chapter indicates that an unstable macroeconomic context, especially high inflation rates, creates large differentials between USD and VND deposit rates, which is one of the main determinants of dollarization. It suggests that a positive gap between VND and USD deposit rates, in addition to macroeconomic stabilization, is conducive to de-dollarization.

Moreover, the chapter also finds that foreign exchange regulations are closely linked to the dollarization status as well as de-dollarization in Vietnam. In other words, some regulations could be associated with higher dollarization status, while others added to de-dollarizing the economy. For example, regulations that allowed residents to place deposits and borrow money in FC from commercial banks could raise FCD, while regulations on enhancing convertibility of VND, controls on foreign exchange net open position of banks, surrender requirements, and other administrative measures in the parallel market could reduce the dollarization index. These findings highlight the fact that the balance between benefits and costs of foreign exchange regulations needs to be considered, especially if they have an impact on the dollarization status in the economy.

Unlike other economies, Vietnam was also affected by goldization. Because of the interconnectedness of dollarization and goldization, de-goldization (e.g., imposing regulations on gold trading, regulations on net open positions in gold assets and liabilities, etc.) functioned as a de-dollarization measure helping authorities to break this link and release devaluation pressures on the dong.

Notes

1. "Goldization" refers to the use of gold as a medium of exchange and a store of value.
2. http://www.ncseif.gov.vn/sites/en/Pages/hethongnganhangvoivan-nd-1644.html, accessed on April 25, 2015.
3. The high inflation rate was not principally associated with the negative impacts of the global financial crisis. It resulted from (i) partly sterilized intervention in the foreign exchange market leading to a significant increase in the money supply, (ii) a rise in the minimum wage, (iii) expansionary monetary policy, and (iv) other external factors such as oil and food prices (Nguyen and Nguyen 2010).
4. The stimulus package approved by the Vietnamese government included the following: (i) A 4-percentage-point interest rate subsidy on new dong-denominated short-term bank loans; (ii) A new credit-guarantee scheme to support commercial bank lending to small- and medium-sized enterprises; (iii) A series of stimulus measures targeting the rural economy including interest-free loans for the purchase of farm equipment and subsidized loans for fertilizer and other agricultural inputs; (iv) Tax breaks for enterprises and individuals; and (v) Reduction in import tariffs on goods used as inputs in domestic production, and an increase in export tariffs on natural resources and import tariffs on some domestically produced goods.
5. Report on Vietnam's Economic and Social Development, 2000–2010, published by the General Statistics Office, page 9.
6. See Decree 63/1998/ND-CP on foreign exchange management and Ordinance on Foreign exchange.
7. The International Monetary Fund (IMF) (2006) has reclassified the exchange rate regime of Vietnam from the category of managed floating

with no predetermined path for the exchange rate to the conventional pegged arrangement category (effective Jan 1, 2005).

8. Currencies from the US, EU, Japan, China, Taiwan, South Korea, Thailand, and Singapore.
9. During the Vietnam War, given the large amount of dollar aide from the US and the existence of US army bases, residents in the South preferred to use the US dollar for buying goods and services instead of using local currency. According to Dacy (1986), during the 20 years of the Vietnam War, the South received about 8.5 billion USD as non-refundable aid (Table 10.2, pp. 200), not including borrowings from the US government for infrastructure and economic development and an annual allowance for the US army located in the South.
10. http://www.tinmoi.vn/Cac-hang-oto-niem-yet-gia-bang-USD-vi-VND-bat-tien-0112186.html, accessed on July 4, 2015.
11. http://m.tin247.com/van_qua_nhieu_doanh_nghiep_mat_hang_niem_yet_gia_bang_usd-3-21429458.html, accessed on July 4, 2015.
12. FPT University was found to quote their tuition fees in US dollars during 2010–2011 (http://laodong.com.vn/kinh-doanh/dai-hoc-fpt-bi-phat-500-trieu-dong-vi-niem-yet-hoc-phi-bang-usd-7863.bld, accessed on July 4, 2015).
13. In Vietnam, depositors are not asked about the source of foreign currencies when depositing at commercial banks. There are both official and unofficial sources of foreign currencies in Vietnam such as export revenues, remittances through both formal and informal channels, smuggling activities, etc.
14. Decision No. 170/1999/QD-TTg, dated August 19, 1999, to encourage and create favorable conditions for overseas Vietnamese to remit their money to their relatives in Vietnam.
15. During 2012–2015, the country faced economic recession as businesses and individuals were unwilling to borrow money from banks. For a bank-based financial system like Vietnam, this situation hindered the country's recovery from the recession. Therefore, by delaying the deadline for ceasing lending in FC (from December 31, 2014 to December 31, 2015), the banking system could expand their credit activities and meet business' objectives.
16. Because of the high demand for foreign currencies, commercial banks and other authorized exchange bureaus did not have sufficient FC to sell in the market. (http://vneconomy.vn/tai-chinh/dau-hieu-cang-thang-

tren-thi-truong-ngoai-te-dau-la-nguyen-nhan-20090514120451771.htm, accessed on October 5, 2015).

17. http://vneconomy.vn/tai-chinh/se-som-xu-ly-nhung-bat-cap-tren-thi-truong-ngoai-te-20090421104948657.htm, accessed on October 5, 2015.
18. See Appendix 1.
19. During 1994–1997, the SBV imposed a ceiling rate for FC loans from 8.5 to 9% (Decision 255/QD-NH7, dated October 18, 1994, and Decision 197/QD-NH1, dated June 28, 1997, on FC loan rates).
20. A similar case was observed in 2010–2011; FC loan rates were 6–8% in comparison with 20–25% for VND loans.
21. According to Decree 95/2011/NĐ-CP, illegal activities in foreign exchange and gold will be punished to a maximum of VND 500,000,000, seven times greater than the stipulation in Decree 202/2004/NĐ-CP.
22. http://www.tinmoi.vn/giao-dich-trai-phep-500000-usd-tai-eximbank-01757956.html. accessed on October 5, 2015.
23. On April 9, 2011, the SBV imposed, for the first time, a ceiling rate of 3% for US dollar deposits. At that time, market rates for US dollar deposits were 5–6%.
24. The interest rate war occurred during 2009–2011.
25. The specific economic entities are export companies and petro-gas companies (Circular 29/2013/TT-NHNN).
26. Vietnam fell into recession in 2011 and was soon faced with a credit crunch. This situation could have resulted due to several reasons: (i) weak demand from residents and nonresidents leading to a drop in the production index. In this case, companies do not want to invest to expand their business, and even if they do want to borrow money from banks, they may not meet bank lending requirements; (ii) commercial banks had large nonperforming loans, so they are unwilling to provide new loans; (iii) high lending costs (high lending rates), etc.
27. By applying an investment and export-led economic growth model, credit growth was found to be a very important determinant of economic growth in Vietnam (To et al. 2013; Pham 2013). In addition, because of the bank-based financial system, the bank lending channel plays a very important role in transferring funds from surplus to deficit entities.

28. Nguyen, D.T. et al. (2013) found evidence of the following successes in goldization policies imposed by the SBV during this period: (i) gold price stability, (ii) less interconnectedness between the foreign exchange market and gold market, (iii) fewer gold smuggling activities, and (iv) higher international reserves.
29. luatkhaiphong.com/Van-ban-Tieng-Anh/Decree-No.-24/2012/ND-CP-dated-April-03-2012-6582.html, accessed on August 1, 2015.
30. See Appendix 1 for further details.

Appendix 1. Calculate of Interest Rate Differentials

Interest parity theory is an exchange rate determination theory which compares the interest rates of two currencies and estimates changes in the exchange rate:

$$R = R^{*} + E(\Delta ER),$$

where R is the domestic interest rate, R^{*} is the foreign interest rate, and $E(\Delta ER)$ is the expected exchange rate change.

However, in most cases, interest rate parity, including covered and uncovered, does not hold because of unrealistic assumptions (See Table 3). This, therefore, will allow us to identify arbitrage opportunities. Profit from arbitrage opportunities is interest differentials that are calculated as follows:

$$\textit{Interest rate differentials} = R - (R^{*} + E(\Delta ER))$$

Table 3 Interest rate differentials in Vietnam

Year	Change in USD's value against VND (1)	USD deposit rate (2)	Total yield of USD deposit rate (3) = (1) + (2)	VND deposit rate (4)	Spread between VND and USD deposit rate (5) = (4) − (3)
1989	377.78	n/a	Greater than 377.78	84	Must be negative
1990	51.16	n/a	Greater than 51.16	48	Must be negative
1991	31.43	9.6	41.03	42	−0.97
1992	−7.02	4.05	2.97	34.1	31.13
1993	3.26	3.2	6.46	20.4	13.94
1994	1.71	3.5	5.21	16.8	11.59
1995	−0.27	4.5	4.23	16.8	12.57
1996	1.23	4.8	6.03	9.6	3.57
1997	10.42	5	15.42	9.6	−5.82
1998	13	5	18	9.6	−8.4
1999	1.066	4.7	5.766	5.25	−0.516
2000	3.28	4.43	7.71	4.45	−3.26
2001	3.7	3	6.7	5.95	−0.75
2002	2.11	3	6.8	9.5	2.7
2003	1.58	3	4.58	5.97	0.93
2004	0.83	3	3.83	6.525	2.695
2005	0.86	3	3.86	7.530	3.67
2006	1.36	3	4.36	7.65	3.29
2007	0.08	3	3.08	7.28	4.2
2008	5.37	3	8.37	11.01	2.64
2009	5.7	3.5–4	9.2–9.7	9.53	(−0.17)–0.33
2010	5.52	4.5–5	10.02–10.52	13.88	3.36–3.86
2011	10.01	2	12.01	14	1.99
2012	0	2	2	8	6
2013	1	1.25	2.25	7	4.75
2014	1	0.75	1.75	5.5	3.75
2015	3.03	0	3.03	5.5	2.47
2016	1.18	0	1.18	5.5	4.32

Source IMF's International Financial Statistics, SBV, *ADB Key Indicators*, Nguyen Thi Hong (2002), and author's calculations

Note Change in USD's value is calculated by taking a change in official exchange rates at time *t* and time *(t − 1)* divided by the official exchange rate at time *(t − 1)*

Appendix 2

See Table 4.

Table 4 De-dollarization and de-goldization policy measures in Vietnam, 1988–2016

Policy measures	Details
1. Legal framework	Regulations on "Foreign exchange management," dated October 18, 1988 Decision 337-HĐBT on foreign exchange management, dated October 25, 1991 Decision No. 48-QD/NH7, dated February 23, 1995, on money transfers to Vietnam from Vietnamese expatriates Decision 173/1998/QD-TTg, dated August 17, 1998, on obligations to sell and right to buy foreign currency imposed on institutions; Decision 180/1999/QD-TTg, dated August 17, 1998, on amendments of Decisions 173/1998/QD-TTg Decision No.170/1999/QD-TTg, dated August 19, 1999 to encourage and create favorable conditions for Vietnamese expatriates to remit their money to their relatives in Vietnam Decree 202/2004/NĐ-CP on "Sanctioning of administrative violations in monetary and banking activities" The Ordinance on "Foreign exchange" (which took effect on June 1, 2006) Decree 160/2006/NĐ-CP on "Guides to implement the Ordinance on foreign exchange" (which took effect on December 28, 2006) Decision 98/2007/QĐ-TTg on "Improving convertible degree of Vietnamese dong and reducing dollarization status" Decree 95/2011/NĐ-CP on Amendments on Decree 202/2004/NĐ-CP
2. Foreign exchange controls	Tight controls on the parallel foreign exchange market Foreign exchange surrender requirements Limit on the amount of foreign currency that residents could bring abroad without custom declaration (maximum of US$3000) (Decision

(continued)

Table 4 (continued)

Policy measures	Details
	1437/2001/QD-NHNN, dated November 19, 2001), 7000 (Decree 160/2006/NĐ-CP), and 5000 (which took effect on August 12, 2011-Circular 15/NHNN)
	Limit on the amount of foreign currency that individuals could buy from commercial banks (maximum of US$100 per day in a foreign country)
	Increase in punishment level for illegal foreign exchange transactions to a maximum of VND500,000,000 (Decree 95/2011/ND-CP, dated October 20, 2011
3. Measures for foreign exchange market stability	Limit on providing foreign currency to import goods that could be manufactured and produced by Vietnamese companies
	Strict control on foreign-currency-denominated deposits and loans:
	+ Restrictions on institutional entities that could borrow foreign-currency-denominated loans from banks
	+ Ceiling foreign-currency-denominated deposit: 3% (4/9/2011); 2% (6/2/2011); 1.25% (6/28/2013); 1% (3/18/2014); 0.75% (10/29/2014), 0.25% (9/29/2015), 0% (12/17/2015)
	+ Increase in reserve requirements for foreign currency deposit from 4% to 6% (4/9/2011) and 7% (6/1/2011)
	Impose daily foreign exchange position to bank's equity from 30% (September 1998) to 20% (Circular 07/TT-NHNN, dated March 20, 2012)
4. De-goldization measures	Closed all gold trading exchanges in Vietnam
	Totally forbidden to borrow and lend in gold
	Imposing daily gold exchange position to bank's equity of 2%
	Government's monopoly role on production of gold bar and on import–export of raw materials for gold bar production
	Introducing the country's national brand for gold bullion (SJC)

References

Balino, T.J.T., A. Bennett, and E. Borensztein. 1999. Monetary policy in dollarized economies. Occasional Paper 171. Washington, D.C.: International Monetary Fund.

Brahm, L.J., and Trong Nhi, Le. 1993. Uncle Ho's posthumous stabilization of the dong. In*Asiamoney*, 194. London, Jul/Aug 1993.

Dacy, Douglas C. 1986. Foreign aid, war, and economic development: South Vietnam, 1955–1975. Cambridge: Cambridge University Press.

Dang, The Tung. 2014. Remittances and economic growth in Vietnam: An ARDL bounds testing approach. MPP thesis, Hitotsubashi Unviversity.

Do, Thi Kim Hao et al. 2014. Impacts of workers' remittance on macroeconomic variables: The case of Vietnam. Research project funded by the Banking Academy of Vietnam.

Dodsworth, J.R., E. Spitäller, M. Braulke, K.H. Lee, K. Miranda, C. Mulder, H. Shishido, and K. Srinivasan. 1996. Vietnam: Transition to a market economy. Occasional Paper 135. Washington, DC: International Monetary Fund.

Galindo, A., and Leiderman, L. 2005. Living with dollarization and the route to dedollarization. Inter-American Development Bank Working Paper No. 526, New York: Inter-American Development Bank.

Hauskrecht, A., and Nguyen, Thanh Hai. 2004. Dollarization in Vietnam. Paper prepared for the 12th annual conference on Pacific Basin Finance, Economics, Accounting, and Business, Aug 10–11, 2004, Bangkok.

Herrera, L., and R. Valdés. 2005. De-dollarization, indexation and nominalization: The chilean experience. *The Journal of Policy Reform* 8 (4): 281–312.

International Monetary Fund (IMF). 2006. *Annual report on exchange arrangements and exchange restrictions.* Washington, D.C.: International Monetary Fund.

Jongwanich, J., and D. Park. 2009. Inflation in developing Asia. *Journal of Asian Economics* 20 (5): 507–518.

Kokenyne, A., J. Ley, and R. Veyrune. 2010. Dedollarization. IMF Working paper no. 188, Washington, D.C.: International Monetary Fund.

Le, Thi Tuan Nghia et al. 2013. Project on exchange rate and interest rate: The case of Vietnam. Ministerial level project, research funded by the State Bank of Vietnam.

Nguyen, Thi Hong. 2002. Dollarization of financial assets and liabilities of the household sector, the enterprises sector and the banking sector in Vietnam. Paper presented at the JICA-State Bank of Vietnam Joint Research Project

Workshop on Dollarization and its effect on monetary and foreign exchange rate policies and the development of financial system: Vietnam, Lao PDR and Cambodia, 5 July 2002, Hanoi.

Nguyen, Xuan Thanh. 2003. *Vietnam: The road to interest rate liberalization.* Fulbright economics teaching program. CE03-53-7.0.

Nguyen, Thi Hong. 2011. Dollarization and monetary policy: The case of Vietnam. *Banking Review*, No. 5/2011 (In Vietnamese).

Nguyen, Van Tien. 2012. *International finance*, 3rd ed. Hanoi: Statistics Publishing House.

Nguyen, Thu Hang, and Nguyen, Duc Thanh. 2010. Macroeconomic determinants of inflation, 2000–2010: The case of Vietnam. Working Paper, VEPR, Hanoi National University.

Nguyen, Duc Trung et al. 2013. Project on solutions to gold market in Vietnam. Ministerial level project, research funded by the State Bank of Vietnam.

Ohno, K. 1999. Exchange rate management in developing Asia: Reassessment of the Pre-crisis Soft Dollar Zone, ADBI Research Paper Series, No. 1.

Pham, Minh Chinh and Vuong, Quan Hoang. 2010. Vietnamese economy: Downs and Breakthrough (Kinh tế Việt Nam: Thăng trầm và đột phá). VNN Publishing, reprint.

Pham, Minh Dien, et al. 2014. Foreign exchange regulation on de-dolarization in Vietnam. Research grant at the Vietnam's economic committee of congress.

Pham, Thi Hoang Anh. 2013. Effectiveness of monetary policy through asset prices channel: The case of Vietnam. Research project funded by the Banking Academy of Vietnam.

Pham, Thi Hoang Anh and Nguyen, Thi Hong Hai. 2013. Assessing Vietnam's exchange rate policy in 2012. *Banking Science and Training Review*. No. 2–3.

Pham, Thi Hoang Anh. 2014. State Bank of Vietnam and exchange rate stability in 2013. *Banking Science and Training Review*. No. 140–141.

Phan, Huy Duc. 1995. Dollarization in Vietnam, an econometric analysis. Working paper at Australian National University.

Reinhart, C., K. Rogoff, and M. Savastano. 2003. Addicted to dollars. NBER Working Paper 10015, Cambridge, MA: National Bureau of Economic Research.

Rosengard, J.K., and Huynh, The Du. 2008. Funding economic development: A comparative study of financial sector reform in Vietnam and China. Paper prepared under UNDP—Harvard Policy Dialogue Papers Series on

Vietnam's WTO Accession and International Competitiveness Research Policy Dialogue Paper Number 2.
State Bank of Vietnam. 2007. Project on improving convertible degree of Vietnamese dong and reducing dollarization degree—Together with decision 98/2007/QĐ-TTg approved by the Prime Minister.
State Bank of Vietnam. 2013. Project on De-dollarization in Vietnam.
To, Ngoc Hung, et al. 2013. Project on Non-performing loans in Vietnam. Ministerial level project, research funded by the State Bank of Vietnam.

Websites visited

https://www.sbv.gov.vn/webcenter/portal/vi/menu/trangchu/tk/cttqt?_afrLoop=1673971245510000#%40%3F_afrLoop%3D1673971245510000%26centerWidth%3D80%2525%26leftWidth%3D20%2525%26rightWidth%3D0%2525%26showFooter%3Dfalse%26showHeader%3Dfalse%26_adf.ctrl-state%3D14pqjezfk6_146. Accessed 5 July 2017
http://www.ncseif.gov.vn/sites/en/Pages/hethongnganhangvoivan-nd-1644.html. Accessed 25 April 2015.
http://gso.gov.vn/default.aspx?tabid=621. Accessed 5 July 2017, annual and monthly Report on Vietnam's Economic and Social Development, 2000–2015.
http://www.tinmoi.vn/Cac-hang-oto-niem-yet-gia-bang-USD-vi-VND-bat-tien-0112186.html. Accessed 4 July 2015.
http://m.tin247.com/van_qua_nhieu_doanh_nghiep_mat_hang_niem_yet_gia_bang_usd-3-21429458.html. Accessed 4 July 2015.
http://laodong.com.vn/kinh-doanh/dai-hoc-fpt-bi-phat-500-trieu-dong-vi-niem-yet-hoc-phi-bang-usd-7863.bld. Accessed 4 July 2015.
http://vneconomy.vn/tai-chinh/dau-hieu-cang-thang-tren-thi-truong-ngoai-te-dau-la-nguyen-nhan-20090514120451771.htm. Accessed 5 Oct 2015.
http://vneconomy.vn/tai-chinh/se-som-xu-ly-nhung-bat-cap-tren-thi-truong-ngoai-te-20090421104948657.htm. Accessed 5 Oct 2015.
www.luatkhaiphong.com/Van-ban-Tieng-Anh/Decree-No.-24/2012/ND-CP-dated-April-03-2012-6582.html. Accessed 1 Aug 2015.

6

Economic Growth, Monetary Policy, and Dollarization in CLMV Countries

Bhanupong Nidhiprabha

1 Introduction

The primary goals of monetary policy are price stability and stable output growth. The CLMV countries—Cambodia, Lao PDR, Myanmar, and Vietnam—have sustained high growth and achieved significant poverty reduction. In the last two decades, the region has become more open to trade, foreign direct investment, and capital flows, from both outside and within the ASEAN region. Market reforms are proceeding gradually, resulting in reduced distortion in foreign markets. Nevertheless, dollarization remains in the CLMV countries.

Dollarization can be classified into payment dollarization and financial dollarization.[1] If we consider payment dollarization, foreign currencies are more often used as a medium of exchange near the borders and in urban areas, rather than in rural areas, with the supply and demand for

B. Nidhiprabha (✉)
Faculty of Economics, Thammasat University,
Bangkok, Thailand
e-mail: bhanupong@econ.tu.ac.th

K. Kubo (ed.), *Dollarization and De-dollarization in Transitional Economies of Southeast Asia*, IDE-JETRO Series, DOI 10.1007/978-3-319-57768-5_6

foreign currencies explaining geographical differences in the level of foreign currency in circulation. When examining financial dollarization, we find that the development of financial institutions is related to dollarized deposits and loans, and differences in the stage of banking development and per capita income levels explain differences in the degree of financial dollarization among CLMV countries to some extent.

As banking habits are slowly established, the demand for cash will fall relative to the demand for bank deposits. With rising income levels, households will save more in the form of bank deposits, either in dollars or in local currencies. This is the issue of asset allocation being dictated by the rate of returns for household portfolios. The key variables determining the allocation of these assets are real interest rates on different forms of deposits, the inflation rate, expected currency depreciation, returns on other assets such as expected changes in gold and land prices.

It is important to understand how these countries can achieve growth while maintaining a certain degree of price stability. What role does monetary policy play in this achievement? This paper asks several questions in seeking to understand the factors underlying such success. First, to what extent does dollarization help or hinder the development process of these countries? Second, what are the challenges for CLMV central banks in the current state of globalization? We ask to what extent, if any, countercyclical policy in the CLMV countries contributes to stabilizing income and price levels.

According to conventional views in the literature, dollarization limits the effectiveness of countercyclical monetary policy. The central bank cannot effectively change the monetary base in the direction and magnitude it wishes in order to stabilize output and employment. Furthermore, the demand for money will not be stable, undermining the relationship between monetary aggregates and output. Information on the exact amount of circulating money supply in the economy is inaccurate, making it difficult, if not impossible, to forecast the outcome of monetary policy expansion or contraction. The velocity of money will be unstable, which results in an unpredictable outcome of changing the monetary base. The multiplier effect of a bond-financed budget deficit is unpredictable because the size of the fiscal multiplier depends on the marginal propensity to consume out of dollar or local incomes.

Another impact of dollarization on macroeconomic policy is the loss of seigniorage revenue from the inflation tax. The loss in inflation tax revenue is small if the expected inflation elasticity of the demand for money is high. Apparently, in a highly dollarized economy, the elasticity of the demand for money must be high with respect to inflation and devaluation expectations. It will be difficult for the government to run a bond-financed budget deficit since government bonds denominated in the local currency will not be as attractive as dollar-denominated bonds.

We reconsider how far these conventional arguments are applicable to the CLMV countries. Section 2 provides a literature review on dollarization in various countries, giving background to the analysis of macroeconomic conditions and problems related to dollarization. Section 3 examines macroeconomic conditions and their relevance to monetary policy, and Sect. 4 discusses the effectiveness of monetary policy in the CLMV countries. Concluding remarks on the roles of monetary policy in the CLMV countries and the case against forced de-dollarization are provided in Sect. 5.

2 Literature Review

2.1 Dollarization and the Banking Sector

Dollarization complicates the business activities of commercial banks by changing the risk structure. Central banks in dollarized economies encounter difficult environments in which to conduct monetary policy. Specifically, in addition to stabilization objectives, central banks must aim for soundness of the banking system, which can be threatened by currency mismatch risk. Herrera and Uyen (2012) find that domestic currency-induced credit risk increases with dollarization in the Peruvian banking industry, while debt dollarization reduces lending risk because banks transfer exchange risk as a hedging mechanism by lending to borrowers in dollars only. Furthermore, in highly dollarized banking systems such as those in Croatia, the Czech Republic, and Slovakia, the high level of foreign currency assets or liabilities on bank balance sheets may create a currency mismatch risk, which could lead to bank failures as a result of sudden exchange rate movements. Central banks in such economies must adjust their currency policies accordingly. Ozsoz et al. (2010) use probit and ordered probit models to forecast central banks' direct interventions in the foreign currency markets as a result of exchange rate volatility. Using data from three transitional economies, they find that central banks' interventions can be predicted by dollarization indicators captured by the ratio of dollar deposits to M2 and monetary base.

Does dollarization affect firms' access to bank credit? Between 1989 and 1993 the government of Paraguay removed most restrictions on financial transactions in domestic and foreign currency. The resulting financial deepening also involved partial dollarization. Serieux (2009) found that partial dollarization led to negative balance sheet effects, which reduced access to investment credit due to a depreciation-induced reduction in firms' net worth as a result of currency mismatches on their balance sheets. This caused a contraction in firms' investment levels when they were faced with real currency depreciation. However, there was also evidence that banks expanded credit more rapidly in the face of currency depreciation. These apparently contradictory movements in credit and investment are due to the lack of a relationship between investment and bank credit. By and large, firms in the CLMV countries rely heavily on bank credit. If dollarization produces negative balance sheet effects on firms and banks, private investment will be curtailed during the period of expected currency depreciation.

Bank performance can also be adversely affected by a high degree of dollarization. With high level of dollarization, profitability, efficiency, and solvency can be impaired if exchange rate fluctuations occur. The dollarization of bank deposits in developing economies may result in a currency mismatch in domestic banking activities, as recent literature has suggested. This may, in turn, increase financial fragility, create balance sheet problems, and affect bank profitability in these economies. Ozsoz (2009) tests the effect of dollarization on bank performance in nine dollarized transition economies. However, no empirical evidence supports the assertions of the currency mismatch theory. The inconclusive results might be related with the following factors. Although there is no direct link between bank profitability and dollarization in these economies, the high level of deposit dollarization lowers the level of provisions set aside for a banks' loan losses. In effect, an inadequate provision for bad loans can inflate bank's profits in the short run and might lead to lower profitability in the long run when the adverse impact of dollarization forces banks to write off their bad debts.

2.2 Dollarization and Inflation

One of the factors contributing to dollarization is the value of the domestic currency. Higher inflation not only affects output growth and resource allocation but also changes the return on holding foreign currencies. When do households switch from foreign to domestic currencies and vice versa? There is an inflation threshold where people switch from domestic currencies to dollar deposits. Empirical evidence provided in Antinolfi et al. (2007) suggests nonlinearity in the impact of inflation on financial intermediation and real economic activity. Their evidence also suggests that high inflation affects financial intermediation through the substitution of dollars "under the mattress" for savings in domestic banks. At low levels of inflation, inflation and real output are positively related. However, when the inflation rate exceeds some threshold, agents substitute dollars for deposits issued by domestic banks, reducing the scale of financial intermediation and investment. As a consequence, at high levels of inflation, capital stock and output become negatively related to the inflation rate.

Different countries would have different thresholds, depending on the elasticity of the demand for domestic currency with respect to expected inflation. This key parameter is a result of historical accidents and bad experiences which caused households to lose faith in the domestic currency during periods of hyperinflation and changes in economic regime. This is particularly true in the case of Cambodia, which might explain why the country has the highest degree of dollarization among CLMV countries.

Financial dollarization in high-inflation countries is usually related to currency hedging activities. Honahan (2008) examines a cross-country dataset on the share of bank deposits denominated in foreign currency. After growing rapidly during the 1990s, the scale of deposit dollarization has slowed or even reversed since 2001. Lower inflation in many countries has reduced the attraction of foreign currency as a hedge. Also, the Argentine crisis of 2001–2002 may have heightened investor awareness of the risk of forced conversion of foreign currency deposits. Nevertheless, a return to higher inflation and fading memories of forced conversions could lead to a resumption of the growth of deposit dollarization, along with the banking risks that this might entail. This study points to the most important determination of financial dollarization: price instability. Thus the fundamental cure for financial dollarization is to maintain price stability to dissuade the private sector from using foreign exchange as a hedging instrument.

Economic integration can underpin price stability, which gives households with confidence in their national currency and contains dollarization. With the establishment of the ASEAN Economic Community, business cycles of the member's countries should become synchronized. The market force of integration should ensure price stability once the CLMV countries are fully integrated within the ASEAN community. Dollarization in these countries will undoubtedly be affected by economic integration, as was the case in Europe. Neanidis (2010) analyzes the effect of European Union (EU) membership on financial dollarization for the Central and Eastern European countries, using a unique monthly dataset that spans about two decades. The results indicate that both the accession processes toward EU membership and EU entry have reduced deposit dollarization and increased loan dollarization. The negative effect on deposit dollarization captures the increased confidence of the private sector in the domestic currency, as the EU admission process is considered a reflection of their government's commitment to policies of long-run currency stability. The positive impact on credit dollarization is the outcome of a greater convergence of exchange rates to the euro and the subsequent anticipation of lower currency risk, which decreases the cost of foreign currency borrowing.

2.3 Dollarization and Exchange Rate Stability

There is an ongoing debate on whether dollarization helps to stabilize exchange rates in emerging economies. If dollarization leads to volatility in exchange rates, fluctuations in foreign exchange rate can affect exports and output growth. Lay et al. (2012) discuss this issue in a highly dollarized country, Cambodia, by empirically examining the relationship between dollarization and exchange rate movements. The GARCH analysis suggests that dollarization induces depreciation of the Cambodian riel in addition to intensifying exchange rate variability. The result is consistent with the argument that dollarization is one of the crucial causes of exchange rate instability.[2]

During the transitional period to market economies in the CLMV countries, there will be anticipated currency depreciation which further heightens the degree of dollarization. Ra (2008) investigates the dollarization of three transitional economies in Southeast Asia, namely, Cambodia, Lao PDR, and Vietnam, which experienced a process of transition and reform of their economies during 1992–2007. The empirical results show that there are positive effects of the expected rate of depreciation in market exchange rates on the holdings of US dollars. The coefficients are significant for only Cambodia and the Lao PDR, not for Vietnam. The effect is strongest for Cambodia, and this may reflect the fact that Cambodia's dollarization is stronger than that of the Lao PDR and Vietnam.

2.4 Crisis Vulnerability, Capital Flight, and Dollarization

Is it possible that dollarization helps rather than hinders the development process? After extremely rapid economic growth during 2000–2007, Cambodia experienced a sudden collapse of growth in 2008–2009. The contraction was short-lived and the country rebounded, thanks to strong exports after the world economy recovered from the global financial crisis (GFC). Hill and Menon (2011) examine the impact of the GFC on Cambodia by highlighting a number of peculiar vulnerabilities, including a narrow economic base, a pre-crisis asset price boom, a fragile financial system, and the limited array of defensive economic policy levers available to the government. The crisis provided the government with an opportunity to place the country's economic growth trajectory on a more sustainable footing by diversifying the economy and creating the preconditions for de-dollarization. It was also a chance to employ policies to improve the business climate and make growth more inclusive. In should be noted that Cambodia experienced high economic growth despite having a high degree of dollarization.

Does dollarization aggravate the twin crises? Currency crises in emerging markets have been accompanied by banking crises, with concentration in bank credit increasing after large devaluations. Luca and Olivero (2012) examine how the presence of imperfect competition and liability dollarization in banking shapes the real effects of the twin crises. Their model, constructed in the presence of the imperfect competition in banking and changes in market structure that occur in the aftermath of crises, reveals that currency devaluations generate more severe twin crises in economies with less competitive banking sectors. This result is consistent with the empirical evidence on the concentration-fragility view, and it shows the importance of prudential regulation that focuses on the market structure in banking. CLMV countries with different degrees of dollarization and different degrees of banking concentration would be exposed to different levels of vulnerability to twin crises. Whether a highly competitive banking sector in Cambodia would be less vulnerable to twin crises also depends on the financial rules and regulations pertaining to bank balance sheets.

Dollarization can originate from external sources through foreign borrowing if there are no capital controls and the private sector can borrow from external sources, which is often associated with currency crises. Offshore dollarization can lead to domestic liability dollarization. Metin-Ozcan and Us (2009) find that rising asset dollarization in Turkey was mainly demand-driven, originating from increasing demand for foreign assets before the 2001 financial crisis. The increasing demand for foreign assets in turn resulted in an increase in foreign-currency-denominated debt, thus causing an increase in liability dollarization. Increasing external funding opportunities for the banking system produced an increase in offshore dollarization, which eventually fed into higher asset dollarization than otherwise would have occurred. The case of dollarization in Turkey points to the importance of capital controls that can sever the link between foreign borrowing and domestic dollarization.

Capital flight is always a threat to countries that limit currency convertibility and maintain unrealistic exchange rates. On the other hand, political risk is also an important factor determining capital flow. With highly dollarized deposits, the capital flight risk associated with overvalued currencies can be mitigated. Ramon-Ballester and Wezel (2008) empirically investigate the extent to which the financial linkages of Latin American banks with other countries are influenced by political risk and deposit dollarization. They find that the sum of banks' foreign assets and liabilities is a function of risk–return considerations and excess domestic credit demand. An increase in political risk is shown to be associated with a build-up of foreign positions by the banking sector, but this adverse effect on the banking system is mitigated in economies with a high share of dollarized deposits. These relationships largely hold when the determinants of foreign assets and liabilities are estimated separately, with risk-induced capital flight being moderated by a high degree of deposit dollarization. Changes in overall country risk, including the risk of macro-collapse, drive official capital outflows. For a wider measure of capital flight, including informal flows, only changes in political risk matter. In each case, deposit dollarization is shown to possess a risk-mitigating property. The results suggest caution with active de-dollarization strategies in highly dollarized economies where political instability remains an issue. If Ramon-Ballester and Wezel's result holds for the CLMV countries, Cambodia will have the lowest risk of capital flight.

2.5 Summary

From this literature review of dollarization from Latin America countries, Europe, and Asia, we have seen the complex nexus between dollarization and macroeconomic variables. Dollarization involves economic growth, inflation, exchange rate volatility, financial deepening, bank balance sheets, and bank performance. One cannot examine the benefits and costs of dollarization and the impact of dollarization on the role of monetary policy without referring to these macroeconomic and financial variables.

3 Economic Development and Dollarization

3.1 Economic Development and Urbanization

Notwithstanding external shocks, real per capita income in Cambodia, the Lao PDR, and Vietnam has trended upward since the early 1980s. These countries have embraced market mechanisms and adopted outward-looking development strategies. Inflows of foreign direct investment (FDI) contributed to capital formation and enhanced labor productivity. The rising tide of FDI in the CLMV countries bodes well for a reduction in economic and political risk.

One of the characteristics of economic development is the degree of urbanization, measured by the urban population as a percentage of the total population. Figure 1 shows the continuous rise in urbanization in the CLMV countries.

The rising trend of urbanization indicates a structural transformation from rural to urban society; as more people live in urban areas, the demand for money for transactions increases. A choice between using domestic currency and using foreign currency for transactions must be made. If income is mainly received in the local currency, naturally people will conduct transactions in the local currency. However, if people receive income in a foreign currency, they might want to use the foreign currency for transaction purposes. International trade, income from tourism, foreign remittance, and cross-border trade transactions many affect payment dollarization.

The rapid transformation of a rural agrarian society to an urban society with booming service and industrial sectors suggests that the structure of the demand for money also changes.[3] Urbanization is related to high economic growth. Because of high economic activity and a declining marginal propensity to consume, the demand for money within urban

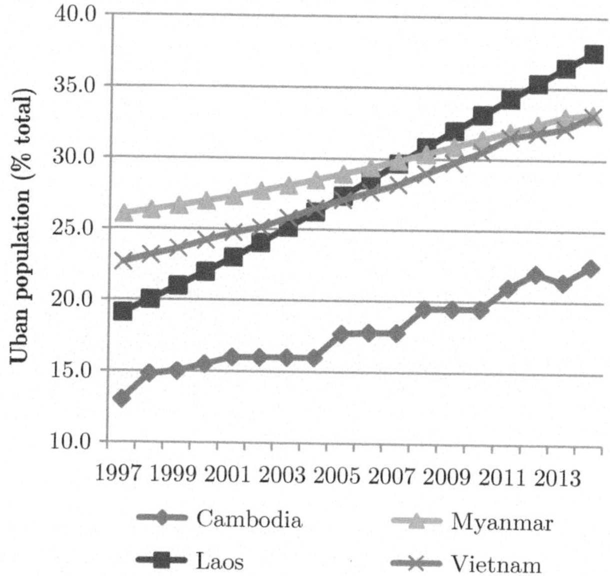

Fig. 1 Urbanization in the CLMV countries. *Source* Key indicators for Asia and the Pacific 2014, Asian Development Bank (ADB)

areas is higher than that within rural areas. Because of increasing linkages between rural and urban areas, the demand for money for transactions increases as the market economy becomes more prevalent as the monetization process becomes widespread. Thus, the demand for money in the whole economy increases.

As real per capita income rises above a certain level, the demand for wealth accumulation exceeds the demand for transactions. Then, the quantity of quasi-money exceeds the quantity of narrow money, and the velocity of broad money declines. The relationship between output growth and velocity is shown in Fig. 2—specifically, the declining velocity and subdued inflation in Cambodia. In effect, expansion of the quantity of money does not always translate into higher inflation. This rapid phase of changing the structure of demand for money is opportune for implementing fiscal policy to finance infrastructure development. This would not cause inflationary pressure because of the declining velocity and the positive output effect generated by infrastructure development.

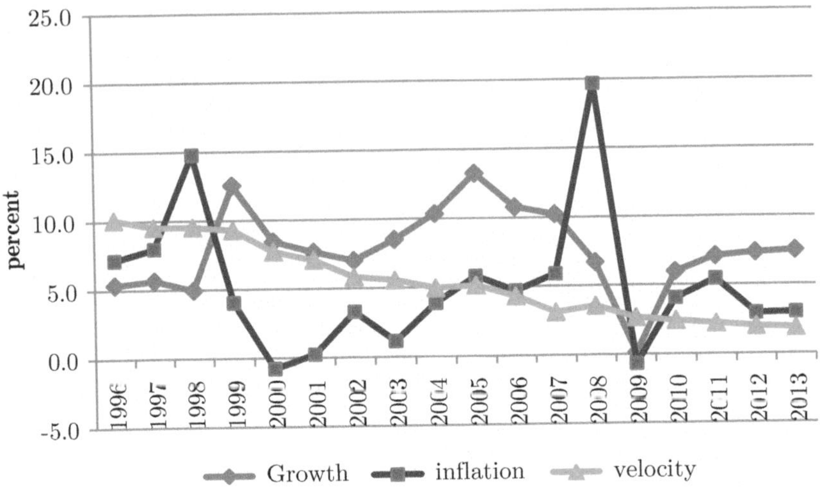

Fig. 2 Declining velocity, output growth, and inflation in Cambodia. *Sources* Key indicators for Asia and the Pacific 2014, ADB, and author's calculation

With appropriate exchange rate policy during this big push for infrastructure projects, CLMV countries will be able to maintain price stability. On the output supply side, the money supply can be regarded as a factor of production. A rising quantity of money also means the quantity of output can be raised as bank credit provides working capital to firms. The linkage between the growth of the money supply and inflation will be weakened during the early stage of economic development.

3.2 International Trade and Dollarization

Trade openness is measured by the value of total trade as a percentage of GDP. It has been established that trade integration is a growth driver in developing countries. The literature on the impact of exports on output growth is well documented. Figure 3 indicates how the CLMV countries have been exposed to globalization and external shocks. An increasing volume of trade implies a higher demand for foreign exchange.

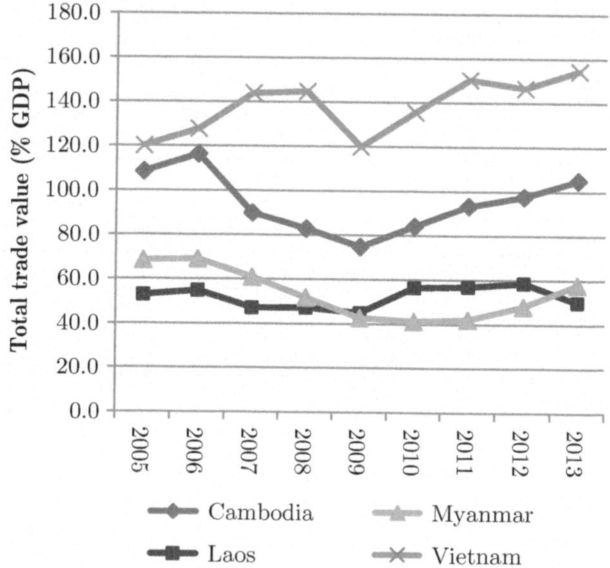

Fig. 3 Trade openness in the CLMV countries. *Sources* Key indicators for Asia and the Pacific 2014, ADB; International Financial Statistics, International Monetary Fund (IMF)

In 2013, the degree of trade openness in Vietnam and Cambodia exceeded 100% of GDP. There is no doubt that exports are growth drivers in the two countries. After the GFC in 2009, the share of international trade in GDP increased steadily. Figure 3 indicates that there is a marked difference of trade exposure among the CLMV countries. The trade exposure in Myanmar and the Lao PDR is still far below that in Vietnam and Cambodia. A measure for de-dollarization would be less complicated in Myanmar and the Lao PDR than in Cambodia.

From Table 1, we see the reason why foreign currency deposits and transactions in foreign currency are still found in the CLVM countries. Especially in Lao PDR, the Thai baht is used for transaction purposes at rates similar to those of the dollar because of its importance in export and import transactions.

Table 1 Top trading partners of the CLMV countries (percentage share of country's total exports/imports).

	Cambodia				Lao PDR			
	Exports to USA		Imports from Thailand		Exports to Thailand		Imports from Thailand	
2013	28.1		27.1		33.2		56.0	
2000	65.8		15.5		17.6		60.8	
	Myanmar				Vietnam			
	Exports to Thailand		Imports from		Exports to		Imports from	
2013	34.9		China	39.8	USA	17.6	China	31.1
			Thailand	20.2				
2000	11.7		China	17.9	Japan	17.7	Singapore	17.2

Source Key indicators for Asia and the Pacific 2014, ADB

We cannot underestimate the importance of the dollar, the baht, and the yuan when used for transactions between the CLMV countries and their major trading partners, in particular in border trade. Using foreign rather than domestic currencies, traders can reduce transaction costs and foreign exchange risk. The rising volume of trade suggests higher demand for transaction purposes. Border trade volumes are smaller than regular international trade volumes. However, these transactions are conducted in shorter periods, with less dependence on trade credit from banks. Furthermore, foreign currencies are held and used because transactions costs are lower than when exchanging them back and forth to domestic currencies when the need arises. Dollarization for international trade transactions is therefore economically justified.

3.3 Financial Deepening, Interest Rates, and Dollarization

Another indicator of economic development is financial deepening. One of the stylized facts of economic development is the financial deepening process captured by the rising ratio of M2 to GDP. When financial institutions in the CLMV countries succeed in establishing banking habits, the demand for financial savings increases faster than GDP growth. The so-called financial deepening process in the CLMV countries is illustrated in Fig. 4.[4]

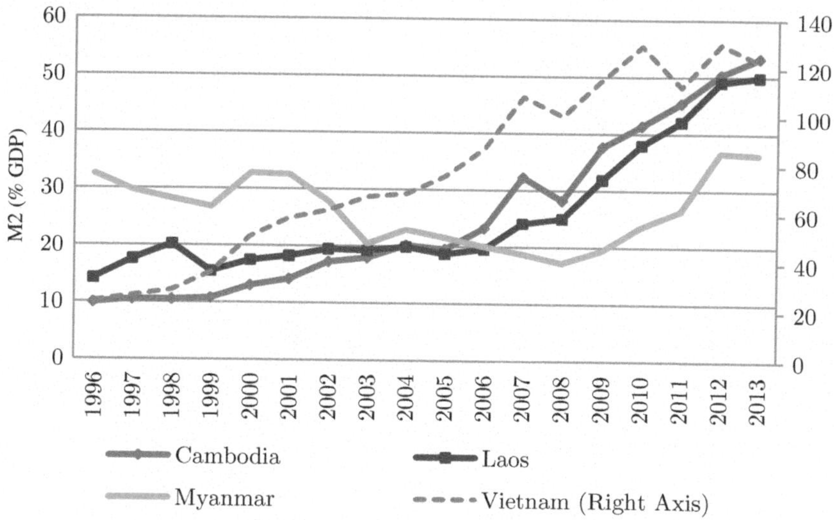

Fig. 4 Financial deepening in the CLMV countries. *Source* Key indicators for Asia and the Pacific 2014, ADB

Rising incomes in the CLMV countries are both an effect and a cause of financial development. On the one hand, because of rising per capita income and positive real interest rates, M2 has risen much faster than output. The soundness of the banking system makes financial savings less risky than before when bank deposits were threatened by bank failure and high inflation. On the other hand, economic growth has become sustainable through the intermediation effect of financial institutions.

Financial savings depend on income level, among other factors, because a rising income level implies a higher propensity to save. Once a banking culture has been firmly established, the ability to save increases, and bank deposits replace non-productive savings outside the banking system.

The other important factor contributing to financial deepening is the incentive to save. With positive real interest rates, M2 increases as a result of substitution between future and current consumption. Figure 5 illustrates the importance of establishing favorable incentives to save in domestic currency in order to create financial deepening. In Vietnam, the rate of change in the broad money supply moved in line with the real

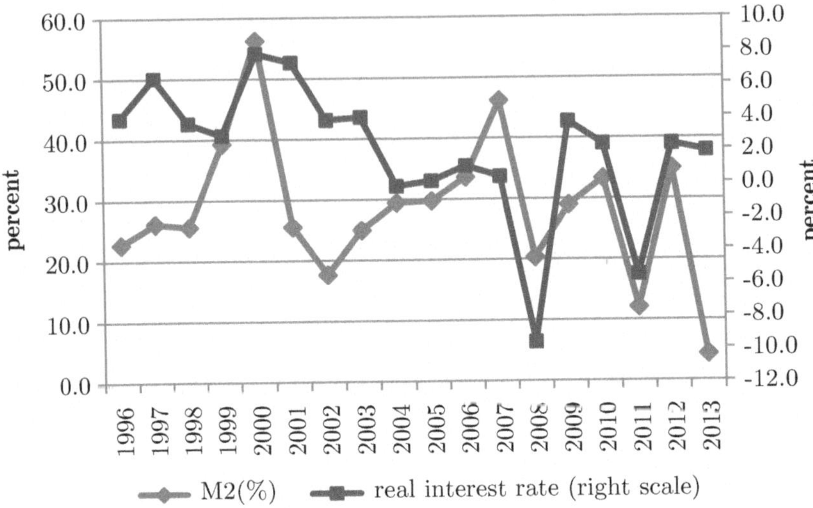

Fig. 5 Real interest rate and financial savings in Vietnam. *Source* Key indicators for Asia and the Pacific 2014, ADB

interest rate. The demand for broad money did not increase steadily without interruption. In 2008, when Vietnam experienced double-digit inflation, the ratio of M2 to GDP declined temporarily as the real interest rate was negative. It is important that when using interest rate ceilings as policy instruments, it does not destroy incentives to save.

If lending and deposit rates are still subject to interest rate ceilings, the central bank can use the ceilings as a policy instrument to alter monetary growth rate and economic activity. Although sophisticated monetary policy instruments are not available in the CLMV countries, ceilings on deposit and loan interest rates can be employed to affect real economic activity. By altering the interest rate structure, bank balance sheets will be affected. The availability of credit is a more powerful means of monetary policy than the interest rate channel. This is because credit rationing is more prevalent in the early stages of financial development, when competition in the financial sector is low. The formal financial institutions are competing more with unorganized money markets.

In the case of dollarization, changing interest rate ceilings can cause portfolio reallocation by households and commercial banks. Note that if the ceiling interest rates are to be effective, they must be established below the equilibrium rate. This point applies for a country with rudimentary financial markets where a system of full-fledged monetary policy instruments is not available. If financial institutions have reached a certain level of sophistication, when central banks have sufficient monetary policy instruments, interest rate ceilings can be abolished. In the meantime, the ceilings can be adjusted upward or downward to ensure that real interest rates remain positive. How soon CLMV countries can liberalize their financial markets depends on the speed of sophistication of financial institutions.

Portfolio reallocation also takes place when the inflation rate rises and increased depreciation is expected. Under high inflation, the rate of return on dollar holdings increases, causing substitution of dollar deposits for local currency deposits in household portfolios. Thus, dollar substitution remains as long as the central bank cannot control inflation or prevent the expected depreciation of the local currency. Furthermore, as in the case of Vietnam, the phenomenon of goldization reflects the demand for inflation-hedged assets.

3.4 Exchange Rate Policy and Inflation

If the trade sector in the CLMV countries is liberalized, inflation will be affected by import prices and exchange rate movements. Vietnam's exchange rate depreciation in 1998 and 2011 led to a rise in the price level.[5] Note that the rate of depreciation is lower than the rate of inflation, implying that despite the high percentage of depreciation, the Vietnamese dong is still overvalued in real terms. The 23% inflation rate in 2008 was the result of food inflation. The global food price crisis in 2008 forced China and India to ban exports of rice. This crisis was a temporary episode of overshooting inflation caused by commodity shortages and expected inflation.[6] When the fear of a food shortage subsided, the inflation rate and expected inflation were curbed.

Price shocks can also stem from increases in import prices arising from transmissions from trading partners. The 1998 Asian financial crisis led to massive depreciation of the baht and imported inflation to neighboring countries. Dynamism of inflation caused by inflation inertia makes it difficult for central banks to alter inflation expectations. An appropriate exchange rate policy is therefore crucial for price stability.

According to Pham and Riedel (2012), high inflation in Vietnam was the result of the untimely conduct of monetary policy and the country's lack of monetary policy instruments. Capital control relaxation also reduced the ability of the State Bank of Vietnam (SBV) to pursue an independent monetary policy. During the GFC, when Vietnam experienced capital flight and speculative attacks, the SBV's announcement of a readiness to sell foreign exchange, in addition to a widening of the trading band, succeeded in demonstrating a greater commitment to defend the dong in the period 2008–2009. According to Takagi and Pham (2011), however, the effectiveness of these policy measures was short-lived.

Depreciation in Vietnam is employed as a means to regain the international competitiveness that has eroded as the result of past periods of high inflation. Expected inflation has been formulated when households adjust price expectations upward. Although the SBV can establish a narrow band for exchange rate movements to calm depreciation expectations, this policy will not work effectively unless the governments maintain price stability by treating the root cause of inflation. In 2015, Vietnam devalued its currency three times and the SBV allowed the dong to trade up to 3% on either side of the central bank fixed rate. The band was widened to allow the dong to depreciate in response to depreciation of the yuan. The dong weakened only 5% in 2015, which was smaller than the depreciation rate of ASEAN's five biggest economies. Nevertheless, supporting the dong was costly for Vietnam's foreign currency reserves. In the third quarter of 2015, the reserves declined by $6.6 billion to $31 billion.

In attempting to curb inflationary expectations, monetary policy may not be effective if the government finances budget deficits by borrowing from the central bank or external sources of funds. According to the IMF country report on the Lao PDR in December 2013, the government had already committed to stop borrowing for new development projects and to refrain from using the Bank of Lao PDR's deficit financing. Apart from that, there was a significant 1-year-pass-through effect of 162%

devaluation of the kip in 1998. Inflation in the Lao PDR jumped to 90% in 1998 and to 115 in 1999, before tapering off to 11.1% in the following year. Since then, the Lao PDR has been able to maintain low inflation and continue the financial deepening process. With price stability, the market pressure on the dollar—kip exchange rate with a band will be lower. Higher flexibility of the exchange rate does not require heavy intervention in the foreign exchange market and therefore a lower international reserves cushion.

Because of the price stability, the ratio of M2 to GDP in Lao PDR increased from 17% in 2000 to 50% in 2013. Thus in the past decade and a half, the Lao PDR has made substantial progress in financial deepening, despite a high amount of foreign currency deposits. In 2001, the Lao PDR experienced its lowest economic growth in a decade as the country was affected by the mild global recession at the time. Since the 4% growth rate in 2001, the Laotian economy has experienced growth rates of more than 6%. In 2009, when other Asian countries were adversely affected by the GFC, the Lao PDR's economy merely slowed to 7.5% growth. The annual growth rate of broad money rarely dropped below 15%, except in 2005. Strong economic growth leads to higher demand for financial savings for wealth accumulation. In 1996 the velocity of money was 10, declining steadily to 2.9. If the velocity of money declines over time, rapid expansion of the money supply, caused by capital inflow, will not necessarily lead to consumer price inflation.

The ability to maintain price stability depends on the central bank's role in managing exchange rate fluctuations. Similar to the Lao PDR and Vietnam, Cambodia's price volatility is related to exchange rate fluctuations. The 27% depreciation of the riel raised inflation to 14% in 1998. Thus Cambodia's nominal exchange rate devaluation constituted a real devaluation, resulting in a gain in international competitiveness. Exports responded by increasing from 5% in 1998 to 12.6% in 1999.

External shocks are another source of price instability. When the US Federal Reserve launched a quantitative easing monetary policy in 2008, massive capital inflows from developed countries moved into Asia, seeking higher rates of return on portfolio investments. Just like other ASEAN countries that witnessed exchange rate appreciation against the US dollar, the riel appreciated by 3% in 2011. As a consequence,

Cambodia was able to maintain price stability because of cheaper imported goods. However, similar to the Lao PDR's experience with the global food price crisis, the inflation rate in Cambodia increased by 19.7% in 2008, when the food price index jumped by 29.9%. Monetary policy was not able to contain external shocks in world commodity prices. In the following year, food prices and consumer prices declined by 0.5 and 0.7%, respectively.

The conclusion from this analysis is that monetary authorities in the CLMV countries have limited power to contain inflation as long as their economies are open to capital flows. Maintaining price stability means establishing a stable exchange rate. The central bank will have to intervene in the foreign exchange markets, and monetary policy will not be effective in the long run unless there are some forms of capital controls. Other administrative pricing policies to contain panics and inflationary expectations are necessary when external price shocks are temporary.

In the early stage of development, if the exchange rate is relatively stable, the low foreign exchange rate risk can reduce export instability and promote investment and growth in the traded sector. However, since the exposure of exports to the world business cycle in the CLMV countries has been increasing, it is not surprising that these countries would succumb to export shortfall during the GFC. Similar to other ASEAN countries, Cambodia's exports collapsed by 10% in 2009 and rebounded to 25.1 and 27.8% in 2010 and 2011, respectively.

There is a trade-off between high growth and price stability. Inflation accelerates when demand outstrips supply as the economy nears full employment. The central bank can let the exchange rate depreciate to cope with rising inflation. The problem occurs when dollar loans accelerate, particularly in the non-traded sector. International competitiveness declines when the real exchange rate (the ratio of trade to non-traded good prices) appreciates. The so-called Dutch disease will be a major threat to the stability of the Lao PDR and Cambodia.

Finally, additional caution peculiar to dollarized economies is that dollarization differs in some respects from the fixed dollar exchange rate system. Under the pegged system, the domestic currency can be under or overvalued, which requires constant intervention in the foreign exchange market to maintain international competitiveness. Under a dollarized economy, the impact of depreciation or appreciation of the dollar has less of an impact than on a non-dollarized economy that trades mainly in the dollar. Nevertheless, the dollarized economy will be subject to fluctuation of the US dollar against major currencies. When the dollar was weakened under the unconventional monetary policy of the US Federal Reserve, dollarized economies benefited from increased competitiveness. On the other hand, when the US Federal Reserve starts normalizing monetary policy, the dollarized economies will be subject to a loss of competitiveness as the dollar appreciates against other currencies.

3.5 Long-Run Growth

When long-term growth is considered, monetary policy cannot be used to raise the growth path, which is dictated by technology and productivity growth. What monetary policy can do is minimize deviations of output from the long-term growth path. In the case of Vietnam, per capita income is on the rise, with minimal deviations from the long-term growth path. But monetary policy can indirectly affect the long-term growth path by providing stability in the macroeconomic environment through the establishment of price stability and realistic exchange rates.

Figure 6 indicates that Vietnam's investment-to-GDP ratio increased from 12.5% in 1990 to 36.2% in 2010, but investments trended downward. Thanks to the role of public investment, the ratio of capital expenditure to current expenditure increased dramatically from 0.35 in 1996 to 0.77 in 2013. Capital formation occurs rapidly when public capital goods are complementary to private capital goods. Monetary policy can accommodate infrastructure development by providing non-inflationary means of financing. Exports have become a stronger growth driver than investment. Thus, the role of the exchange rate in growth sustainability has become more important.

It should be noted that quality of investment cannot be ignored and that excessive investment in the non-traded sector, especially property sector, can lead to a rapid decline in international competitiveness.

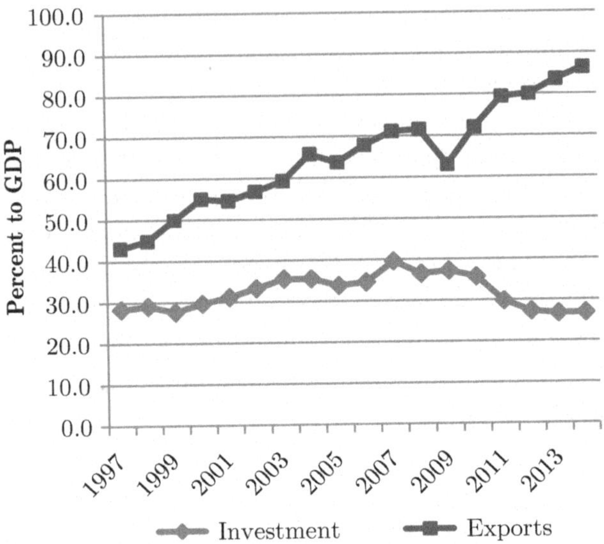

Fig. 6 Vietnam's growth drivers. *Source* Key indicators for Asia and the Pacific 2014, ADB

Macro-prudential policy must therefore be implemented to make sure that dollar loans do not add to effective speculation in property markets and that dollar deposits are utilized such that they do not create currency mismatch risk. In some CLMV countries, loan-to-value (LTV) regulations have been implemented. The Central Bank of Myanmar has imposed LTV of 50% for commercial banks to prevent speculation in Myanmar's property sector. Other regulations on banking supervision and monitoring can be imposed gradually because commercial banks require time to adjust to new rules and the central banks need to increase their supervision capability. In addition to a liquidity reserve ratio, capital adequacy can be imposed to ensure bank solvency while the central bank's role as lender of last resort is limited by dollarization. To prevent speculation and the consequences of Dutch disease, the central banks can impose a waiting period between buying and selling the property to cool down the property markets.[7]

4 Effectiveness of Monetary Policy in the CLMV Countries

4.1 Monetary Policy Instruments in Underdeveloped Financial Markets

Given the constraints imposed by synchronization of the business cycle and inflation, and the lack of conventional monetary policy instruments, CLMV central banks may opt to use available means of controls, which can enhance bank solvency and promote financial development. Interest rate ceilings on deposit rates can be used to alter the funds loanable to the private sector. The gap between ceilings on local currency and foreign currency can be powerful in reshuffling portfolio allocation in households and the banking sector. As long as the ceiling on the deposit rate does not create financial shallowing caused by a negative real interest rate, the central banks can indirectly affect loan growth volume by changing the amount of available loanable funds.

CLMV central banks also have to maintain the soundness of the banking sector using available means of controls. A credit growth limit can be engineered through the imposition of a maximum loan-to-equity ratio, so that bank solvency will not be impaired despite the lack of a lender of last resort in the central bank. Also, with a booming economy, banks can use their larger profits to enhance equity and provide provisions for bad debt. To enhance bank solvency and infrastructure development, legal reserve requirements should include government bonds in addition to cash reserves and deposits at the central bank.

When the money market is not fully developed, the central bank cannot effectively intervene by changing the discount rate or altering key short-term interest rates. Furthermore, there is no close link between short-term policy rates and the lending rates of commercial banks. Instead, the central bank can adjust the ratio of the reserve requirement and the percentage composition of the reserves as a signal of a monetary policy stance.

As inflationary expectations lead to anticipated currency depreciation, temporary ceilings on key commodity prices can be used to calm the inflation spiral caused by temporary commodity price shocks. The maximum prices imposed must be temporary in nature so as not to cause shortages of goods and production inefficiency in the long run. This ceiling can be used to accompany monetary policy particularly for countries which are prone to high inflation and when disinflation policy is obstructed by inflation inertia.

4.2 Business Cycle Synchronization

As the CLMV countries become more integrated to the world economy, they cannot be shielded from external shocks. Exchange rate policy must be flexible enough to provide a cushion for fluctuations in external demand and changes in commodity prices. Figure 7 illustrates how CLMV inflation rates move in line with their major trading partners: China and the ASEAN-5 countries (Indonesia, Malaysia, Philippines, Singapore, and Thailand). Dollarization and maintaining stable exchanges rate with major trading partners make the CLMV countries

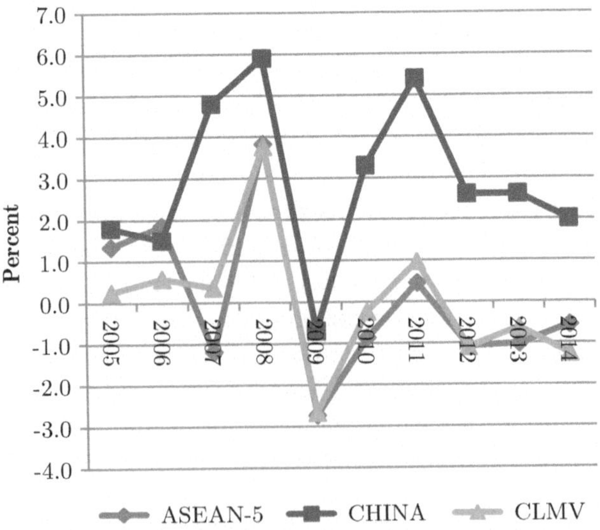

Fig. 7 Synchronization of regional inflation. *Sources* Key indicators for Asia and the Pacific 2014, ADB, and author's calculation

vulnerable to imported inflation, unless the central banks choose to allow a higher degree of exchange rate flexibility. The consequences of trade liberalization within the region are inflation, exports, and output growth synchronization (Nidhiprabha 2015a).

China's imports are crucial factor in determining exports of ASEAN countries. A growth slowdown in China spells trouble in ASEAN economies, because of the growing network trade and product fragmentation in the region. Consequently, there are repercussions from the deceleration of growth in ASEAN-5 economies for the CLMV countries. When export growth rates in ASEAN are synchronized, their GDP growth rates also fluctuate in tandem (Fig. 8). The GFC led to a collapse in exports in 2009 and caused a collapse in the output of the ASEAN-5 and CLMV economies. We observed a V-shaped recovery in 2010 and a double-dip in growth rate in 2011. As China's expansion slowed in 2014 and 2015, adverse consequences on ASEAN economies have become more pronounced. The extent of the damage depends on the trade exposure and China dependency of each ASEAN country (Nidhiprabha 2015b). ASEAN economies, whether they are dollarized or not, would succumb to violent fluctuations of world trade volume.

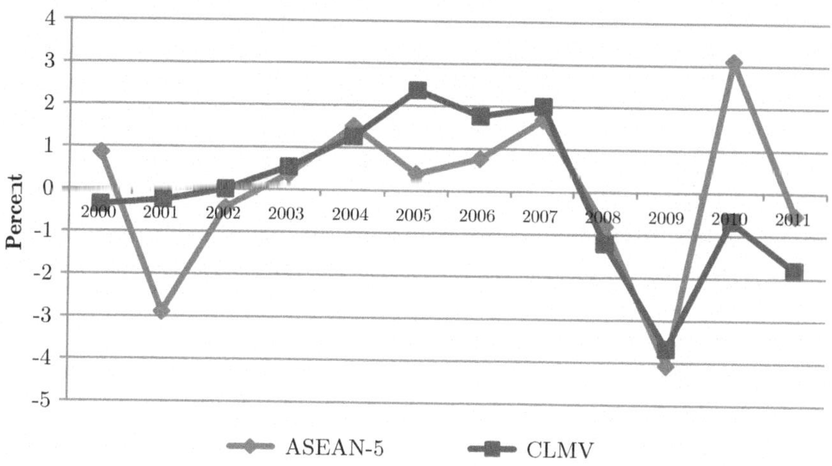

Fig. 8 Growth synchronization: Principal GDP growth components of the CLMV countries and ASEAN-5. *Sources* Key indicators for Asia and the Pacific 2014, ADB, and author's calculation

Domestic demand in the CLMV countries must be stimulated by expansionary monetary policy and fiscal policy to counter the consequences of slumps in the world business cycle. It is imperative to understand that expansionary monetary policy has a long lag and the private sector's responsiveness to credit availability also depends on consumer confidence and investor sentiment.

In terms of the objectives of monetary policy, price stability should be given the highest priority, and all else being equal, a decline in dollarization follows when price stability is achieved. Low inflationary expectations lead to lower expected currency depreciation. The substitution effect away from foreign deposits to local currency deposits results in a natural decline of foreign currency deposits to the M2–GDP ratio, as observed in the Lao PDR and Vietnam. The fact that Cambodia has the highest rate of deposit dollarization can be explained by persistent habits caused by historical accident. Compared with the other CLMV countries, Cambodia must have had very elastic demand for the dollar with respect to expected inflation and riel depreciation.

5 Concluding Remarks

With or without dollarization, the ability of central banks in the CLMV countries to control the money supply is impaired by undisciplined fiscal authorities, and the lack of monetary instruments, and business cycle synchronization between CLMV and ASEAN-5 economies. The main transmission channel of monetary policy is the availability of credit rather than the policy interest rate, exchange rates, and asset prices. Nevertheless, available monetary policy instruments are interest rate ceilings and commercial banks' reserve requirement.

Without capital controls, monetary policy will be ineffective in targeting exchange rate in the long run, with or without dollarization in the first place. Under those circumstances, there is nothing much to gain from forced de-dollarization in order to gain monetary policy effectiveness. Dollarization can be as beneficial as any anchor currency used in the Optimal Currency Areas. With the ASEAN Economic Community blueprints by the end of 2025, the use of the dollar or a proxy dollar (an anchor currency pegged relative to the dollar) can enhance trade and investment through reduced exchange rate risk and lowered transaction costs for exchanging goods and services.

The loss in the effectiveness of monetary policy under dollarization is over-stated, and the argument that dollarization impairs the central bank's role as lender of last resort might be exaggeration. As we have observed, Cambodian banks hold a large amount of excess reserve to protect themselves from bank runs. We can argue that dollarization discourages moral hazard leading to overlending as no banks will be too big to fail. If excess reserves are abundant, does it mean the interest rates are high to discourage domestic investment? It should be noted that investment depends not just on the cost of borrowing but also on the availability of credit and a stable investment environment that reduces the risk premium. On top of that, if dollarization can reduce price instability it can also indirectly provide favorable environment for investors.

On the contrary, dollarization is crucial for the early stage of economic development in the CLMV countries. During the time when banking habits have yet to spread to rural areas, commercial banks simply perform tasks such as deposit taking and have considerable excess reserves. As the economy develops with sustained per capita income growth and undergoes structural transformation from a predominant agriculture sector to a predominant manufacturing sector, the demand for loans will exceed disposable deposits. The interbank market will become active and provide opportunities for the central bank to employ short-term interest rates as policy instruments. Before a sophisticated banking environment is established, monetary policy in the CLMV countries will never be effective as a stabilization policy tool.

Rather than attempting to force de-dollarization in the name of national pride, CLMV central banks should be more concerned with Dutch disease. If property prices in dollarized economies are increased by asset price speculation fueled by excessive property credit, the non-traded sector will expand at the expense of the traded sector. Without proper credit controls, the economy will be approaching a Minsky moment.

Loan dollarization and deposit dollarization create the atmosphere of a fixed exchange rate, thereby seemingly eliminating foreign exchange risk, and encouraging investors to take on riskier projects. Then, excessive and inefficient investment can retard growth in the long run. If currency mismatch risk is accentuated by borrowing and lending in different currencies, speculation in the booming non-traded sector can threaten the sustainability of growth. Does dollarization really reduce exchange risk against currencies other than the dollar? A dollarized economy will experience fluctuations in the dollar similar to those experienced by its trading partners. But if its major trading partners tend to keep their exchange rates in line with the dollar, a highly dollarized economy will indeed suffer less severe exchange rate turmoil than less dollarized economies.

A gradual approach to de-dollarization is more appropriate than a big-bang approach or forced de-dollarization. After all, the CLMV countries have experienced growth and price stability despite the existence of dollarization for the last two decades. A natural approach, dictated by the desire to hold domestic currencies, is more practical without losing the benefits gained from dollarization in the past. In time, when the private sector develops banking behavior and prudential culture, and the CLMV governments have sufficient time to develop financial and capital markets and prudential regulations, financial instruments will be available and suitable for the central banks to alter the interest rate and the quantity of money.

When should a country earnestly embark on de-dollarization? Since the CLMV economies are at different levels of financial development, the timing of de-dollarization depends on a stable macroeconomic environment and the benefits and costs of the process. Habitual use of the dollar for transactions and wealth accumulation would make the costs of de-dollarization higher than its benefits. It will take longer in some CLMV countries than in others to get to the stage where the benefits of de-dollarization exceed its costs. On the other hand, Myanmar, at the cross-road of dollarization, should find the cost of de-dollarization to be lower than that of Cambodia.

Dollarization is a historical accident that people in Cambodia, the Lao PDR, Myanmar, and Vietnam have learned to live with. In time, when people see the benefits from holding their own currencies, they will eventually switch to local currencies as long as price stability and exchange rate stability prevail.

Notes

1. There is another classification, real dollarization. See Chap. 1 for classification of dollarization.
2. According to Chap. 2, in Cambodia, the poor tend to earn incomes in riel. Dollarization could therefore be a constraint on poverty reduction since it tends to affect the living standards of the poor through depreciation of the currency and intensified volatility of exchange rates.
3. From 1996 to 2013, the urban population in the Lao PDR increased from 18.3 to 35.3%. For the same period, Vietnam's urban population rose from 21.1 to 32.2%.
4. It should be pointed out that the broad money to GDP ratio will reach a plateau when bond and equity markets are developed to an extent that other means of savings can be offered to the private sector.
5. According a simulation model by Goujon (2006), the sharp 25% depreciation in 1997/1998 led to an additional cumulative inflation of 13% in Vietnam.
6. The world export price of white rice per metric ton sharply increased from 481 dollars in February 2008 to 1015 dollars in August 2008.
7. It should be noted that the equity-to-loan ratio sets a maximum level of loan extension. Rather than putting a ceiling on loan growth, the central banks can adjust the capital adequacy ratio in response to boom and bust cycles. In the long run, banking habits and financial development depend on the solvency of the entire banking sector.

Acknowledgements The author wishes to thank Hidenobu Okuda and Koji Kubo for their valuable comments

References

Antinolfi, G., C.M. Landeo, and M. Nikitin. 2007. Dollarization and the inflation threshold. *Canadian Journal of Economics* 40 (2): 628–649.

Goujon, M. 2006. Fighting inflation in a dollarized economy: The case of Vietnam. *Journal of Comparative Economics* 34: 564–581.

Herrera, A.A., and J.G. Uyen. 2012. Currency-induced credit risk in a dollarized economy. *Emerging Markets Finance and Trade* 48 (5): 105–114.

Hill, H., and J. Menon. 2011. Reducing vulnerability in transition economies: Crises and adjustment in Cambodia. *ASEAN Economic Bulletin* 28 (2): 134–159.
Honohan, P. 2008. The retreat of deposit dollarization. *International Finance* 11 (3): 247–268.
Lay, S., M. Kakinaka, and K. Kotani. 2012. Exchange rate movements in a dollarized economy: The case of Cambodia. *ASEAN Economic Bulletin* 29 (1): 65–78.
Luca, Alina C., and Maria Pia Olivero. 2012. Twin crises in emerging markets: The role of liability dollarization and imperfect competition in banking. *Review of Development Economics* 16 (1): 72–94.
Metin Ozcan, K., and V. Us. 2009. What drives dollarization in Turkey? *Journal of Economic Cooperation and Development* 30 (4): 29–50.
Neanidis, K.C. 2010. Financial dollarization and European Union membership. *International Finance* 13 (2): 257–282.
Nidhiprabha, B. 2015a. The global financial crisis and macroeconomic policy in Southeast Asia. In *Handbook of Southeast Asian economics*, ed. Ian Coxhead, 385–407. Abingdon: Routhledge.
Nidhiprabha, B. 2015b. The ASEAN business cycle and China's slowdown. *The Philippine Review of Economics LII* 2: 203–221.
Ozsoz, E. 2009. Evaluating the effects of deposit dollarization in financial intermediation in transition economies. *Eastern European Economics* 47 (4): 5–24.
Ozsoz, E., E.W. Rengifo, and D. Salvatore. 2010. Deposit dollarization as an investment signal in transition economies: The cases of Croatia, the Czech Republic, and Slovakia. *Emerging Markets Finance and Trade* 46 (4): 5–22.
Pham, T., and J. Riedel. 2012. On the conduct of monetary policy in Vietnam. *Asian-Pacific Economic Literature* 26 (1): 34–45.
Ra, H. 2008. Modeling the dollarization: A case study for Cambodia, Laos, and Vietnam. *Global Economic Review* 37 (2): 157–169.
Ramon-Ballester, F., and T. Wezel. 2008. International financial linkages of Latin American banks: The effects of political risk and deposit dollarization. *Journal of Business and Economic Studies* 14 (2): 1–24.
Serieux, J. 2009. Partial dollarization, exchange rates, and firm investment in Paraguay. *Developing Economies* 47 (1): 53–80.
Takagi, S., and T.H.A. Pham. 2011. Responding to the global financial crisis: Vietnamese exchange rate policy, 2008–2009. *Journal of Asian Economics* 22: 507–517.

7

Banking and Dollarization: A Comparative Study of Cambodia, Lao PDR, and Vietnam

Hidenobu Okuda

1 Dollarization Under Globalization

As the world economy continues to globalize, dollarization is prevalent and is even growing among developing economies, especially formerly planned economies. Dollarization increases the exposure of individuals and entities to exchange rate risk and can therefore be a potential source of macroeconomic and financial instability.

So far, theoretical and empirical studies on financial dollarization have mainly focused on the behavior of households and firms. The minimum variance portfolio approach explains household behavior as a portfolio choice problem in which agents choose the currency composition of their portfolio that minimizes the variance of returns.[1] The credit risk paradigm explains the behavior of firms as the result of optimal decisions by risk-neutral agents in the presence of default risk accompanied with moral hazard/asymmetric information.

H. Okuda (✉)
Graduate School of Economics, Hitotsubashi University, Tokyo, Japan
e-mail: hokuda@econ.hit-u.ac.jp

K. Kubo (ed.), *Dollarization and De-dollarization in Transitional Economies of Southeast Asia*, IDE-JETRO Series, DOI 10.1007/978-3-319-57768-5_7

Theoretical and empirical studies have not given sufficient weight to the role of banks in dollarization. Instead, banks have been treated as small supporting players that react passively to the progress of dollarization. However, because they play a pivotal role in financial transactions in developing (emerging) economies, understanding the behavior of banks in dollarization is of great interest to both researchers and policy-makers.

This paper conceptually analyzes the role of banks in dollarization and examines the banking industry in Cambodia, the Lao PDR, and Vietnam as specific examples. Section 2 describes the primary issues relating to banking operations in a dollarized economy. Section 3 sketches the behaviors of banks in cross-border dollarization using the simplified portfolio allocation model of Luca and Petrova (2008), which consists of households, firms, and banks. Section 4 observes the distinctive characteristics of bank behaviors in Cambodia, Lao PDR, and Vietnam in the analytical framework set in Sect. 3. Section 5 examines the similarities and differences in the banking of the three countries and discusses the determinants of those. Section 6 examines the role of banks in the dollarization driven by domestic financial intermediation in the Cambodian case. Section 7 summarizes the discussions and provides concluding remarks on policy implications.

2 Banking Under Dollarization

2.1 Perceptions of Banks Under Dollarization

Previous studies have examined the different roles of banks in the progress of dollarization from multilateral viewpoints.

1. Banks as supporting players passively corresponding to dollarization

Some studies have examined the effects of dollarization on bank performance in developing economies. According to the experience of selected countries in the past decade, dollarization had a negative effect on the profitability of banks in dollarized economies.[2] In addition, in these countries, dollarization put downward pressure on the quality of bank loans, resulting in higher loan defaults. These observations suggest that dollarization deteriorates fragility in financial intermediation in partially dollarized economies.

2. Banks as active players promoting dollarization

Some papers focused on the active role of banks in promoting dollarization in emerging markets. Banks often have an open facility to increase funds by accumulating foreign liabilities in transition countries.[3] Many banks are now subsidiaries of foreign banks in these countries and have ample access to foreign sources of funding from their parent banks. These banks borrow from abroad to fund domestic credit growth. Interest rate differentials between loans in foreign and local currencies are a key factor behind credit dollarization. It is often recognized that subsidiaries of foreign banks are driving up fast credit growth in their attempt to capture market shares.

3. Specific propositions of equilibrium dollarization in banks

The progress of dollarization depends on the interaction between households and bank behavior in the deposit-taking market. At the same time, it depends on the interaction between firms and bank behavior in the credit market, too. The choices of households to keep their savings and firms to borrow dollars from banks are generated through their transactions with a financial institution, stemming from the bank's providing accounts and undertaking lending in that currency. However, management behavior of banks depends strongly on the proactive management policy of the bank itself.

A group of papers has aimed at specifying the effects of dollarization on bank behaviors. Catao and Terrones (2000) made suggestions about specific properties of bank behavior for banks operating in dollarized economies. In general, equilibrium dollarization in banks changes with external interest rates and devaluation risk, while the direction of change depends on the initial level of dollarization, degree of competition in domestic—and foreign-currency-denominated loan markets, bank's cost structure, and the availability of collateral (or cost of loan enforcement).[4]

2.2 Problematic Behaviors of Banks Under Dollarization

Banks play an active role in promoting dollarization in emerging markets due to several possible circumstances. First, banks may excessively promote foreign currency loans, neglecting borrowers' currency mismatch risk, in order to use the funds absorbed by dollar-denominated deposits in the domestic market. In this case, the ratio of dollar-denominated loans to total loans is expected to be higher than the ratio of foreign-currency-denominated revenue to total revenue of companies.

Second, to take advantage of the cheap dollar-denominated funds gathered abroad, banks may actively promote dollar-denominated loans. In Eastern European countries, foreign banks borrowing with low cost of funds from abroad have expanded dollar-denominated loans recklessly (Basso et al. 2007), which is one factor that promotes the dollarization of these countries. In this case, the amount of foreign debt exceeds the amount of overseas assets for each bank. At the same time, the amount of foreign-currency-denominated loans comes to exceed the amount of foreign-currency-denominated deposits.

Third, when low-cost overseas funds are available, banks may lose the motivation to absorb domestic deposits using the operating expenses. In this case, absorption of banks' foreign currency deposits remains at a low level. Also, when operating expenses of local-currency-denominated loans are high, banks are likely to avoid local-currency-denominated loans, to the extent possible. In this case, compared to the potential demand for local currency loans, actual supply of local currency loans would be small and sluggish.

Finally, as banks' provision of financial intermediation and payment services in dollars promotes real and payment dollarization based on network externality, the development of such a banking system propels the dollarization of the whole economy. Through the linkage between financial and real dollarization, banks function as a core player in the self-propelled dollarization of an economy as a whole.

The progress of dollarization depends on the interaction between households' portfolio choice and banks' fundraising in the deposit market, as well as the on interaction between firms' fundraising and banks credit-extending behavior in the loan market. Decisions made by households, firms, and banks are all affected by not only financial dollarization, but also real and payment dollarization.

Real and payment dollarization is explained by the network externality of currency transaction. The more widely the currency is used in transaction, the smaller the accompanied cost of transaction in that currency. As real dollarization progresses, individual households and firms want to increase the portion of dollar assets. At the same time, as real dollarization progresses, it is expected that for the households and the dollar-denominated deposit and loans are good natural hedge to change in exchange rates. In addition, as real dollarization progresses, covariance between domestic price and foreign exchange change increases in a small open economy. These factors have a positive impact on the demand for foreign-currency loans and deposit holding. Therefore, real and payment dollarization and financial dollarization have a mutually promoting relationship, and the level of credit and deposit dollarization will increase over time.

3 Banking and Dollarization

3.1 Luca and Petrova-Type Portfolio Allocation Model

By using Luca and Petrova (2008), we can sketch banking in the framework of a static one-period portfolio allocation model that contains a continuum of banks, firms, and households. The agents of each type are identical and their numbers are normalized to unity. We assume that all of them are risk-averse and all transactions are conducted under competitive circumstances.[5] The choice of medium exchange is a social convention and can be explained by network externality.[6] If economic agents are given the choice among currencies for payment, they are likely to prefer the currency that is already widely used in the economy. The more widely the dollar is accepted as a means of payment, the more preferably the economic agents will choose the dollar as a medium of exchange. We assume that all banks, firms, and household use local currency as the medium of exchange and the unit of account.

3.1.1 Bank

At the beginning of the period, a representative bank raises deposits from households in domestic and foreign currencies and makes loans to domestic firms in domestic and foreign currencies. The bank borrows or lends additional funds in domestic and foreign interbank markets. At the end of the period, the firm repays bank loans. The bank repays domestic depositors and interbank loans.

In a dollarized economy, the balance sheet of the bank can be represented by the equation $L_b + L_b^* + B + B^* = D_b + D_b^* + K$. The bank's credit items consist of dollar-denominated loans L_b^*, local-currency-denominated loans L_b, dollar-denominated liquid assets B^*, and local-currency-denominated liquid assets B. The bank's debit items consist of dollar-denominated bank deposits D_b^*, local-currency-denominated bank deposits D_b, and local-currency-denominated paid-in capital K. The initial exchange rate in terms of domestic currency is set to be equal to 1. The nominal rate of depreciation of domestic currency at the end of the period is ε. The profit of the bank is given by $\Pi_b = r_L \cdot L_b + r_L^*(1+\varepsilon) \cdot L_b^* + r \cdot B + r^*(1+\varepsilon) \cdot B^* - r_D \cdot D - r_D^*(1+\varepsilon) \cdot D^*$, where r_D and r_D^* denote the interest rate on domestic and foreign currency deposits, r_L and r_L^* denote the interest rates of domestic and foreign currency loans, and r_B and r_B^* denote domestic and foreign interbank market rate.

The risk-averse bank chooses its optimal net open dollar position $L_b^* + B^* - D_b^*$ to maximize the objective function $E[\Pi_b] - \frac{1}{2}\delta\, Var[\Pi_b]$,[7] subject to the balance sheet constraint, given the coefficient of bank's risk aversion $\delta > 0$.

Because arbitrage conditions require that $r_L = r_D = r_B$ and $r_L^* = r_D^* = r_B^*$,[8] the bank's optimal net open dollar position $L^* + B^* - D^*$ is determined by the first-order condition as follows:

$$L_b^* + B^* - D_b^* = \frac{1}{\delta\, \sigma_\varepsilon^2\, r^{*2}} \left[r_L^* (1 + E(\varepsilon)) - r_L \right]. \tag{1}$$

The bank's optimal net open dollar position is high, if the volatility of the return in dollar σ_ε^2 is low, the expected relative return to dollar-denominated loan is high, and the level of the bank's risk aversion is low.

3.1.2 Firm

A representative firm borrows from the bank in local currency and dollars to purchase one unit of input to produce y units of the final good. Because local currency is used as the medium of exchange and the unit of account, the firm's profit is $\Pi_f = y \cdot P - r_L \cdot L_f - r_L^* \cdot (1 + \varepsilon) \cdot L_f^*$. L_f^* and L_f are dollar and local currency borrowings, and r_L^* and r_L are the gross interest rates on dollar and local currency borrowing. P is the price of the final good, which is correlated with the exchange rate.

The risk-averse firm maximizes its objective function $E\left[\Pi_f\right] - \frac{1}{2}\gamma\, Var\left[\Pi_f\right]$ by choosing the optimal demand for dollar borrowings L_f^*, subject to the budget constraint $w = L_f + L_f^*$, where $\gamma > 0$ is the coefficient of the firm's risk aversion.

The firm's optimal demand for dollar loans is determined by the first-order condition:

$$L_f^* = \frac{1}{\gamma \sigma_\varepsilon^2\, r_L^{*2}} \left[\gamma \sigma_{\varepsilon P}^{\ 2}\, y\, r_L^* - \left\{ r_L^* (1 + E(\varepsilon)) - r_L \right\} \right]. \tag{2}$$

If the covariance between the exchange rate and domestic prices $\sigma_{\varepsilon p}$ is high, the optimal demand for dollar borrowings is high, because the dollar-denominated borrowing is a good natural hedge to change in prices. If the volatility of dollar borrowing payment σ_ε^2 is low, the firm's optimal demand for dollar borrowings is high. If the expected exchange depreciation is high, the firm's optimal demand for dollar borrowing is low, because the expected relative cost of borrowing in dollars increases.

3.1.3 Household

A representative household makes dollar and local currency deposits at the beginning of the period and withdraws them to purchase one unit of good at the end of the period. The profit of the household is $\Pi_h = r_D \cdot D_h + r_D^* \cdot (1+\varepsilon) \cdot D_h^* - P$, where D_h^* and D_h are foreign and domestic currency deposits and r_D^* and r_D are the gross interest rate on foreign and domestic deposits. P is the price of goods, which is correlated with the exchange rate.

The risk-averse household chooses the demand for foreign currency deposits to maximize the objective function $E[\Pi_h] - \frac{1}{2}\mu\, Var[\Pi_h]$, subject to the budget constraint $h = D_h^* + D_h$, where μ is the coefficient of risk aversion.

The first-order condition gives the household's optimal demand for foreign currency deposits:

$$D_h^* = \frac{1}{\mu\, \sigma_\varepsilon^2\, r^{*2}} \left[\{ r_L^*(1+E(\varepsilon)) - r_L \} + \mu\, \sigma_{\varepsilon p} r^* \right]. \qquad (3)$$

The household's optimal demand for dollar deposit is high, if it has dollar-denominated expenses or if the covariance between the exchange rate and domestic prices $\sigma_{\varepsilon p}$ is high, which means the dollar-denominated deposit is a good natural hedge to change in prices. The optimal demand for dollar deposit is high if the volatility of returns to dollar deposits σ_ε^2 is low. The expected exchange depreciation raises the optimal demand for dollar deposit, because the expected relative return of depositing in dollars increases.

3.1.4 Banking Under Dollarization

Substituting the demand for dollar borrowing L_f^* for the supply of dollar loans L_b^* and substituting the demand for dollar deposits D_h^* for the supply of dollar deposits D_b^*, the equilibrium level of external foreign currency assets holdings of the bank is[9]

$$B^* = \frac{1}{\sigma_\varepsilon^2 r^*}\left(\frac{1}{\delta} + \frac{1}{\gamma} + \frac{1}{\mu}\right)\left[r_L^*(1+E(\varepsilon)) - r_L\right] - \frac{\sigma_{\varepsilon P}^2(y-1)}{\sigma_\varepsilon^2 r_L^*} \quad (4)$$

The impacts of determinants on dollar loans, dollar deposits, and the net dollar open position are summarized in Table 1. The level of external foreign currency asset B^* depends on the arbitrage condition that the foreign currency lending and deposit interest rate equalizes to the foreign interbank interest rate, determined exogenously. The level of dollarization is also affected by the government regulations constraining the balance sheet of banks.[10]

So far, all economic agents are assumed to use local currency as the unit of account and medium of exchange. However, if, like in the Cambodian economy, all three functions of money are replaced by the dollar, then real and payment dollarization as well as financial dollarization has occurred.[11] In this economy, for all agents (firm, household,

Table 1 Affects of determinants on dollarization

	Firm's demand for foreign currency loan, L_f^*	Household's demand for foreign currency deposit, D_h^*	Bank's net open foreign exchange position, $L_b^* + B^* - D_b^*$
The expected interest rate difference, $r_L^*(1+E(\varepsilon)) - r_L$	negative effect	positive effect	positive effect
Tthe volatility of exchange rate, σ_ε^2	negative effect	negative effect	negative effect
The covariance between the exchange rate and domestic prices, $\sigma_{\varepsilon p}$	positive effect	positive effect	n.a
The coefficients risk aversion of firms, household, and bank, γ, μ, δ	negative effect	negative effect	negative effect

Source Author

and bank), using and holding local currency is almost like using and holding foreign currency. For Cambodia, P indicates the price in dollars and ε indicates the nominal rate of depreciation of the dollar at the end of the period. Therefore, the influence of the determinants on the choice between currencies differs from the above-mentioned portfolio allocation model. When the volatility of the foreign exchange rate is high, economic agents prefer the dollar to local currency. When covariance between the foreign exchange rate and domestic prices that are actually denominated in dollars is high, they prefer local currency to the dollar. When economic agents become more risk-averse, they prefer the dollar to the local currency, the Khmer riel (KHR). The signs of determinants in Table 1 shall be reversed.

3.1.5 Patterns of Bank Portfolio

Bank portfolio can be classified into four cases. In Fig. 1, the 45° line represents the portfolio that holds $L^* + B^* - D^* = 0$. When bank portfolio is in the area above (below) this line, net open dollar position of the bank is positive (negative).

The first case is that the net open dollar position is positive and net foreign asset is negative: $L^* + B^* - D^* > 0$ and $B^* < 0$. The amount of lending in dollars exceeds the sum of dollar borrowing abroad and dollar deposits in local market. The gap between the two is financed by local currency deposit. The bank bears the foreign exchange risk accompanied with the conversion of local currency deposits into dollar loans.

The second case is that the foreign exchange net open position is negative and net foreign assets are negative: $L^* + B^* - D^* < 0$ and $B^* < 0$. Bank loans in dollars are financed by raising dollar deposit in local market and borrowing abroad. The bank does not bear the exchange rate risk arising from conversion of local currency deposits into foreign currency loans.

The third case is that the foreign exchange net open position is positive and net foreign asset is positive: $L^* + B^* - D^* > 0$ and $B^* > 0$. The bank loans and foreign asset holdings are financed by dollar deposits and

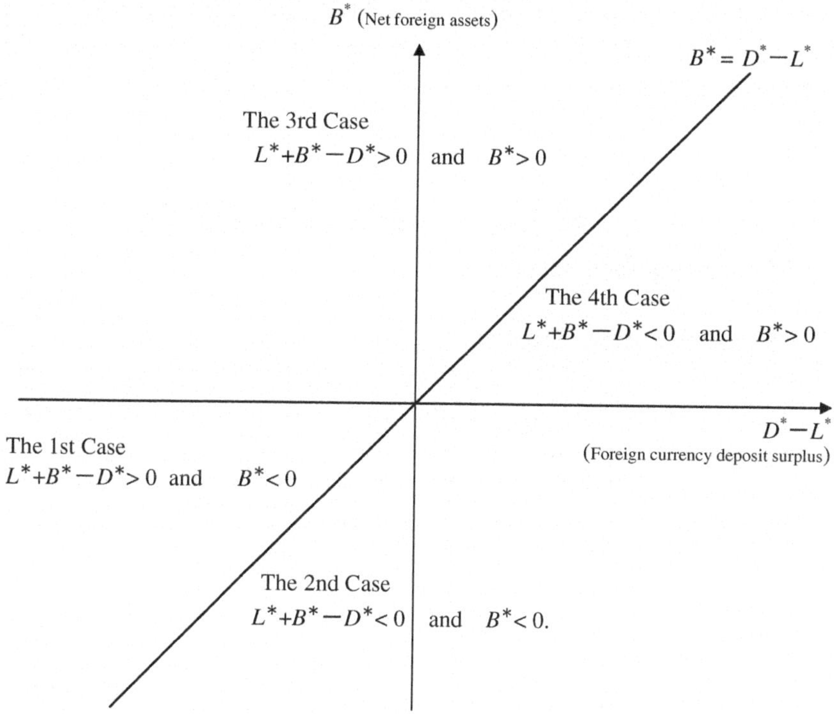

Fig. 1 Patterns of bank portfolio. *Source* Author

local currency deposits tapped in the local market. The bank bears the foreign exchange risk accompanied with the conversion of local currency deposits into dollar loans and foreign assets.

The fourth case is that the foreign exchange net open position is negative and net foreign asset is positive: $L^* + B^* - D^* < 0$ and $B^* > 0$.

Bank loans in dollars and foreign asset holdings are financed by dollar deposits in the local market. The exchange rate risk accompanied with conversion of local currency deposits into foreign currency loans does not occur.

4 Banking Sectors in Countries in the Lower Mekong Region

4.1 Bank Balance Sheets

The balance sheets of the banking sector of countries in the lower Mekong region during several years before and after 2010 show several changes in their dollar-denominated deposits, dollar-denominated loans, and the net foreign assets, and the net open dollar-denominated position during several years.[12]

1. Cambodia

In Cambodia, the macroeconomic conditions were strong, and dollarization was the highest among the three countries. Dollar-denominated deposits comprised more than 80% of total deposits, and the percentage share of dollar deposits to total bank assets varied around 50% in the range between the second half of 40% and the first half of 50% (Fig. 2). Almost all bank lending to the domestic private sector was denominated in dollars, and the share of dollar-denominated loans to total bank assets decreased from nearly 70% to in the 50%. The amount of dollar-denominated deposits always exceeded that of dollar-denominated loans.

In Fig. 3, the amount of net foreign assets and the difference between dollar deposits and loans are measured as a percentage of the total bank assets. Net foreign assets, which were mostly denominated in dollars, were generally positive. The amount of dollar-denominated deposits exceeded that of dollar-denominated loans and the amount of net foreign assets was positive around 5% on average. In Fig. 4, the net open foreign exchange position and the difference between dollar deposits and loans

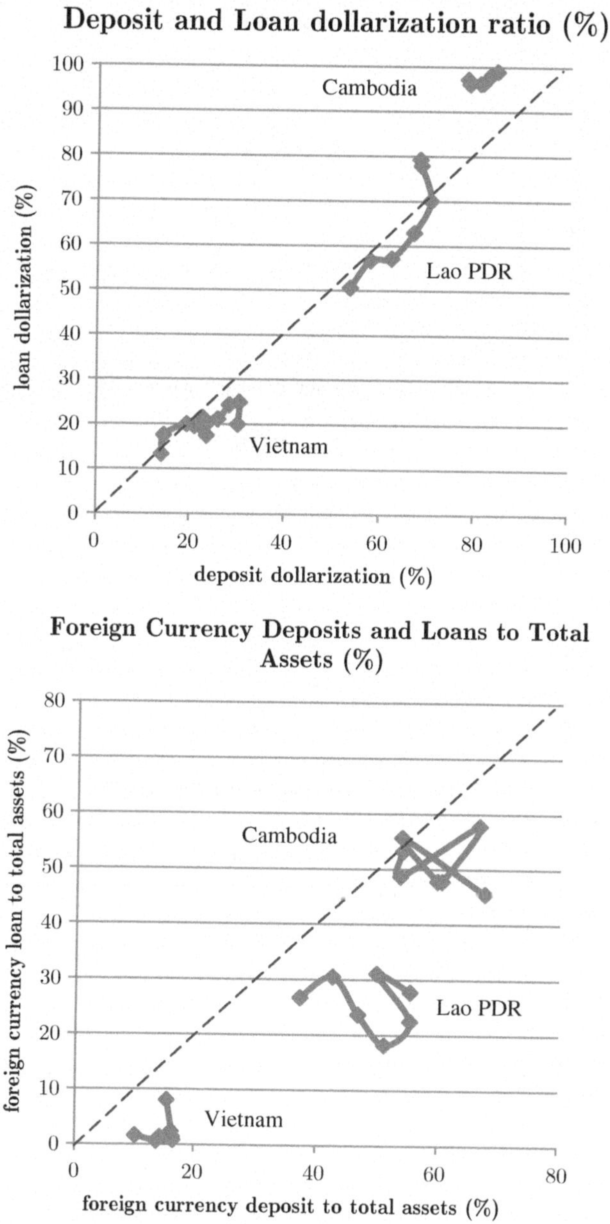

Fig. 2 Ratios of deposit and loan dollarization

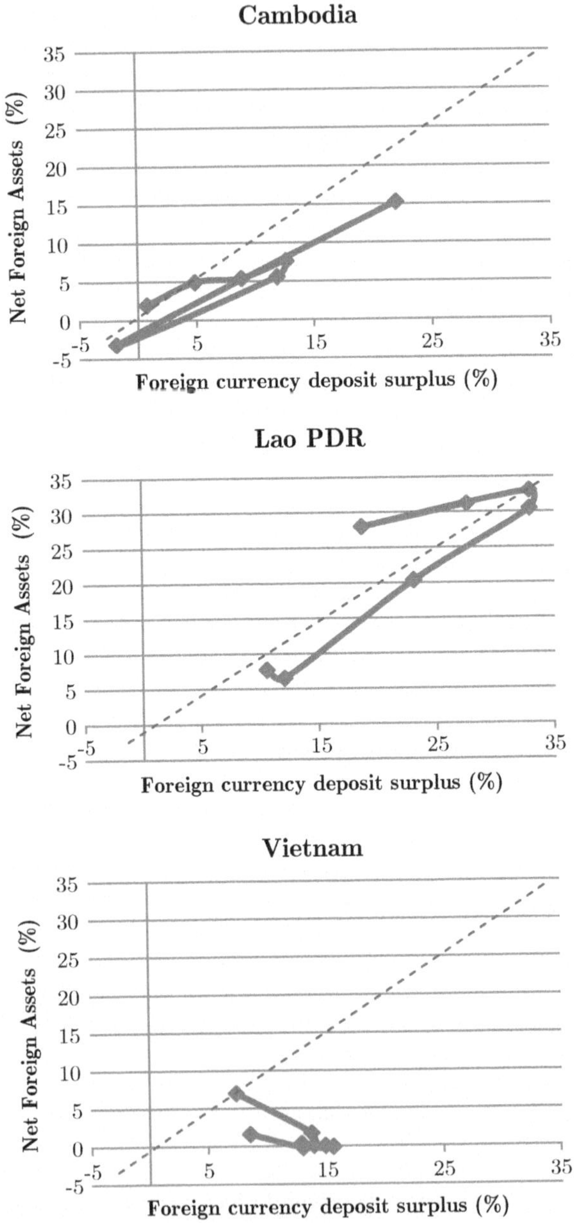

Fig. 3 Net foreign assets of banks

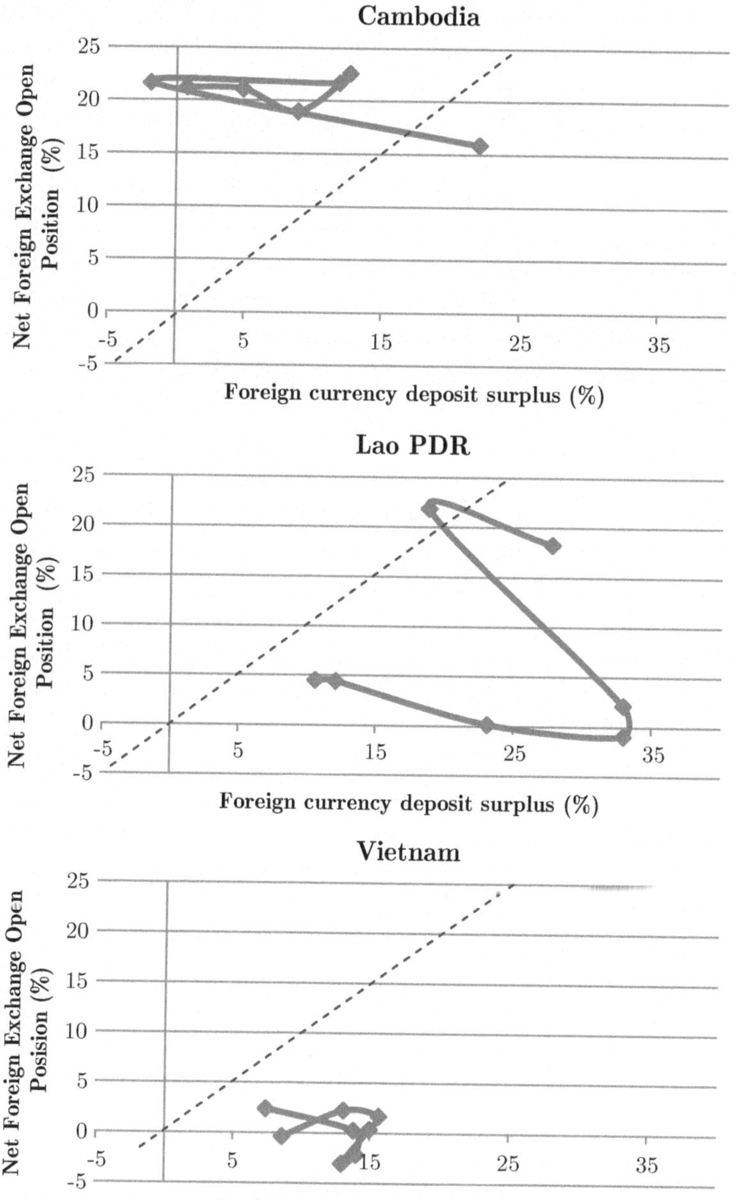

Fig. 4 Net open foreign exchange position of banks

are measured as a percentage of the total bank assets. When the dollar-denominated reserves deposited at the central bank are included in the dollar-denominated assets of banks,[13] the net open dollar-denominated position became significantly positive.

Significant financial disintermediation occurred in Cambodia. Domestic loans were slightly more than 50% of total assets. There were strict liquidity rules for Cambodian banks to protect against their failure, and the liquidity ratio across the banking sector was above 70%. For each bank to hold a reserve fund of dollar assets above the level mandated by the government would create disintermediation by reducing the amount of funds available to be lent by financial institutions.

2. Lao PDR

In Lao PDR, as the macroeconomic situation, which had deteriorated as a result of the global financial crisis, recovered gradually, the dollarization ratio of deposits was significantly reduced. The ratio of dollar deposits to total assets was reduced by about 10% from above 55% to below 40%.

However, there was no significant change in the dollarization ratio of loans, and the ratio of dollar loans to total bank assets was nearly 30%. The amount of dollar-denominated deposits was significantly reduced during the period, while the level was always higher than that of dollar-denominated loans. Looking at the supply and demand balance of domestic private dollar funds, dollar funds were essentially in surplus.

Net overseas assets denominated in dollars were positive, and their share of the total assets of the banks was reduced from 30 to 10% or less. Net open dollar-denominated positions to the private sector changed from positive to negative, and their percentage of the total assets of the bank changed from a few % positive to a few % negative. However, as in Cambodia, when dollar-denominated deposits at the central bank were added, the net open dollar-denominated position was significantly increased, and became almost positive. Similar to Cambodia, financial disintermediation was significant in the Lao PDR, where the ratios of claims on the central bank to total assets reached around 25%.

3. Vietnam

In Vietnam, dollarization ratios of both deposits and loans were lower compared to those in the other two countries, and they tended to decrease. Although the dollarization ratio of deposits was higher than the dollarization ratio of the loans, the difference between them decreased gradually, and they were almost the same level in 2013. The ratio of dollar deposits to the total assets of the bank decreased from more than 20% to over 10%. Likewise, the percentage ratio of dollar loans to total bank assets was reduced to the mid-teens. The dollarization ratio of deposits was more reduced than that of loans, and the ratio of the two was almost the same in 2013. While both dollar-denominated deposits and dollar-denominated loans dropped, the former level was always higher than the latter, and domestic private dollar funds were essentially in surplus.

The percentage of net foreign dollar-denominated assets accounting for the total assets of banks decreased significantly from about 10%, and temporarily turned negative. The ratio of the net open dollar position to the private sector share of the bank's total assets was smaller compared to that of the other two countries and moved modestly around zero. The net open dollar-denominated position increased slightly as dollar-denominated reserves deposited at the central bank were added, and the position moved around zero modestly.

4.2 Features Observed in Countries in the Mekong Region

The balance sheets of banks in Cambodia, Lao PDR, and Vietnam demonstrated the following features.

First, in Cambodia, Lao PDR, and Vietnam, net foreign dollar-denominated assets of the banking sector were generally positive, and the use of overseas dollar funding was not the factor that promoted the domestic dollar-denominated loans.[14] In this regard, the circumstances of the three countries were different from the circumstances of dollarization of the Eastern European countries that Basso et al. (2007) indicated.

Also, in Cambodia, Lao PDR, and Vietnam, the banks absorbed ample domestic dollar funds in the form of dollar-denominated bank deposits. For this reason, the domestic dollar-denominated loans were fully financed by the domestic dollar-denominated deposits. However, in Lao PDR and Vietnam, the dollarization ratio of deposits as well as dollar loans to the dollar deposit ratio tended to decrease gradually alongside the stabilization of the economy.

It should be noted that the dollar-denominated loans changed less than the dollar-denominated deposits in the event of economic changes. In Lao PDR, as the economy recovered from the macroeconomic turmoil caused by global financial crisis, dollarization ratios were reduced for both deposits and loans. In this process, the reduction of dollar-denominated deposits was greater than the decrease in the dollar-denominated loans.

In Cambodia, Lao PDR, and Vietnam, net overseas dollar-denominated assets tended to move with the difference between the domestic dollar-denominated deposits and dollar-denominated loans in each country. That is, when the difference between the domestic dollar-denominated deposits and dollar-denominated loans increased, the net overseas dollar-denominated assets also increased by that amount. When that difference was reduced, net overseas dollar-denominated assets were reduced by that amount. The difference between the change in the domestic dollar-denominated deposits and dollar-denominated loans was adjusted simply by increasing or decreasing the holdings of overseas assets.

The ratio of the net open dollar-denominated position that included dollar-denominated deposits at central banks to the total assets of banks was positive in Cambodia and Lao PDR, but was close to zero in Vietnam. The magnitude of changes in ratio during this period was the largest in Lao PDR and was smaller in Cambodia and Vietnam. These results show that the Cambodian banking sector wanted to hold a high level of dollar-denominated assets, and that the Vietnam banking wanted to hold only a marginal amount of dollar-denominated assets. The results also show that the desired level of holdings of the net open foreign exchange position decreased substantially during the period.

Finally, in Cambodia and the Lao PDR, financial disintermediation was significant. The ratios of claims on the central bank to total assets reached about 25% in Cambodia and the Lao PDR. In Vietnam, the claims on the central bank were less than 7% of the total assets and the level of financial intermediation was basically normal. One of the most serious disadvantages of dollarization is that the role of banks as suppliers of funds is greatly reduced because the function of the central bank as a lender of last resort has been undercut.

5 Factors Affecting Banking in Countries in the Lower Mekong Region

5.1 Financial Regulations and Macroeconomic Circumstances

The behaviors of banks were affected by the macroeconomic situation. Major macroeconomic determinants of dollarization according to Kubo (2014) and discussed in Sect. 3 are summarized in Table 2 for Cambodia, the Lao PDR, and Vietnam. There was a substantial interest rate differential in deposit interest rates and loan interest rates between the dollar and the local currency. In all three countries, dollar interest rates were lower than the local currency interest rates. When we look at the foreign exchange rate, exchange rates were relatively stable but moved up and down in two directions of depreciation and appreciation in Cambodia, while exchange rate was in the persistent trend of appreciation in the Lao PDR. In contrast, in Vietnam, the exchange rate fluctuated widely but moved persistently in only one direction of depreciation; furthermore, in Vietnam the CPI and exchange rate fluctuated widely. When we look at the consumer price indexes, Cambodia and the Lao PDR both were relatively stable in the high single digits. The correlation between the CPI and exchange rates was quite small in Cambodia and negative in the Lao PDR. In contrast, in Vietnam, the CPI fluctuated widely and the correlation between the CPI and the exchange rate was higher than in Cambodia and the Lao PDR.

Table 2 Macroeconomic environments in Cambodia, Lao PDR, and Vietnam

	Cambodia	Lao PDR	Vietnam
Expected interest rate differential $r_L^*(1+E(\varepsilon)) - r_L$	Negative[a]; KHR was appreciated against USD in 2010, 2011, 2012	Negative; Kip was appreciated against USD in 2006, 2007, 2008, 2010	Negative; Dong was persistently depreciated against USD
Fluctuation of CPI (coefficient of variation)	0.017 smaller than other two	0.067 smaller than Vietnam larger than Cambodia	0.109 larger than other two
The correlation between CPI and exchange rate (correlation coefficient)	−0. 093 negative and small	−0.856 negative	0.957 larger than other two
Firm's risk aversion (γ)	Large; payment was dollarized	Medium; payment was not dollarized	Medium; payment was not dollarized
Bank's risk aversion (δ)	Large; no lender of last resort	Smaller than Cambodia; lender of last resort existed	Smaller than Cambodia; under the protection of government
Household's risk aversion (μ)	Small; payment was dollarized	Larger than Cambodia; payment was not dollarized	Larger than Cambodia; payment was not dollarized

Source Author

Notes 1. The values of σ_ε^2 and $\sigma_{\varepsilon p}$ are not useful statistic for comparing the degree of variation, since the means differ widely among three countries. Therefore, for normalization, the fluctuation of CPI and the correlation between CPI and exchange rate are measured by coefficient of variation and correlation coefficient. The values of the two statistics are calculated month to month base during the period from 2007 to 2013. 2. In Cambodia, where the dollar is widely used as a medium of exchange and unit of account, P means price in dollar and ε means the nominal rate of depreciation of the dollar at the end of period

[a]In the recent years after 2012, the USD lending rates have been almost same as the KHR lending rates, while the USD deposit rates have been slightly lower than the KHR deposit rates. It seems that, under these interest rates, dollar loans and dollar deposits were favorable to neither firms nor depositors

The behavior of banks was also strongly affected by the substantially different historical developments of financial regulations among the three countries.[15] Financial regulations affected the network externality of the dollar as well as portfolio allocations in dollars. Dollarization in Cambodia spontaneously occurred over a period of more than 20 years under a very liberal economic and financial system.[16] Dollarization in Cambodia began as the UN Transitional Authority attempted to revive the economy. The dollar was trusted and utilized for a wide variety of payment systems. Subsequently, with the spread of the currency and increase in financial activity, more people came to utilize the dollar to make payments, and thus "payment dollarization" developed along with the economy. The dollar took on the roles of value storage, medium of exchange, and unit of account. In Cambodia, the government acquiesced to the use of the dollar, and there were no legal restrictions upon dollar savings or the free exchange between the dollar and the local currencies. Furthermore, there were no legal impediments to the dollar being a network externality.[17] When a currency is acting as network externality even if the rate of inflation decreases and the value of the domestic currency improves, it will not weaken the role of dollar holdings. This is because both the dollar and the domestic currencies retain their value in the same manner; thus, more savings will continue to be in dollars because of its essential role in expressing value and payments compared to the domestic currency. Samreth (2011) sought through an empirical study to point to this network externality as being a powerful factor in explaining dollarization.[18]

In contrast to Cambodia, in the Lao PDR and Vietnam, dollarization was at a peak at the time macroeconomic stability was severely damaged.[19] Recently, dollarization was reduced to around 50 and 20% in the Lao PDR and Vietnam, respectively. Dollarization halted as their economies stabilized and the inflation rate began to fall, and local currencies were once again used in place of the dollar. However, it should be noticed that the governments of the Lao PDR and Vietnam substantially pursued "de-dollarization" policies under a favorable economic climate in the 2000s. For instance, in Vietnam, banks were not allowed to extend foreign currency loans to companies without revenue in foreign exchange in April in 2011. Additionally, in these countries it is prohibited to use foreign currency to settle domestic transactions, or to display prices in foreign currency.

5.2 Cambodia

In Cambodia, the government acquiesced to the use of the dollar, and there were no legal restrictions upon dollar savings or free exchange between the dollar and the local currency.[20] Furthermore, there were no legal impediments to the dollar being a network externality. Because the dollar was used widely as a unit of account, there were strong network externalities. The potential demand for dollar-denominated deposits and loans was not suppressed by the financial regulations.

Among the three countries, Cambodia had the most stable foreign exchange rate, and there was a correlation between the exchange rate and prices. Since the Cambodian economy had been highly dollarized since the early 2000s, economic entities (firms, households, and banks) used the dollar as a unit of account and a means of payment in almost all transactions except in the case of very small trades. Under these circumstances, both firms and households were hesitant to hold KHR deposits or take KHR loans. With this in mind, it was predictable that, among the three countries, the ratios of dollarization of both deposits and loans were the highest in Cambodia. When the USD was depreciated in 2010, 2011, and 2012, the ratio of deposit dollarization decreased but the ratio of loan dollarization slightly increased.

Because of the significant dollarization of the balance sheet of banks in Cambodia, the central bank could not function as the lender of last resort. For this reason, there were strict liquidity rules for Cambodian banks to protect against their failure. Private banks held large amounts of dollar-denominated deposits at the central bank in preparation for a systemic risk, and the liquidity ratio across the banking sector was above 70%. As a result, their net open dollar-denominated position including reserves was persistently very large. The high dollarization of loans and deposits accompanied by holdings of large external liquid assets was predictable. The change in exchange rates affected the net open foreign exchange position of banks. When the US dollar depreciated in 2010, 2011, and 2012, net foreign assets increased slightly.

5.3 Lao PDR

The Laotian government began a de-dollarization policy in the 2000s. It imposed regulations on dollar-denominated bank lending and prohibited pricing in dollars. As a result, the function of the dollar as a currency was constrained to some extent. This was one of the factors explaining why the proportion of dollar-denominated loans to total assets of banks was stable, and that the proportion of dollar-denominated deposits to total assets of banks decreased significantly during the period of observation.

In contrast to Cambodia, because legal restrictions on dollar payments and dollar pricing have been imposed in the Lao PDR, the network externality of dollarization has been restrained by government regulations, making foreign currency holding less favorable.[21]

The variance of foreign exchange rate σ_ε^2 was much lower in the Lao PDR than in Vietnam, but a little bit higher than in Cambodia. However, while the openness of the economy of the Lao PDR was high, the covariance between the foreign exchange rate and prices $\sigma_{\varepsilon P}$ was as low as that in Cambodia and lower than in Vietnam. The relatively low correlation between the exchange rate and prices had a negative impact on dollarization, while the low variance of the exchange rate had a positive impact on dollarization.

This situation is different from that of Vietnam, since the exchange rate moved in both directions of depreciation and appreciation in Lao PDR. It would have been difficult for the economic entity to predict the direction of the change in the exchange rate. This would have made firms and households hesitant to take loans and hold deposits in dollars. When the USD depreciated in 2006, 2007, 2008, and 2010, the ratio of deposit dollarization continued to decrease.

Changes in exchange rates also affected the net open foreign exchange position of banks. When the USD depreciated in 2010, 2011, and 2012, net foreign assets decreased. In addition, because the Lao PDR is a small open economy, its ability to conduct independent financial policy has been restricted and it has faced difficulties in sustaining a stable financial system. These factors would make banks as well as firms and households sensitive to risk.

5.4 Vietnam

Both the volatility in exchange rates σ_{ε}^2 and the correlation between exchange rate and prices $\sigma_{\varepsilon P}$ were larger in Vietnam than in the other two countries. The high correlation between exchange rate and prices had a positive impact on dollarization, while the high variance of exchange rate had a negative impact on dollarization.

The foreign exchange rates of the dong lowered consistently over a long period. This implies that the firms, households, and banks could have easily expected a further depreciation of the exchange rate. With this in mind, the dollar-denominated deposits of households and the net open dollar-denominated positions of banks could have been much larger than the actual observed level.

The low level of deposit dollarization as well as the small net open foreign exchange position could be due to the strong government control over banks in Vietnam.[22] In particular, as the dollar loans were restrictive compared to other countries, the amount of dollar-denominated loans was constrained significantly. To avoid a balance sheet mismatch, the bank would be hesitant to accept dollar deposits. In addition, because foreign currency pricing and payment were illegal in Vietnam, the network externality of dollar usage was restricted substantially. These controls suppressed the dollarization of deposits and loans, and lowered the net open foreign exchange position of banks.

6 Dollarization and Domestic Financial Intermediation

As opposed to Eastern European cases, credit dollarization is domestically financed by deposit dollarization in the lower Mekong countries. This is because an abundant amount of dollars in cash is held by residents and firms in these countries, so banks can easily raise the needed amount of foreign currency funds from the local deposit market at low cost. In addition, in the Lao PDR and Vietnam, contrast to Cambodia, the government clarified the non-favorable position to bank lending in dollars to local firms that did not have income in dollars.

However, due to the different causative factors, banks play a positive role in promoting dollarization in Cambodia. First, banks functioned as a pivot to expand payment dollarization in rural area by providing foreign currency deposits (FCD) for settlement of domestic transactions. Second, banks drove the domestic financial intermediation in dollars, which is generally a flow of surplus dollar funds from urban areas to rural regions.[23]

6.1 Region-Wide Differences in Dollarization

Similar to the case in neighboring countries but distinct from that in Central European countries, domestic credit dollarization in Cambodia matches domestic deposit dollarization. As shown in the previous sections, it is not true that foreign banks are driving up fast credit growth in their attempt to capture market shares.[24] The ratio of foreign assets to total assets is 20.8%; however, the ratio of foreign debt to the sum of total debt and capital is 15.3%. Therefore, foreign-currency-denominated loans were covered fully by the local funds procured in the foreign currency.

The fact that Cambodian banking is not dependent on external borrowing is also supported by the data on the loan-to-deposit ratios of select individual banks. Table 3 shows the loan-to-deposit ratios by currency of nine major banks are lower than unity. Either domestic banks or foreign-owned banks match the currency composition of their assets and liabilities. Foreign borrowing by banks is not used to fund domestic credit growth. The provision of dollars in Cambodia has been locally financed, and we do not observe the phenomenon in which the provision of dollars has increased via financing from overseas, as is observed in European emerging countries.

Table 3 Loan to deposit ratios of major banks by currency in Cambodia

Name	Ownership	Denominated by foreign currency	Denominated by Riel	Total loans to total deposits
ACLEDA	Domestic	0.845	0.820	0.843
CNB	Domestic	0.679	0.008	0.664
CPB	Foreign	0.715	0.00	0.711
ANZ	Foreign	0.572	0.00	0.564
FTB	Domestic	0.513	0.064	0.481
BIDC	Foreign	1.536	0.00	1.536
MY	Foreign	0.447	—	0.447
VB	Domestic	0.337	0.00	0.336
UCB	Domestic	0.572	0.010	0.572

Source Interview at National Bank of Cambodia
Note If capital ownership ratio of foreigners is greater than or equal to 50%, referred to "foreign."

Table 4 Currency circulation by region in Cambodia

	USD	KHR	Baht	Dong
Phnom Penh	87.3	12.7	0.0	0.0
Takeo	26.3	73.6	0.0	0.1
Svay Rieng	55.1	36.6	0.0	8.3
Kampong Cham	39.0	60.9	0.0	0.1
Battambang	25.2	59.8	14.9	0.0
Pailin	28.8	33.0	37.5	0.0
Banteay Meanchey	18.4	28.8	52.8	0.0
Siam Reap	67.4	32.2	0.4	0.0
Sihanouk Ville	25.8	50.5	23.7	0.0
Koh Kong	19.0	36.5	44.6	0.0
Steung Treng	34.6	65.2	0.2	0.0
Cambodge	46.5	42.5	10.4	0.6

Source Khou (2014)

However, the level of dollarization differs significantly between urban and rural regions. As shown in Table 4, the rate of dollarization is high in urbanized areas such as Phnom Penh but low in the countryside, while being high in areas doing business overseas.[25] The cities are affected by all three of these dollarization dimensions because they are located near factories of export industries such as textiles and are the primary consumers of imported goods. This provides corroboration for Cambodia's dollarization being strongly correlated to the "payment dollarization" founded on its network externality.

6.2 Dollarization Driven by Domestic Bank Lending

Attention must be paid to the movement of capital within Cambodia, which is generally a flow of surplus dollars from urban areas to rural regions. As Table 4 shows, circulation of foreign currencies varies significantly by region. In rural areas where demand for funds exceeds their supply, KHR is widely used. Because the lending interest rate is higher in rural areas than urban areas, banks or other financial institutions tap funds in the form of dollar deposits in urban areas and extend loans denominated in dollars in rural areas. Rural branches of financial institutions borrow dollar-denominated funds from urban areas and drive credit dollarization in rural areas.

The stock market in Cambodia is largely undeveloped, and the primary role of financial intermediaries is discharged by commercial banks, specialized banks, and microfinance institutions. As shown in Table 5, these financial intermediaries are of two types. One largely deals in

Table 5 Composition of deposits and loans by currency for selected banks in Cambodia

	ACLEDA	ANZ royal	PRASAC
Deposits	Riel 9% Dollar 89% Baht 1%	Dollar almost 100%	Riel 10% Dollar 89% Baht 1%
Loans	Riel 9% Dollar 89% Other currency 2%	Dollar almost 100%	Riel 2% Dollar 93% Baht 5%
Notes	Domestic commercial bank. Operating 238 offices across country. Intermediating surplus funds from urban to rural area	Foreign commercial bank. Tapping domestic deposits in dollar and extending loans to primary borrowers such as foreign exporting companies in dollar	Microfinance institution. Intermediating funds centering on dollar from urban to rural agricultural area

Source Data provided in interviews at each institution

dollars but also uses funds in KHR, utilizing savings as capital to conduct lending in both currencies. The other works exclusively in dollars, using dollar savings to lend the same. For instance, ACLEDA Bank, which has evolved from a microfinance institution and deployed 238 offices across the country, intermediates funds in both riel and dollars. However, PRASAC and the ANZ Royal Bank, which were owned substantially by foreign capital, act solely as dollar intermediaries within Cambodia. While these two kinds of financial institutions have different compositions of deposits and loans, currency-wise, both of them serve to accelerate dollarization by flowing surplus dollars from urban areas to rural regions.

7 Concluding Remarks

The activities of financial organizations have received attention in recent years as a determining factor in dollarization. This paper describes the primary issues relating to banking operations in the dollarized economy and sketches the discerning characteristics of bank behavior in Cambodia. According to our observation of three Mekong region countries—Cambodia, Lao PDR, and Vietnam—the dollarization of three countries was not driven by the rapid inflow of overseas dollar funds intermediated through banks, such as in the cases observed in Central and Eastern Europe countries. Furthermore, the expansion of dollar-denominated loans in these countries was fully financed by bank intermediation of domestic dollar funds. The different level of dollarization of each country seemed to correspond to the different macroeconomic environment in each country. In addition, characteristics of the banks in each country were greatly affected by the financial regulations, the introduction of strict regulations on dollar-denominated pricing, and the restriction of the purpose of dollar-denominated loans, which had a significant effect in reducing dollarization.

In Cambodia, the bank played a positive role in promoting dollarization in two ways, compared to Lao PDR and Vietnam. First, because the dollar was used widely as a measure to settle accounts and as the unit of accounts in Cambodia, the network externality of the dollar had a large influence in promoting dollarization. Second, banks drove credit dollarization in rural areas by intermediating dollar surplus funds from urban areas to rural areas.

In lower Mekong countries, banks should have made the best portfolio allocation considering the accompanied risk and return. According to our observations, there are some suggestions for policy-makers to contain loan dollarization and to expand the usage of local-currency-dominated financial services. First, macroeconomic stability is essential to reversing the increasing trend of deposit dollarization. Because banks seemed to match local dollar deposits with local dollar loans, once the increase in local dollar deposits is suppressed, the progress of loan dollarization can be effectively contained.

Second, no matter how costly it is, prohibiting the official utilization of dollars is effective to weaken the network externality of dollarization. Introducing strict measures against "dollarized payment", such as forbidding the display of prices in dollars, should be effective. In addition, stringent regulations on bank operations are effective in reducing the dollarization of deposits and loans.

Third, if holding of net overseas dollar assets is restricted by regulation, banks are likely to grant domestic dollar loans to match their domestic dollar deposits. Since this may result in further loan dollarization, the regulation on net overseas dollar position should be lifted. In general, stringent prudential regulation makes banks more hesitant to grant loans to firms that cannot naturally hedge currency risk with their cash flow in dollars.

Finally, as Luca and Petrova (2008) suggested, if there are well-developed forward and futures markets for foreign exchange where banks can hedge exchange risk effectively, they are less likely to shift currency risk to firms by granting loans in dollars. This restrains loan dollarization. Similarly, if the central bank provides to banks with currency swap, the banks will become less likely to avoid currency risk through dollar deposits and more likely to grant loans to firms in local currency.

Notes

1. This approach assumes that local-currency-denominated assets have uncertain returns due to domestic inflation, whereas foreign-currency-denominated assets have uncertain returns due to real exchange rate risk.
2. Several studies such as Demirguc-Kunt et al. (2000) and Ozsoz (2007), using bank-level data for selected countries during recent years, examined empirically the effects of dollarization on bank performances.
3. See Basso et al. (2007).
4. More specifically, first, if the initial dollarization levels are low, the fall of external interest rates increases dollarization in banks. Second, if loan default is solely a function of idiosyncratic shock, domestic currency devaluation risk increases dollarization in banks. Third, if loan default is a function of external interest rates and exchange risk, greater devaluation risk increases dollarization further in a highly dollarized economy; however, it decreases dollarization in a low dollarized economy. Finally, equilibrium dollarization tends to be higher when the domestic credit market is more competitive and collateral is more available.
5. This is distinct from the credit risk paradigm, where risk-neutral agents choose the optimal fundraising behavior in the presence of default risk and asymmetric information, as this model does not include the credit risk explicitly. It is also distinct from the minimum variance portfolio approach, where domestic inflation and the exchange rate change and domestic and foreign currency interest rates are determinants of financial dollarization, and this model does not include inflation factor explicitly.
6. See Kiyotaki and Wright (1989) for details. Valev (2010) briefly reviews linkage between network externality and dollarization.
7. Financial institutions are commonly recognized to be risk-neutral and to maximize their profit under budget constraints and government regulations. However, in emerging market economies, banks are prevented from adequately diversifying risks because forward markets are underdeveloped.
8. The capital adequacy requirement is implicitly assumed to be satisfied in the sense that the requirement is nonbinding. This problem is mentioned later.
9. This is true if the lending interest rates are higher than interbank interest rate by the operating cost of granting loans $t_L^* > 0, r_L^*/r^* = 1 + t_L^*$. Or, similarly, if the deposit interest rates are lower than interbank interest

rate by the operating cost of taking deposits $t_D^* > 0, r_D^*/r^* = 1/(1+t_L^*)$. If we consider the operating cost of granting loans and taking deposits, the equilibrium level of external foreign currency assets holdings is slightly different from (10). However, this does not substantially affect the following arguments.

10. When we consider the bank's cost of taking deposits and lending loans, these operating costs affect the level of *B*. For instance, if the cost of extending foreign currency loan to firms is high, the level of external foreign asset is positive and large. This can happen when the information asymmetry is large and the bank cannot easily find good borrowers in the local credit market. If the cost of taking foreign currency deposits from local residents is high, the level of external foreign asset is small or even negative.
11. In the case of Cambodia, to the extent that more people used dollars than their local currency, higher utility from more people using the dollar led to more people using the currency (Eichengreen et al. eds. 2005).
12. In this section, we use data and information that was collected from the IMF *International Financial Statistics and IMF County Report on Article IV consultation*. See Table 6 in Appendix 1.
13. When the dollar-denominated assets of banks do not contain the dollar-denominated reserves at the central bank, the net open dollar-denominated position of Cambodian banking sector was slightly negative.
14. Financial intermediation of individual banks in Cambodia is described in Appendix 2.
15. The regulations on dollarization in Cambodia, the Lao PDR, and Vietnam are described in Appendix 2. Also see Unteroberdoerster (2004) for banking regulations in lower Mekong countries.
16. The major difference between Cambodian dollarization and the conventional pattern of dollarization is that Cambodian dollarization began during the process of rebuilding the financial system from scratch after it had been temporarily destroyed by the Khmer Rouge. In conventional dollarization, due to the lack of trust in the domestic currency caused by political and economic instability, asset substitution occurs from assets denominated in local currency to those denominated in dollars, resulting

in "financial dollarization". Subsequently, with further economic instability, the role of the domestic currency in the economy was further reduced, and "payment dollarization" was reached, wherein the foreign currency began to be used to settle transactions. Further deterioration in the economy prompted the local currency to lose even its function of measuring value, and ultimately, "real dollarization" resulted in a phenomenon wherein the foreign currency is used to display prices as well (Nicolo et al. 2005). Also see Duma (2011) for more details.

17. Using Eastern European examples, through an investigation into transactions, Valev (2010) directly investigates the importance of network externalities in currency selection.
18. However, there seems to be a conceptual problem triggered by the Samreth substituting network externality for a hysteresis effect.
19. Dollarization was at a peak in the Lao PDR and Vietnam, in the early 2000 and 1990, respectively.
20. Financial regulations are described in Chap. 2 by Odajima.
21. Financial regulations are described in Chap. 3 by Keovongvichith.
22. Financial regulations are described in Chap. 5 by Pham.
23. Policy measures for changing Cambodian Bank Behaviors are described in Appendix 3.
24. See Table 6 in Appendix 1.
25. Also see Chap. 2 by Odajima.
26. These questions and answers concerning dollarization were provided to the author by Koji Kubo in January 2016.
27. Transactions within rural villages are conducted in riels. In this case, the dollars earned from the sale of livestock agricultural produce to the cities are converted into riels to be used in the villages. Access to bank deposits is limited, and gold is widely used as a means of saving. See Chap. 2 by Odajima for details.
28. 16 Kinoshita and Hayashi (2014) "Utilization of local currency UDIS in dollarization policy countries," Kinyu-zaisie-jijo (April 7, pp. 34–37) describe the operation of regional currencies within officially dollarized economies in South America. See Quispe-Agnoli and Whisler (2006) for official dollarization.

29. According to Garcia-Escribano and Sosa (2011), implementing de-dollarization solely through the achievement of macroeconomic stability is problematic, but regulations that raise the value of the national currency against the dollar and ones that are more favorable to domestic currency transactions than dollar ones are effective in realizing de-dollarization. Persistent dollarization in Cambodia is described in Menon (2008) and International Monetary Fund (2011).

Appendix 1: Foreign Currency Portfolio of Banks

See Table 6.

Appendix 2: Regulations on Dollarization in the CLMV Countries[26]

See Table 7.

Table 6 Foreign currency portfolio of banks in Cambodia, Lao PDR, and Vietnam

(1) Cambodia							
	Net open foreign exchange position (including foreign currency reserve)	Net foreign assets	Foreign currency loan	Foreign currency deposits	Foreign currency reserve in dollar	Dollarization ratio	
						Deposit	Loan
2007	−6.8 (15.9)	15.2	45.6	67.6	22.7	80.8	96.3
2008	−1.3 (21.6)	−3.1	55.7	53.8	22.9	78.2	97.2
2009	−6.3 (21.7)	5.6	47.8	59.7	28.0	78.6	96.2

(continued)

Table 6 (continued)

(1) Cambodia

	Net open foreign exchange position (including foreign currency reserve)	Net foreign assets	Foreign currency loan	Foreign currency deposits	Foreign currency reserve in dollar	Dollarization ratio	
						Deposit	Loan
2010	−5.0 (22.6)	7.6	47.8	60.5	27.6	81.4	96.4
2011	−3.5 (19.0)	5.4	57.8	66.6	22.4	80.9	111.8
2012	0.1 (21.1)	4.9	48.7	53.6	21.0	83.1	98.3
2013	1.2 (21.2)	2.0	53.2	53.9	20.0	84.4	99.0

(2) Lao PDR

	Net open foreign exchange position (including foreign currency reserve)	Net foreign assets	Foreign currency loan	Foreign currency deposits	Foreign currency reserve in dollar	Dollarization ratio	
						Deposit	Loan
2004	3.5 (18.3)	31.2	27.8	55.4	14.8	68.2	79.3
2005	9.2 (21.9)	28.0	31.1	49.9	12.7	68.5	77.9
2006	0.1 (2.2)	33.1	22.5	55.5	2.1	70.6	70.1
2007	−2.5 (-0.9)	30.5	18.2	51.2	1.6	67.1	62.9
2008	−2.8 (0.2)	20.3	23.7	46.9	3.0	62.3	57.2
2009	−5.6 (4.4)	6.5	30.5	42.6	10.0	57.8	56.7
2010	−2.9 (4.5)	7.7	26.7	37.3	7.4	53.6	50.6

(3) Vietnam

	Net open foreign exchange position	Net foreign assets	Foreign currency loan	Foreign currency deposits	Foreign currency reserve in dollar	Dollarization ratio	
						Deposit	Loan
2006	2.4	8.0	15.4	21.0	n.a.	26.1	21.1
2007	0.3	2.4	16.2	18.3	n.a.	22.9	21.4
2008	−2.1	1.4	15.4	18.9	n.a.	23.8	20.1
2009	−3.0	1.4	14.3	18.7	n.a.	23.7	17.5
2010	0.4	1.5	16.4	17.5	n.a.	21.1	19.6
2011	1.7	0.8	16.5	15.6	n.a.	19.5	20.0
2012	2.3	0.7	13.7	12.1	n.a.	14.6	17.5
2013	−0.4	1.6	10.2	12.2	n.a.	14.1	13.3

Sources IMF Country Report on Article IV consultation with Cambodia, Lao PDR, and Vietnam (various issues)

Note Share of total assets in percentage (%)

Table 7 Regulations on dollarization in the CLMV countries

	Sources of FCD	Settlement of domestic transactions using FCD (Domestic account transfer of FCD)	Ceiling on FCD interest rate	Reserve requirement on FCD	Foreign currency loans	Net open position of commercial banks	Quotation of prices in foreign currency
Cambodia	No restriction	No restriction	No ceiling (In March 1995, interest rates were liberalized, which abolished the floor on deposit interest rate.)	1993–2007: same for FCD and LCD (8% in 1997-2007) 2008: 16% for FCD, 8% for LC 2009–2013: 12–12.5% for FCD, 8% for LCD	No restriction	Prakas on Monitoring Banks' and Financial Institutions' Net Open Position in Foreign Currency (August 2007), 20% of bank's net worth for a single currency and for the sum of all foreign currency, long or short	No control
Lao PDR	No restriction	No restriction	No ceiling (There were the ceiling on lending rates and floor on deposit rates until around the mid-1990s.)	1989–2001: same for FCD and LCD (12% in 1995–2001) 2001: 12% for FCD and 6% for LCD	BOL regulation (No. 792/BOL) in September 2013 has restricted FC loans only to firms with FC revenues. Before September	Regulation on foreign currency exposure (No. 818/BOL: October 2010), long or short position, 20% of tier-one	Decree No 53/CM (September 1990) on Foreign Currency Management and Precious Metals prohibited the use of FC for

(continued)

Table 7 (continued)

	Sources of FCD	Settlement of domestic transactions using FCD (Domestic account transfer of FCD)	Ceiling on FCD interest rate	Reserve requirement on FCD	Foreign currency loans	Net open position of commercial banks	Quotation of prices in foreign currency
				2006: 10% for FCD and 5% for LCD	2013, no control (Both households and firms took FC loans, regardless of FC revenues.)	capital for a single currency, and 25% for the sum of all foreign currencies	domestic transactions, but it was not enforced strictly. In March 2008, the Decree was upgraded to Presidential Decree (No1/P) for stringent enforcement with penalties.
Myanmar	Until April 2012, foreign exchange of foreign sources can be deposited after aplicable tax	No restriction	State banks: in practice 1% Private banks: non-interest bearing account only	No reserve requirement on FCD; 10% for local currency deposits, cut to 5% in October 2015	Foreign Exchange Management Law (August 2012) allows banks to lend in FC to borrowers with FC revenues, but it had not been practiced.	Foregin Exchange Management Regulation (September 2014) 30% of bank capital	In July 2015, Central Bank instruction to government agencies to quote prices/charges in local currency. In practice, quotation of prices are tolerated.

(continued)

Table 7 (continued)

	Sources of FCD	Settlement of domestic transactions using FCD (Domestic account transfer of FCD)	Ceiling on FCD interest rate	Reserve requirement on FCD	Foreign currency loans	Net open position of commercial banks	Quotation of prices in foreign currency
Vietnam	No restriction since October 1988 (Decision 170/1999/QD-TTg: August 1999 abolished income tax on remittances from abroad, resulting in a hike in FCD of households.)	Not permitted (Circular 16/2014/NHNN (August 2014) states residents and non-residents having FC accounts at licensed banks are allowed to receive and transfer FC to others holding FC accounts. But this is not applicable for settlement of domestic transactions.)	No ceiling until April 2011	Higher rates on FCD, but rates are different by maturities of deposits and discretionary upon banks. From August 2011, rates on FCD are twice as high as rates on VND deposits: for most banks, VND deposits with maturity less than 1 year 3%, over 1 year 1%, FCD with maturity less than 1 year 8%, more than 1 year 6%.	Since April 2011, SBV has restricted FC loans only to firms with revenues in FC. Before April 2011, Decision 418/2000/QĐ-NHNN7: FC loans could be granted with SBV Govenor approval, FC loans were permitted for imports, repayments to foreign lenders, and projects designated by the government.	September 1998: 30% of bank's equity in both long and short sides for all foreign currencies March 2012: 20% of equity in both long and short sides for all foreign currencies	1990s: Banned, but not enforced strictly. 2006: Ordinance on Foreign Exchange. 2011: Decree 95/2011/ND-CP specified and increased the penalty for quoting prices in FC to a maximum of VND 500 million.

Source Compiled by author

Appendix 3: Policy Measures for Changing Cambodian Banking Behaviors

Khou et al. (2017) discusses more generally policy measures for de-dollarization in Cambodia. Also see De Zamaroczy and Sa (2002) and Duma (2011).

Expansion in the Use of the Riel as a Regional Currency

In Cambodia, the spread of financial services in rural areas and in small companies within urban areas is insufficient, and there exists strong potential demand for such services. Because agricultural villages and smaller firms have little access to funds or income in dollars, the riel becomes comparatively important to them.[27]

In reality, most of these potential customers struggle to access formal financial institutions, and if they are able to, the only services available involve transacting in dollars. Therefore, the provision of financial services in riels would boost economic activity if these potential needs could be met.[28]

Specifically, we would expect a "financial rielization" due to an expansion in the attractiveness of holding savings in riels, which would emerge with the provision of finance for the development of agricultural villages and smaller firms in that currency. Provision of payment and financial services in riels for regions, industries, and firms targeted by government policy would be economically rational, since domestic transactions in agricultural produce are as of now unfamiliar with the present dollarized financial system. Through the expansion of finance in riels, which would create a riel-denominated payment network, we may expect further expansion in the use of the riel due to its network externalities.

The expansion in "payment rielization" and "financial rielization" would be effective in mitigating the financial constraint on economic activities in rural areas and small and medium firms, but a number of prerequisite conditions need to be fulfilled for such a policy to be a success. First, care must be taken to avoid depreciation of the riel in order to maintain trust in the currency, and implementation of policies for macroeconomic stability is essential to maintain the exchange rate of the riel against the dollar. For Cambodia, it is strongly desired that strict fiscal discipline is maintained so that the expansion in the use of the riel does not relax it and invite the issuance of government bonds to cover deficits.

Second, it is important that households, firms, and financial institutions hold the appropriate proportions of both currencies (by using riels balance currencies appropriately) to enable them to avoid the effects of changes in the exchange rate on their balance sheets. It is vital that financial intermediations in particular modulate capital, supply, and investment funds in dollars and riels appropriately. Currently, because financial institutions in Cambodia have their assets and liabilities almost entirely in dollars, the possible negative effects on their balance sheet are limited. Should the degree of dollarization be reduced in the future, that is, should the almost fully dollarized economy become a partially dollarized one, the management of assets and liabilities for these financial intermediations shall become more complicated than it is at present.

Third, for firms and financial institutions to avoid a mismatch in the currencies they hold, it is vital that a futures market is set up to enable smooth exchange transactions between dollars and riels, and an interbank market is established to enable them to adjust their balance of funds.

Government intervention and path dependency

According to institutional economics, since path dependency affects the process of development in economic institutions, great resistance emerges when such institutions are altered. Growth in use of the riel in Cambodia would cause tremendous friction by changing the economic system. Cambodia's economic institutions, characterized by "real dollarization," "payment dollarization," and "financial dollarization," constitute a stable system that has the character of a Nash equilibrium, with the network externality of dollar payments as its underpinnings. Government policies to increase the use of the riel would cause great friction through institutional change, and the possibility of strong reactionary forces seeking to restore the current development path is high.

If the use of the riel is to be expanded within the current dollarized system, the support of the state is essential. The "Action Plans and Measures to Promote the Use of the Riel," published by the Cambodian government in 2013, aim to expand use of the riel in the future and have a general road map for its implementation. However, the relation between the main points is unclear and the plan remains unfeasible in the absence of numerical targets. Dollarization was also present in Cambodia's neighbors, Vietnam and Lao PDR, but both have greatly reduced the degree of dollarization in recent years. This was not just due to the stabilization of the economy, but by raising the appreciation of the exchange rate of the riel against the dollar and introducing strict measures against "dollarized payment," such as forbidding the display of prices in dollars. These measures seem to have been effective in reducing the network externality of dollar use.[29] Cambodia too should begin to investigate the specifics of such measures and when it would be best to implement them.

References

Basso, H., and et al. 2007. Financial dollarization: The role of banks and interest rates. Working Paper Series No. 748, European Central Bank.

Catao, Luis, and Marco Terrones. 2000. Determinants of dollarization: The banking side. IMF Working Paper WP/00/146.

Demirguc-Kunt, A., and H. Huizinga. 2000. Financial structure and bank profitability. World Bank Policy Research Working Paper No. 2430.

De Nicolo, Gianni, Patrick Honohan, and Alain Ize. 2005. Dollarization and bank deposits: Causes and consequences. *Journal of Banking & Finance* 29: 1697–1727.

De Zamaroczy, Mario, and Soponha Sa. 2002. Macroeconomic adjustment in a highly dollarized economy: The case of Cambodia. IMF Working Paper WP 02/92.

Duma, Nombulelo. 2011. Dollarization in Cambodia: Causes and policy implications. IMF Working Paper WP/11/49.

Garcia-Escribano, Mercedes, and Sebastian Sosa. 2011. What is driving financial de-dollarization in Latin America? IMF Working Paper WP/11/10.

International Monetary Fund (IMF). 2011. Cambodia: Staff report for the 2010 Article IV consultation. IMF Country Report No. 11/45.

Khou, Vouthy. 2014. Cambodia's monetary policy: Dollarization, managing national currency supply and exchange rate stability. Paper presented at the conference of Japan Association of Asian Study at Keio University, May 31.

Khou, Vouthy and Hidenobu Okuda. 2017. Policy Implications. In Special Issue Dollarization in Cambodia: The Results of NBC-JICA Joint Research and Policy Implications. Hitotsubashi Economics 10 (2): 117–128.

Kiyotaki, Nobuhiro, and Randall Wright. 1989. On money as a medium of exchange. *Journal of Political Economy* 97: 927–954.

Kubo, Koji. 2014. Dollarization in ASEAN latecomers: Framework of analysis. Paper presented at the workshop on Dollarization and De-dollarization in ASEAN Latecomers held at Thammasat University, Oct 20–21, in Bangkok, Thailand.

Luca, Alina, and Iva Petrova. 2008. What drives credit dollarization in transition economies? *Journal of Banking & Finance* 32: 858–869.

Menon, Jayant. 2008. Cambodia's persistent dollarization. *ASEAN Economic Bulletin* 25: 228–237.

Ozsoz, Emre. 2007. Bank performance in dollarized economies. Paper presented at the 7th Global Conference on Business and Economics.

Quispe-Agnoli, M., and E. Whisler. 2006. Official dollarization and the banking system in Ecuador and El Salvador. *FED Atlanta Economic Review* 91 (3): 55–71.

Unteroberdoerster, Olaf. 2004. Banking reform in the Lower Mekong countries. IMF Policy Discussion Paper PDP/04/5.

Valev, N.T. 2010. The hysteresis of currency substitution: Currency risk vs. network externalities. *Journal of International Money and Finance* 29 (2): 224–235.

Index

A

Asian financial crisis, 5, 78, 81, 101, 134, 136, 139
Asset substitution, 2, 10–13, 27, 43, 73, 85, 90, 99–101, 101, 105, 106, 111, 131
Association of Southeast Asian Nations(ASEAN), 167, 172, 185, 186, 191, 192
Automated Telling Machine (ATM), 94, 141

B

Banking behavior, 194
Banking system fragility, 21
Bank intermediation, 197, 224
Bank of Lao PDR (BOL), 74
Bank run, 109, 193
Barter, 39, 43
Border trade, 79, 180
Broad money, 3, 4, 6–8, 15, 16, 18, 33, 42, 74, 78, 80, 101, 106, 110, 125, 181
Business cycles, 172

C

Cambodia, 1–5, 8, 9, 11, 14–16, 18, 19, 21, 25–27, 33–35, 38, 39, 41–44, 53, 56, 61, 68, 173, 174, 176, 177, 179, 185, 186, 194, 198, 206, 208, 212–215, 217–219, 221, 223
Capital flight, 98, 173, 175, 184
Carry trade, 36
Cash-based economy, 14
Central and Eastern Europe, 36, 37, 172, 197
Central Bank of Myanmar, 106, 112, 121, 122, 188

K. Kubo (ed.), *Dollarization and De-dollarization in Transitional Economies of Southeast Asia*, IDE-JETRO Series, DOI 10.1007/978-3-319-57768-5

Convertibility, 11, 92, 93, 136, 138, 146, 152, 156
Cost of dollarization, 175, 176, 180, 182, 188, 190, 192–194, 197–201, 212–214, 217–225
Credit risk, 21, 94, 169
Cross-border deposits, 106, 112, 115, 116, 120, 125
Cross-border trade. *See* border trade,
Currency convertibility, 1, 2, 26, 27, 118, 175
Currency crisis, 174
Currency mismatch, 23, 67, 170, 188, 194
Currency substitution, 2, 10, 12, 24, 25, 35, 43, 44, 73, 100, 101, 102, 106, 131
Current international transactions, 11, 26, 119

D

De-dollarization, 2, 3, 10, 24–27, 35, 42, 53, 56, 75, 90, 92, 97, 101, 106, 124, 131, 132, 146, 149, 156, 174, 179, 193, 194
De-dollarization policy, 74, 90, 101, 105, 126
Demand deposit, 81, 89, 90, 101, 109
Demand for money. *See* money demand,
Demonetization, 107
Deposit dollarization, 110, 125, 141, 142, 145, 156, 171, 172, 175, 192, 201, 218, 220
Depreciation,
  depreciation of domestic currency, 202
Dollarization, 204, 205, 212–215, 217–222, 224, 225
Dollarization index, 3–5, 7, 8, 12, 13, 16, 106, 139, 140, 156
Domestic account transfer (of FCDs), 9, 100, 101, 113, 125

E

Eastern Europe, 3, 13, 200, 214, 220, 224
Exchange rate risk, 21, 37, 67, 122, 186, 197, 208
Exchange rate unification, 118

F

Financial deepening, 7, 19, 26, 44, 170, 175, 180, 181, 185
Financial disintermediation, 4, 22, 212
Financial dollarization, 9–11, 19, 26, 43, 44, 74, 98, 140, 167, 168, 172, 205
Financial re-intermediation, 21, 167
Fiscal discipline, 20
Fixed deposit, 26. *See also* Fixed-term deposit; term deposit
Foreign banks, 83, 118, 120, 121, 199, 200, 221
Foreign currency banknote, 1, 2, 4, 9–11, 13, 14, 16, 18, 26, 74, 109, 112, 113, 117–119, 126
Foreign currency borrowing, 35–37, 58, 140, 172

Foreign-currency-denominated assets, 1, 2, 8, 10, 11, 24, 27, 102, 121
Foreign Currency Deposits (FCDs), 33, 73, 74
Foreign currency in circulation, 12, 13, 16, 27, 131, 132, 140, 168
Foreign Currency Loans (FCLs), restrictions on foreign currency loans, 92, 94
Foreign Direct Investment (FDI), 147, 176
Foreign Exchange Certificates (FECs), 117
Foreign exchange management, 2, 96, 112, 118, 119, 136, 143
Foreign reserves, 94. *See also* Foreign exchange reserves
Foreign trade settlement, 105, 126

G

Global Financial Crisis (GFC), 173
Gold, 9, 39, 43, 57, 131, 132, 138, 141, 142, 144, 148, 154–156
Goldization, 9, 132, 138, 154, 155, 157, 183

H

Hysteresis, 5, 11, 12, 37, 44, 81

I

Inflation, 4, 5, 10–12, 14, 20, 24, 25, 43, 74, 78, 79, 81, 92, 98, 105, 107, 108, 131, 132, 135, 142, 149, 171, 175, 177, 183–186, 189, 190, 192, 217
Interest rate ceiling (interest rate cap), 152, 182, 192
Interest rate differentials, 35, 131, 144, 145, 199
International Monetary Fund(IMF)
Article VIII of the IMF, 147

L

Lao PDR, 212–215, 217, 219, 224
Latin America, 2, 3, 175
Legal tender, 9, 107, 132
Lender of last resort, 21, 188, 189, 193, 218
Liquidity ratio, 22, 152, 212, 218
Liquidity risk, 21, 122, 126
Loan dollarization, 131, 141, 145, 153, 156, 193, 218, 225
Local currency outside bank, 4. *See also* Local currency in circulation

M

M2, 48. *See also* Broad money
Managed float, 78, 118, 122, 123
Medium of exchange, 79, 141, 167, 202, 203, 216
MicroFinance Institutions (MFI), 40, 223
Minimum variance portfolio (approach, model, hypothesis), 35, 197
Monetary policy, 3, 24, 27, 54, 92, 96, 121, 132, 136, 149, 167–169, 176, 182–187, 189, 192, 193
Monetization (from barter), 39, 43

Monetization (of fiscal deficits), 107
Money demand, 168
Money supply, 24, 34, 140, 168, 178, 185, 192
Mono bank, 39, 77
Multiple exchange rate, 135
Myanmar, 167, 179, 194

N

National Bank of Cambodia (NBC), 35
Net open position, 100, 132, 155, 157, 206
Network externality, 35, 201, 217–219, 223, 225

O

Official (de jure) dollarization, 8
Official exchange rate, 40, 77, 78, 107, 136, 137
Open position, 205. *See also* Open foreign exchange position, net open position

P

Parallel exchange rate, 142. *See also* Parallel market exchange rate
Partial (de facto) dollarization, 8
Pass-through, 24, 184
Payment dollarization, 25–27, 43, 118, 126, 167, 200, 201, 205, 223
Payment system, 10, 92, 95, 102
Political risk, 175, 176
Precautionary demand (for foreign exchange), 43, 102
Price quoting, 97. *See also* Quoting price
Private transfer, 132. *See also* Net private transfer
Prudential regulation, 23, 109, 174, 194

R

Real dollarization, 9, 43, 69, 201
Real interest rate.*See* real return of deposits,
Real Time Gross Settlement (RTGS), 95
Remittances, 39, 118, 143
Reserve requirement, 21, 100, 121, 189, 192
Reserve requirement ratio, 22, 100, 153

S

Savings deposit, 81, 83, 90
Savings mobilization, 2, 8, 22, 110
Seigniorage, 169
Settlement, 1, 9–12, 25, 45, 95, 105, 106, 116, 121, 125, 126, 221
State Bank of Vietnam (SBV), 131, 184
State Economic Enterprises (SEEs), 112
State-Owned Commercial Banks (SOCBs), 74, 83
Store of value, 2, 9, 89, 154
Surrender requirement, 113, 156

T

Tax payment (in local currency), 96, 116
Term deposit.*See* Fixed deposit,
Time deposit.*See* Fixed deposit,
Trade openness, 178
Transitional economies, 1, 3, 105, 106, 173

U

Underdeveloped banking system, 4, 22, 23
United Nations Transitional Authority in Cambodia (UNTAC), 15, 39, 40
Unit of account, 2, 9, 43, 79, 202, 205, 216, 218
Usability of local currency, 94, 102
US economic sanctions, 116. *See also* US sanctions

V

Valuation effect (of depreciation on dollarization), 13
Velocity (velocity of money), 168, 177, 185
Vietnam, 1, 3–6, 9, 11, 15, 16, 18, 21, 45, 110, 131–133, 135, 136, 138, 149, 154, 156, 173, 179, 183–185, 214, 215, 219, 221

The manufacturer's authorised representative in the EU is Springer Nature Customer Service Centre GmbH, Europaplatz 3, 69115 Heidelberg, Germany. If you have any concerns regarding our products, please contact ProductSafety@springernature.com

Printed and bound by CPI Group (UK) Ltd, Croydon, CR0 4YY
22/09/2026
02221067-0006